How to:

Buy, Own and Sell a Boat
(Without Going Broke)

By: John Schneider and Don Woodwell

To Doris, for her patience

and

To Donna, for her love and support

How to:

Buy, Own and Sell a Boat
(Without Going Broke)

by: John Schneider and Don Woodwell

Published by:
ProStar Publications, Inc
P.O. Box 341668
Los Angeles, CA 90034

Copyright 1990 by John Schneider and Don Woodwell
Printed in the United States

ISBN 0-930030-55-9

Book Design: Roger Gordon

PUBLISHED BY
ProStar Publications, Inc.
Publishers of the Pacific Boating Almanac
and other marine books. Catalog on request.
P.O. Box 341668
Los Angeles, CA 90034

In Canada:
Gordon Soules Book Publishers
1352-B Marina Drive
West Vancover, B.C. V7T 185

PREFACE

The most oft quoted (and hackneyed) saying in the pleasure boat industry goes something like this: "The two happiest days in a boat owner's life are the day he buys that boat and the day he sells it." While we still all laugh at that saying when we hear it, unless it contained some seed of truth, it wouldn't be such a best seller.

Those who do take the plunge into boating often end up miserable with their decision. Not because the sport wasn't enjoyable; more likely because boating turned out to not be affordable, legal and tax hassles arose, the boat was poorly insured ... whatever.

People in the boat business are fond of saying that boat buying is an emotional and impulsive experience, with much talk of a phenomenon known as "buyer's remorse", a deal killer that sets in quickly if a prospective owner thinks about the purchase too long. It's as if the only way a boat can be bought is without advance thought and consideration, implying that a purchase cannot be rational, structured and planned. Rubbish! Unfortunately, many purchases are carried out in just this manner, but it does not have to be.

The sad fact is that a lot of would be boatsmen don't get into the sport because of all the "bad news" stories they hear — from friends and relatives, the media, or the guy in the next office. Perhaps no one can tell them how to experience **successful** boat ownership. And what can be more frightening than becoming a bad news story yourself? Indeed, buying a boat does represent a major expenditure of capital that will consume a substantial amount of discretionary income far into the future. In this sense, it is as significant to buy as a house, and is deserving of the same effort.

There are hundreds, perhaps thousands, of books written on the subject of boating covering a wide range of topics from designing and building to cruising and cooking. But it occurred to us that nowhere in a single volume was there a comprehensive guide to buying and owning a boat that addressed the many topics related to ownership **outside** the straight product issues. Topics such as financial planning, insurance, registration, legal considerations and so forth.

This book, then, attempts to present in logical order all the facets which the average buyer will encounter in purchasing a boat, whether it be a 28 foot sailboat or a 75 foot motor yacht. The discussion is implicitly slanted toward larger boats, those costing in excess of $30,000. Smaller boats, because they don't cost as much, require less planning. Nevertheless, many of the topics apply to smaller boats as well.

We will not provide any details or recommendations on the type of boat you should buy (other than demonstrating some interesting size/cost trade-offs) and only in one appendix do we describe some basic design differences intended as background for the less experienced buyer.

The book was written for both the first time owner and the experienced yachtsman. The former will find it a useful guide in directing planning while covering all the bases. The latter may discover interesting ideas for restructuring ownership and preparing for the next boat. Both will hopefully find it interesting as we have endeavored to keep it easily readable although not at the expense of necessary detail and description.

Our goal in setting all this down in written form is simple. We want to change that old saying to reflect the more positive elements of this most enjoyable of leisure activities: "The two happiest days in a boat owner's life are the day he buys his first boat and the day he buys the next boat!"

Don Woodwell   John Schneider

TABLE OF CONTENTS

CHAPTER 1

INTRODUCTION: There Are Many Choices

An Overview: Setting Boat Ownership Objectives And Strategies

Each person has his own vision of what "boating" means. Some see it as the ultimate getaway vacation — lounging on the aft deck of a sixty foot Italian motor yacht in the harbor at Saint Tropez sipping champagne and watching the people go by. South Pacific dreamers are tanning themselves under a brilliant sun in an emerald lagoon surrounded by white Tahitian sand and lightly swaying palm trees.

Others see boating as a Sunday afternoon cruise to Catalina Island with some close friends or a fishing trip out of Ensenada. Atlantic coast residents may cruise to the Bahamas, race in the Chesapeake Bay, or power out to the Baltimore Canyon for some early summer fishing.

Unfortunately, few of these dreams will be fulfilled. You may not lack desire, just money (so you think). There are but two issues involved in boat economics: How to plan the finances for a boat purchase, and the ongoing cost of its upkeep. In most cases, this is due to a lack of the right how-to information, and the belief that you have to be rich to own that dream boat. There are few good books on the subject, and scarce magazine articles. Financial planners can't help because of the uniqueness of this field. Besides that, owning a boat is not a conventional investment. It involves love and enjoyment for the sport. Professional financial advisors, including accountants, don't normally give financial boating advice, so the prospective boat owner needs to turn elsewhere, or figure it out for himself.

Good help is hard to find

Where can you turn for help? How about the money lenders? After all, they are always working with prospective buyers, and consequently, they should know what steps to take in financing a boat. True, lenders can tell potential buyers what personal financial data they need to qualify for a loan. But they can't advise buyers about the costs of keeping up the boat, which can be the biggest financial headache in boat ownership. Money lenders can provide only a partial answer. Someone must have the rest of the answers to questions about the financial responsibilties of ownership, but who?

Marina operators should be able to give you some idea of the ongoing costs, particularly maintenance. It doesn't matter if you buy a fiberglass or wooden boat, it still needs to be maintained. Glass boats may have less hull and deck maintenance, but the mechanical and electrical systems (not to mention sails and rigging) still need to be kept up. A good boatyard mechanic can help you project the average annual costs for the size boat you are considering. After trying several yards, perhaps a general outline of the annual costs may emerge. But don't count on it.

Relax. This book provides, in one place, the information you need to define your financial status, secure a loan, anticipate your ongoing costs, and understand the other requirements of ownership such as regulations, insurance and taxes. Although we may not be able to make the best of your dream come true, you will be in a better position to understand how much of that dream you can or cannot afford.

Set your objectives

Buying and justifying the right boat means finding the boat that suits your boating objectives. The choice is not simply between power and sail. Selecting just the right package of features on whatever boat you buy only results from knowing just how you plan to use her. It is even more important to define your needs before buying your first boat. Experienced boaters know what they like and dislike. But they still need to refine their boating objectives based on how they plan to use their new boat in the future.

A visit to any boat show — most of which feature hundreds of boats on land or in water, thousands of accessories, and dozens of services — points out that no new boat purchase is simple. For that matter, neither is buying a used boat. Publishers of used boat listings will gladly provide you with lengthy lists of all types previously owned boats. Where do you start?

Four components — seaworthiness, comfort, speed and cost — are compromised in every boat. Your objectives point out which of these is most important to you. Exhibit 1-1 shows how different vessels stack up based on the relative weight that buyers typically give to each of the four components of boat design.

Exhibit 1-1

	Seaworthiness	Comfort	Speed	Cost
SAIL:				
Meter type racer	20%	5%	70%	5%
Ocean racer	35%	20%	30%	15%
Family cruiser	25%	20%	20%	35%
POWER:				
Ocean racer	25%	10%	50%	15%
Express cruiser	15%	10%	25%	30%
Trawler cruiser	30%	30%	10%	30%
Houseboat	10%	45%	15%	30%

Courtesy of: Edward S. Brewer, N.A. and Jim Betts, Understanding Boat Design , published for the YACHT DESIGN INSTITUTE, Brooklin, Maine, by INTERNATIONAL MARINE PUBLISHING COMPANY, Camden, ME, 1980

Compromise obviously is the name of the game. The weight you place on one factor changes the balance of the other components. Rarely can you gain in one design area without sacrificing in another. For the most part, boating is a family activity. Many of us are interested in both sport (fishing, racing, and water skiing, for example) and cruising to some extent. A boat that can meet both needs provides greater flexibility in its uses.

Many of the variations in design and cost are determined by whether you operate on relatively quiet inland lakes and rivers, or on the potentially more turbulent coastal waters or offshore.

Compromises in design are frequent in order to accommodate varied boating interests, too. For example, avid fishermen appreciate open deck spaces. But cruising mariners like enclosed cabins, especially when the weather is bad. Design variations might allow for frequent fishing from a cruiser by providing the right amount of openess along with adequate interior cabin space. If only occasionally do you get the urge to race your sailboat on weekends, you may have to weigh competitive hull characteristics against those of a cruising boat design. Sail and powerboat builders are constantly seeking to find the right balance for their customers. This makes the selection broad, but the choice difficult.

Another important aspect to consider before selecting a boat is how frequently you expect to use it. If you're an avid fisherman and you'll be on board every weekend, your needs will be different than if you fish infrequently. Overnighters need fewer accommodations than vacationers who may spend a week or two onboard. If your boating waters are close to your home, then day trips may be your thing. A portable head and small vee berth may be adequate for comfort.

A family of ten won't be comfortable on a day trip, or even safe, on a 20 footer. Space for such a crowd may be cramped even on a 35 foot boat. The longer the trip, the more living space seems to shrink. If your family needs space around them to feel comfortable then allow about seven to ten feet of boat length per person. Quarters that are too confined can turn a contented family into an unhappy group that can't wait to get off the boat.

Select the largest boat that meets your objectives the first time through the selection process. This will give you more space as well as greater flexibility in the ways you can meet your overall objectives. All things being equal, unless you want to keep on the conservative side because of your inexperience in handling a large boat, go for the one with the most usable space. At this time you may wish to review Appendix A for more design considerations.

How much should you pay?

Fall and mid-winter boat shows provide some of the best opportunities to negotiate a deal on spring delivery for a new boat. Dealers and builders are anxious to close out the current model year or stack up orders for the new boating season. Several dealers in your area may be competing for your order which may make it easier to realize some significant savings. Typically, the best profit margins are on the add-on equipment which is an incentive for dealers to load up your new boat. Select just the right equipment to meet your needs without inflating the price of the boat beyond your reach.

As in any large purchase, you need to compare not only different boats but the list of optional equipment that comes with each. Competing manufacturers will list those features and options that they include in the price and those that are extra. These lists are a good place to start as they provide a base against which to compare what each builder is providing for the money they are asking. Compare the base prices first, then the built in features, and finally the options. Next, list and price the equipment that is not provided in the price of the boat. The builder's options and dealer's equipment can quickly add up to a sizeable percentage of the base price. This makes it essential that you eliminate equipment options that do not satisfy your boating objectives. Costly equipment like generators and air conditioners should be included prior to financing the boat so they can be included in the loan.

Depending largely on the make and type of boat you may pay up to 20% more than the base price in options and equipment to bring it to a "sail away" condition. Time well spent now in making all the comparisons will better assure you that you have selected the best boat to meet your financial objectives and boating dreams.

Develop a procedure by which you can compare the various features of different manufacturer's models. A simple one page chart with the features in the first column and the alternatives at the head of subsequent columns is a big help as in Exhibits 1−2a and 1−2b.

Exhibit 1-2a

Power Boat Selection Chart

This chart is designed to help you choose the power boat whose design and features most closely meet your needs, and can be afforded, financed, and insured.
(1) Prioritize the hull and deck design elements, power plant, accommodations, etc. in terms of importance, in this way: high = 3, medium = 2, low = 1, and no priority = 0. The higher the number, the more desireable the design feature or the better the quality of the materials or equipment.
(2) Select boats that are appealing to you and rank their features from 1 (low) to 10 (high).
(3) Multiply the priority by the feature rankings to establish the weighted ranking in points.
(4) Sum these points in each column to determine the total points per boat. The highest total points is likely to be your best choice.
(5) You may choose to modify these criteria depending on your particular needs.

To illustrate, we have provideds three boats and ranked them hypothetically.
  Boat A: New, fiberglass 28' cruiser, twin I/O gas engine
  Boat B: Three year old fiberglass 32' sportfish, twin inboard diesels
  Boat C: Eight year old fierglass 40' convertible, twin inboard diesels

Selection criteria		Alternative Selections						
		Boat A		Boat B		Boat C		
	Priority	rank	points	rank	points	rank	points	
Objectives								
Fishing	3	5	15	8	24	6	18	
Cruising	2	8	16	7	14	9	18	
Racing	0	n/a		n/a		n/a		
Water skiing	0	n/a		n/a		n/a		

(continued on next page)

Exhibit 1 – 2a (continued)

Alternative Selections

Selection criteria	Priority	Boat A		Boat B		Boat C	
		rank	points	rank	points	rank	points
Vessel performance							
Inland lakes/rivers	0	n/a		n/a		n/a	
Coastal waters	3	7	21	7	21	8	24
Offshore waters	2	4	8	6	12	8	16
Seaworthiness	2	7	14	7	14	7	14
Comfort	2	7	14	6	12	8	16
Speed	2	9	18	6	12	4	8
Costs							
Financing	3	7	21	2	6	8	24
Insurance	1	7	7	4	4	7	7
Maintenance	2	8	16	3	6	6	12
Storage or slip	2	9	18	7	14	5	10
Age	2	10	20	6	12	2	4
Hull type							
Displacement	0	n/a		n/a		n/a	
Semi-displacement	2	n/a		n/a		7	14
Planing	3	8	24	8	24	n/a	
Dimensions							
Length overall (between 30' and 40')	3	1	3	7	21	8	24
Beam (over 10')	3	1	3	5	15	8	24
Hull construction and condition							
Fiberglass	3	10	30	n/a		9	27
Aluminum	2	n/a		n/a		n/a	
Wood	1	n/a		8	8	n/a	
Steel	1	n/a		n/a		n/a	
Cement	0	n/a		n/a		n/a	
Power/drive							
I/O gas	1	8	8	n/a		n/a	
I/O diesel	2	n/a		n/a		n/a	
Inboard gas	2	n/a		n/a		n/a	
Inboard diesel	3	n/a		8	24	6	18
Outboard	0	n/a		n/a		n/a	
Twin screw	3	10	30	10	30	10	30
Single screw	1	n/a		n/a		n/a	

(continued on next page)

Exhibit 1 – 2a (continued)

Selection criteria	Priority	Boat A		Boat B		Boat C	
		rank	points	rank	points	rank	points
Fuel capacity (over 200 gallons)	3	3	9	6	18	9	27
Fuel consumption (less than 25 gph)	2	9	27	5	15	2	4
Accommodations							
Cabin layout	2	5	10	6	12	8	16
Cockpit	3	5	15	9	27	6	18
Galley	2	4	8	6	12	9	18
Heads	2	4	8	6	12	9	18
Water supply (over 75 gallons)	3	2	6	6	18	9	27
Electrical system	2	8	16	5	10	5	10
Electronics							
Radios	3	6	18	7	21	7	21
Navigational	3	6	18	6	18	7	21
Radar	3	7	21	7	21	8	24
Suitable for charter	0	n/a		n/a		n/a	
Builder	2	9	18	2	4	8	16
Dealer	2	9	18	4	8	7	14
Total			**478**		**469**		**542**
Rankings:			2		3		1

Boat C is clearly the number one selection based on the accumulated points. While this may hold true, there are practical and subjective evaluations that could alter the purchase decision. Maybe Boat C will not reduce its price enough to fit in with your financial plan. In that case, you would be faced with closely ranked boats A and B. But while they are rated almost the same, Boat B may "feel better" for fishing. This closeness in ranking may necessitate additional assessment of these two boat alternatives. The ranking chart lets a prospective buyer more objectively sort the options, but it does not give all the answers.

Exhibit 1-2b

Sailboat Selection Chart

This chart is designed to help you choose the sail boat whose design and features most closely meet your needs, and can be afforded, financed, and insured.

(1) Prioritize the hull and deck design elements, power plant, accommodations, etc. in terms of importance, in this way: high = 3, medium = 2, low = 1, and no priority = 0. The higher the number, the more desireable the design feature or the better the quality of the materials or equipment.

(2) Select boats that are appealing to you and rank their features from 1 (low) to 10 (high).

(3) Multiply the priority by the feature rankings to establish the weighted ranking in points.

(4) Sum these points in each column to determine the total points per boat. The highest total points is likely to be your best choice.

(5) You may choose to modify these criteria depending on your particular needs.

To illustrate, we have provideds three boats and ranked them hypothetically.

Boat A: New, fiberglass 26' fin keel sloop, outboard gas engine
Boat B: Five year old fiberglass 28' centerboard cutter, inboard diesel
Boat C: Twelve year old fiberglass 32' shoal draft cutter, inboard diesel

Alternative Selections

Selection criteria	Priority	Boat A rank	Boat A points	Boat B rank	Boat B points	Boat C rank	Boat C points
Objectives							
Cruising							
Day	3	8	16	8	16	7	21
Extended	2	4	8	6	12	8	16
Cruising/racing	1	7	7	7	7	5	5
Vessel performance							
Inland lakes/rivers	0	n/a		n/a		n/a	
Coastal waters	3	7	21	7	21	8	24
Offshore waters	1	4	8	6	12	8	16
Seaworthiness	2	7	14	7	14	7	14
Comfort	2	5	10	6	12	8	16
Speed	2	9	18	6	12	4	8
Costs							
Financing	3	5	15	8	24	8	24
Insurance	1	6	6	7	7	7	7
Maintenance	2	8	16	6	12	4	8
Storage or slip	2	9	18	7	14	5	10
Age	2	10	20	6	12	2	4

(Continued on next page)

Exhibit 1 – 2b (continued)

Selection criteria	Alternative Selections					
		Boat A		Boat B		Boat C
	Priority	rank	points	rank	points	rank	points
Dimensions							
Length overall (between 20' and 30')	3	8	24	7	21	2	6
Beam (greater than 8')	3	4	12	7	21	9	27
Draft (less than 4')	2	4	8	7	14	7	14
Hull construction and condition							
Fiberglass	3	10	30	9	27	7	21
Aluminum	0	n/a		n/a		n/a	
Wood	0	n/a		n/a		n/a	
Steel	1	n/a		n/a		n/a	
Cement	0	n/a		n/a		n/a	
Auxiliary power							
Inboard gas	2	n/a		n/a		n/a	
Inboard diesel	3	n/a		8	24	6	18
Outboard	1	10	10	n/a		n/a	
Fuel capacity (over 20 gal)	1	1	1	5	5	7	7
Fuel consumption (less than 3 gph)	1	10	10	5	5	2	2
Type rig							
Sloop	3	9	27	n/a		n/a	
Cutter	2	n/a		7	14	n/a	
Ketch	0	n/a		n/a		n/a	
Other	0	n/a		n/a		n/a	
Number of sails	1	7	7	4	4	3	3
Condition of sails	2	10	20	7	14	2	4
Accommodations							
Cabin layout	2	5	10	6	12	8	16
Cockpit	3	5	15	6	18	9	27
Galley	2	4	8	6	12	8	16
Heads	2	4	8	6	12	9	18
Water supply (over 40 gallons)	3	2	6	6	18	9	27
Electrical system	2	8	16	5	10	5	10

(continued on next page)

Exhibit 1 – 2b (continued)

Alternative Selections

Selection criteria	Priority	Boat A		Boat B		Boat C	
		rank	points	rank	points	rank	points
Electronics							
Radios	3	6	18	7	21	7	21
Navigational	3	6	18	6	18	7	21
Radar	3	7	21	7	21	8	24
Suitable for charter	0	n/a		n/a		n/a	
Builder	2	9	18	2	4	8	16
Dealer	2	9	18	4	8	7	14
Totals:			482		478		485
Rankings:			2		3		1

In this case, there is no clear favorite. Unfortunately, in the real world, decisions are often this difficult to make.

Purchasing previously owned boats

Age differences between new and used boats are important but style or construction as well as wear and tear may be more significant. The asking price of a used boat is determined largely by the current market for that type and age of boat, and the cost of the equipment on board. New boats are not usually equipped with all the electronics, furnishings, sails and other equipment that previously owned boats often have. For this reason, the price for quality used boats may be higher than a comparable new one of the same make. Thus, if a realistically priced boat that meets your needs is an infrequently changed model in good condition it may be worth buying.

But who is selling it? Does he clearly state his selling price and, if asked, will he tell you why he is selling the boat? All cost and equipment records should be readily obtainable. The seller's terms should be simple and straightforward, and he should want to work with you and close the deal to mutual advantage. Other considerations of buying (or selling) a used boat are discussed in Chapter 9.

Thinking About Boat Financing

Once you grasp your needs and begin looking at different types and sizes of boats, you'll begin to whittle away at those features that don't stack up. The difference in cost between alternatives will begin playing a major role in your decision making. On new boats, you will undoubtedly undergo "sticker shock". The price of boats no longer is guaged in dollars per foot. Nowadays, the cost goes up as the volume of the boat increases. Exhibits 1-3, 1-4, and 1-5 show the total cost and cost per pound for new boats.

Exhibit 1-3
Total Cost and Cost Per Pound for New Boats

Exhibit 1-3(A)

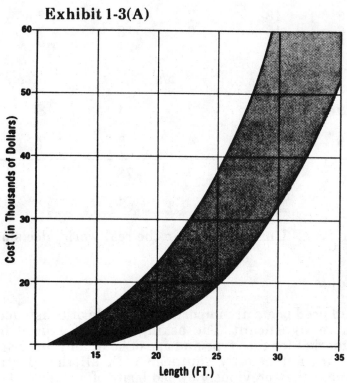

Fiberglass Outboard Boats
Length (FT.) vs. Cost (in Thousands of Dollars)

Charts on these pages represent the new purchase price of U.S. stock and semistock fiberglass boats. The purchase price is shown two ways: (1) As a function of the total cost vs. the boat length (2) As a function of the cost per pound of displacement vs. the boat length. The shaded area represents about 70% of the market with roughly 15% above and 15% below the shaded area. The center line in the cost per pound of displacement is the median cost where 50% of the boats cost more and 50% cost less.

Exhibit 1-3(B)

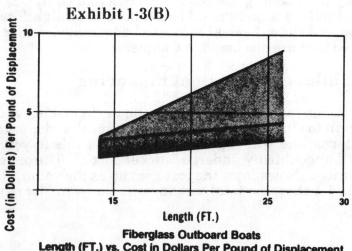

Fiberglass Outboard Boats
Length (FT.) vs. Cost in Dollars Per Pound of Displacement

Exhibit 1-4
Total Cost and Cost Per Pound for New Boats

Exhibit 1-4(A)

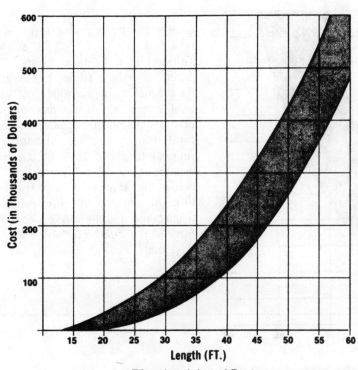

Fiberglass Inboard Boats
Length (Ft.) vs. Cost (in Thousands of Dollars)

Charts on these pages represent the new purchase price of U.S. stock and semistock fiberglass boats. The purchase price is shown two ways: (1) As a function of the total cost vs. the boat length (2) As a function of the cost per pound of displacement vs. the boat length. The shaded area represents about 70% of the market with roughly 15% above and 15% below the shaded area. The center line in the cost per pound of displacement is the median cost where 50% of the boats cost more and 50% cost less.

Exhibit 1-4(B)

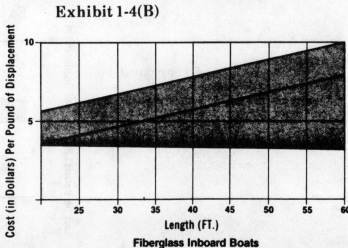

Fiberglass Inboard Boats
Length (FT.) vs. Cost in Dollars Per Pound of Displacement

Exhibit 1-5
Total Cost and Cost Per Pound for New Boats

Exhibit 1-5(A)

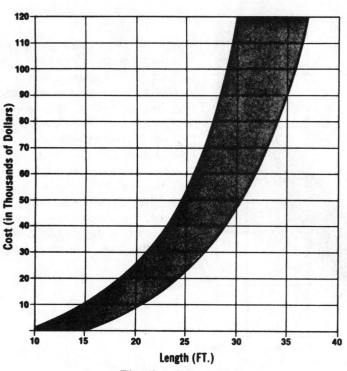

Fiberglass Stern Drive Boats
Length (Ft.) vs. Cost (in Thousands of Dollars)

Charts on these pages represent the new purchase price of U.S. stock and semistock fiberglass boats. The purchase price is shown two ways: (1) As a function of the total cost vs. the boat length (2) As a function of the cost per pound of displacement vs. the boat length. The shaded area represents about 70% of the market with roughly 15% above and 15% below the shaded area. The center line in the cost per pound of displacement is the median cost where 50% of the boats cost more and 50% cost less.

Exhibit 1-5(B)

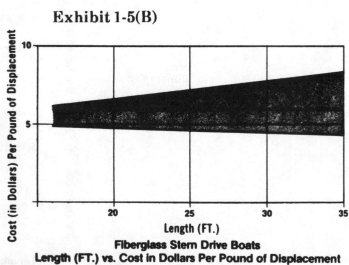

Fiberglass Stern Drive Boats
Length (FT.) vs. Cost in Dollars Per Pound of Displacement

Exhibit 1-6
Total Cost and Cost Per Pound for New Boats

Exhibit 1-6(A)

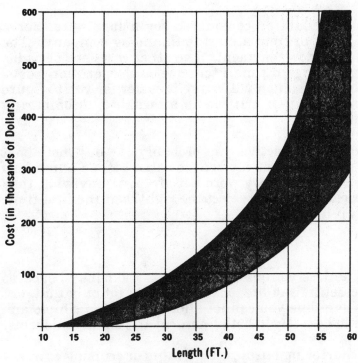

Fiberglass Production Sailboats
Length (FT.) vs. Cost (in Thousands of Dollars)

Charts on these pages represent the new purchase price of U.S. stock and semistock fiberglass boats. The purchase price is shown two ways: (1) As a function of the total cost vs. the boat length (2) As a function of the cost per pound of displacement vs. the boat length. The shaded area represents about 70% of the market with roughly 15% above and 15% below the shaded area. The center line in the cost per pound of displacement is the median cost where 50% of the boats cost more and 50% cost less.

This information is copyrighted by Robert Snow Means, Co., Inc. It is reproduced from Boating Cost Guide with permission.

Exhibit 1-6(B)

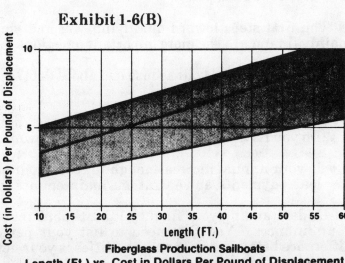

Fiberglass Production Sailboats
Length (Ft.) vs. Cost in Dollars Per Pound of Displacement

Even used boats, particularly ones noted for quality construction, are not inexpensive. Unlike automobiles, many boats don't lose their value rapidly, particularly those over 30 feet. The price of smaller boats, 30 feet or less, more closely reflects their age.

The trick, though, is not to be deterred by the sticker or asking price of the boat. Think about how much you can afford to pay each month rather than the sticker price. If you view the price of a boat as a one time cost, you'll never begin boating on the scale of your dreams. Not only that, but tying up a large chunk of money in a boat is not a good investment.

Any purchase price over $5,000 should be considered for a loan — either a personal loan through your local bank or from a marine financing company. The only large one time cost should be the downpayment. The other costs are periodic, and include monthly payments and ongoing maintenance and operation costs. Thinking about marine finances in this fashion will make it easier for you to figure out if every boat that meets your selection criteria is affordable. Comparing financing alternatives becomes easier, too.

In short, with the proper financial perspective, you probably can buy more boat than you think. The average boatowner keeps his boat for about three and a half years. People might not upgrade so often if they were not afraid to buy what they really needed in the first place. Most people can select the right boat the first time, but they do not know how to justify it financially.

Justifying boat ownership

A boat may be hard to justify unless you plan to run it as a business, such as chartering. Homes and cars are essentials of life, boats are not. Not only that, but boats are very expensive. This is one time you cannot afford to make a simple and uninformed decision. It will prove to be costly in both finanical and emotional terms.

If you opt for setting up a boat chartering business for fishing or cruising as a way to justify your purchase, there are several financial and tax benefits. These may defray some costs of ownership. On the downside, however, you can't use your boat as often as you might like since the IRS limits your personal use. There are many ramifications of running a boat rental business, both positive and negative. We'll look at these in Chapter 8.

The first steps toward qualifying you and your family for boat ownership are mainly financial. The more important questions concern your financial limitations:

▸ How do you and your spouse feel about debt?

▸ Can you qualify for a loan?

▸ Do you have enough cash to handle the downpayment?

▸ Is your annual income enough to cover your ordinary living expenses, monthly loan payments, and operations/maintenance costs?

Understanding your financial limitations requires you to do some homework on your finances. You first need to list your personal assets and liabilities. The difference between assets and liabilities is your net worth which gives the financing company an indication of your relative financial stability. This relates directly to your capabilty to carry the loan. Further, it gives you more of a cushion in the event of a financial setback. Next, you must analyze both your annual and monthly income and expenses. The resulting cash flow picture is particularly beneficial not only in determining your ability to make monthly loan payments, but also to handle other monthly costs.

Developing an overall financial plan

A financial plan will help you define your limitations, and provides a base for carefully and logically analyzing your financing options. The financial plan (detailed in Chapter 2) helps you get a better grip on your personal finances, qualify yourself to a finance company by using a sales plan, and mentally prepare yourself and your family for the boat purchase. In short, it will put you in the right frame of mind as you begin looking around for a good banker or financing company. The overall objective of the financial plan, of course, is to help you justify the purchase of the largest boat consistent with your boating needs and your financial limitations.

Loan processing is not complicated if you have done your financial homework, and if you are convinced you're doing the right thing. First, find and select one or more prospective lenders. They are easy to find in boating magazine ads and at boat shows. Set up the preliminary financial criteria by which you can choose the lender. Some criterion include approximate monthly payment, term of loan, downpayment percentage, interest rate, type of plan such as fixed or adjustable rate, etc. In your preliminary search for a lender, compare your needs against what the finance company has to offer.

Next, complete your financial sales plan in detail, and choose one company with whom you want to work. Your final selection may be based particularly on where they are located and on recommendations of others who have borrowed from them. Your broker or dealer may have some very good recommendations as to which lenders can be of greatest help to you. The outcome of your discussions with the lender should give you a clearer view of your financial limitations. You may be surprised to find that you have fewer limitations than you thought, and may be able to afford more boat than you considered possible.

As soon as you qualify for a loan, you can more actively work toward selecting your dreamboat. Chapter 3 and 4 help you become more specific in your loan choices. As the choices begin to narrow down, then you can start a second round of negotiations with the boat dealer or broker. The suggested retail price is only the starting point. It may be set higher than competing boats or dealers. Although you won't be bargaining for a 35 foot cruising sailboat as you would a Mexican vase in Tijuana, there always is some flexibility in prices. By all means, negotiate early. Be aware that discounts are available on new boats, and you should take advantage of these so as to get the best possible deal. Boat shows are a particularly good place to negotiate as competitors are sitting side-by-side, and they may be more willing to strike a deal. You can also get special prices on equipment, financing, and other boat items at shows.

Dealers And Builders

Boat shows are a great place to meet the builders and dealers, too. If the show is in your boating area many of the local dealers representing several manufacturers will be in attendance. Discuss your objectives with them, and get their ideas as to what sort of boat would best meet your needs. In this way, you can possibly learn which of them is in tune with your thinking and want to place you in the right boat. In the next few paragraphs, there are several other points that you might want to cover with both builders and dealers alike.

Dealers

A dealer with a good reputation for handling warranty claims, for not padding a boat with unnecesary gear, for helping to find financing, and for being interested in his customers is what you should seek. Other considerations may include lines of boats represented by the dealer, his sales competence and the quality of service he provides after the sale. It may be more fun to search for the boat and not the dealer of your dreams, but if the boat is delivered late or not delivered at all, you will realize that you should have spent more time checking on the integrity of the builder and dealer, and understanding their relationship.

Know what commitment you are making when you make a deposit and under what conditions you are entitled to get it back. Money passed over as a deposit is subject to certain specific and usually stated conditions, and is binding to the purchase of a boat. If the buyer subsequently cancels his order, defaults on payments, fails to take delivery, or in any way violates his side of that contract, then he stands to lose that deposit. On the other hand, if (1) the dealer fails to deliver his boat; (2) delivers it late; (3) does not meet other conditions of the contract; or (4) the buyer cannot obtain financing, then the buyer is entitled to the return of his deposit. Typically deposit money is placed in escrow pending the outcome of the transaction. In any case, be sure that you have a signed contract with clearly stated terms and conditions (have your lawyer review it if you are not sure of the wording). Verbal agreements should be confirmed in writing, too.

Builders

Talk with a member of the builder's sales or customer service department before you place an order for his product. When you have a signed agreement to buy a boat, check with the builder to make sure the dealer actually passed on that order. Once the dealer took your money, he should have ordered your boat with it. The builder may be reluctant to give you information about the boat's manufacture but periodically check the progress of your boat if possible.

Although builders and dealers may have no legal connection, a variety of working arrangements can be set up between them. Nevertheless, your contract is between you and the dealer. The builder sells the boat to a dealer who adds the commission onto the factory price and sells it to you. Variations in this three way operation make it essential to keep records at each step.

The warranty process is one area that mandates that you keep good records not only of work done, but also who does it. First, discuss the warranty terms with the dealer before you take delivery of the boat. If the dealer modifies any of the terms, write out the new terms and have him initial the changes. If the dealer seems vague about warranty settlements or dismisses the possiblity that you will have any, take your business elsewhere. You can almost bet on having numerous warranty claims the first three months of ownership. It is advisable to leave your new boat in the dealer's slip until the bugs get worked out, especially if your boat is a new model. Otherwise, you may need warranty work at some location remote to the dealer.

Accomplishing this work means returning the boat to the dealer which will probably be time consuming and inconvenient not to mention the loss of money moving it there. On a warranty claim, do not authorize repair or replacement without the manufacturer's approval unless you are prepared to pay for it yourself. If you find yourself in a situation where you must submit an invoice for reimbursement for warranty work already done and paid for, insist that the invoice you obtain itemize the warranty work and invoice it separately from any other work done.

Final Steps To Making Your Purchase

When you finally settle on the right boat and equipment, bring the dealer/broker and finance company together on a mutually agreeable settlement date. If you have done your financial homework, obtained the best loan terms and the lowest dealer/broker price, you will close the deal. Pick up the keys to your dream boat, and you will be realizing the enjoyment of ownership aware that you did afford more boat than you ever thought possible.

In order to ensure that you do not miss any step in the purchasing process, review the chart shown in Appendix B.

CHAPTER 2

FINANCIAL PLANNING: Getting It Together

How much boat can you afford? Rule 1: Buy the largest boat you can afford that meets your objectives, but no larger; Rule 2: Don't put all your discretionary income into your boat purchase.

There are two key reasons for these rules. First, maintenance and monthly payments are major recurring costs. Second, you have other uses for your money. You need a reasonable buffer between your ongoing boat expenses and other home and family needs. This will take the pressure off owning the boat. Besides, other financial opportunities may come along in which you might want to invest. It probably isn't worth giving up everything for a boat no matter how much you want one. On the other hand, with a little careful planning you may be able to have your cake and eat it, too.

Mention planning and people lose interest. Planning doesn't have to be boring, however. Instead, it makes borrowing money easier, gives visibility to your assets and liabilities, and lets you know what boats you can afford.

How To Prepare A Financial Sales Plan

Understanding your net worth and cash flow are important to you. They are even more important to your marine finance company. After all, it's their money that you are borrowing, and they need some assurance that it will be repaid. Further, the numbers are not all they need to know. They want to believe that their investment is not a high risk venture, that your income is reasonably stable, and the boat is protected by insurance. The question is, how do you convince them that you are a minimum risk person? This is largely done with a financial sales plan. After you have collected all the pertinent financial data they want, you need to figure out how to best communicate this information to the finance company. If you do this right, your chances of qualifying yourself will improve significantly.

Your balance sheet should be prepared on the conservative side. Typically, you are paying for this boat as an individual and not a corporation or claiming it as a business asset. Therefore, keep the assets and liabilities personal. Otherwise, they may not truly reflect your net worth. Similarly, income from sideline activities such as consulting, writing or other such businesses are often not considered by the financier. You may be counting on such income to provide the cushion between your personal living costs and the boat expenses. The loan officer, however, wants to see a solid organization behind your current earnings. Usually he will discount sideline income. Your future earnings over the next five years may be reasonable to you, but loan officers may ignore them because they are too speculative. What they want to know is your current salary, and the likelihood that it will continue at the same rate. The length of time that you have worked for your company and its reputation for employment stability will have an affect on the loan decision. If you feel that one or both these factors may adversely affect your chances to qualify for a boat loan, then include some positive statements about your company and its current status in the letter that accompanies your loan application.

Discuss your plan with a marine banker

Include a cover letter with your credit package. This is your chance to tell why you should get the loan. Explain that you've done your homework and are convinced you are qualified. Tell them what kind of boat you want to buy and when, and specify the loan terms you are willing to accept. This is a business deal and should be treated as such. You're paying good money for the use of their money so don't feel they are doing you a favor by making the loan. Finance companies have as much to gain as you do since this is a competitive market to them. If they don't get your business, some other company probably will. Consequently, most finance companies will try to help you attain your goals if they're realistic.

Once you complete all the financial statements, write the cover letter and fill out the application. The attached "Yacht Financing Application" (Exhibit 2-1) illustrates the type of data most often requested by marine bankers. The entries in the application may be redundant to your balance sheet and income-expense statement, but this is the key document from which decisions are made by the lender based on your qualifications. Sign the cover letter and application, attach your financial statements and tax returns, and send the package to the finance company you selected.

Exhibit 2-1

Yacht Financing Application

CREDIT APPLICATION

APPLICANT — Personal Employment and Financial Data

Print Name _____ Drivers Lic. No. _____ Soc. Sec. No. _____
LAST   FIRST   MIDDLE

Date of Birth _____ Place of Birth _____ Home Phone No. _____

U.S. Citizen: Yes ☐ No ☐   Marital Status: Married ☐ Unmarried ☐ Separated ☐   No. of Dependents _____ Ages _____

Present Home Address _____ Years _____

Former Home Address _____ Years _____

Nearest Relative (Not living with you) _____ Phone No. _____
              NAME   ADDRESS

ARE YOU: Self-employed? ☐   Employed by a firm principally owned by you? ☐   Otherwise employed? ☐

Employer _____ Address _____

Position _____ Type of Business _____

Phone No. _____ Years Employed _____ Annual Salary $ _____

Previous Employer _____ Address _____ Years _____

Other Income Source (s) _____ Annual Amount $ _____
(Alimony, child support or separate maintenance payments are optional and need not be revealed if the Applicant does not choose to rely on such income in applying for credit.)

RENT ☐ **FIRST MORTGAGEE OR LANDLORD:**   Name _____

OWN HOME ☐ _____ Address _____
          ACCOUNT NUMBER

| Monthly Payment $ ____ | Value of Real Estate $ ____ | Purchase Price $ ____ | Current Balance $ ____ | 2nd Mortgage Payment $ ____ | Current Balance $ ____ |

DEPOSIT ACCOUNTS   Institution   Location   Account Number   Balance

Checking Account _____

Savings Account _____

Money Market Fund _____

Other _____

OPEN LOANS / GUARANTEES / AND OTHER FIXED MONTHLY OBLIGATIONS (Including Alimony or Child Support Payments)   Attach separate sheet if needed.

Creditor	Branch	Contact Officer	Purpose	Account No.	Orig. Amt.	Unpaid Bal.	Mo. Payt.
			AUTO				

Are you a guarantor or co-signer on any other loan? Yes ☐ No ☐   Have you ever filed for bankruptcy or reorganization? Yes ☐ No ☐

NOTICE: Any financial institution or finance company to which Applicant or Co-Applicant (or Seller or Broker on behalf of Applicant or Co-Applicant) may apply for financing on the Boat described in Section B is hereby authorized to investigate the credit history and capacity of Applicant or Co-Applicant. Any proposed creditor may request a consumer report concerning the Applicant or Co-Applicant in connection with this credit application or any future credit update or renewal. The Applicant and/or Co-Applicant may ask whether the creditor obtained such a consumer report. If such a report has been obtained, the Applicant and/or Co-Applicant may request the name and address of the consumer reporting agency which provided the consumer report to the creditor.

_____   _____   _____   _____
SIGNATURE OF APPLICANT   DATE   SIGNATURE OF CO-APPLICANT   DATE

COMPLETE ALL SECTIONS OF THIS APPLICATION WHICH APPLY TO YOU

BOAT DATA

New ☐ Used ☐ Manufacturer _____ Year_____ Model_____ Length _____

If Used, How Documented? Federal ☐ State Title ☐ Foreign ☐ Homeport _____ Official Number or State I.D. # _____

Hull: Wood ☐ Fiberglass ☐ Metal ☐ Engine Manuf. _____ Diesel ☐ Gas ☐ Single ☐ Twin ☐ _____ H.P./Eng.

Selling Price $ _____ Cash Down Payment $ _____ Trade-In $ _____ Amount to Finance $ _____ Years: _____

Trade-In Description _____
        YEAR   MANUFACTURER   MODEL   ENGINE(S)

Anchorage: Summer _____ Winter _____

Purchased From _____
     SELLER'S NAME   ADDRESS   PHONE NO.

Purchased Through _____
     BROKER'S NAME   ADDRESS   PHONE NO.

Use: Owner Pleasure Use ☐ Live Aboard ☐ Full-time Charter ☐ Part-time Charter ☐ Other ☐ _____
(Attach all available information and forms of contract for any independent charter management plans for boat.)

Where Boat Can Be Inspected _____ Phone No. _____

Yacht Insurance _____
     AGENT OR BROKER   PHONE NO.

_____
     CARRIER (IF KNOWN)   POLICY NO.

Name (s) In Which Boat Will Be Owned _____

In about a week, follow up on the telephone with the key loan officer. Discuss your letter and application with him, and ask if he needs any further information. Supply the data requested as soon as possible, and work closely with him until he has a firm grasp of your financial situation. If possible, go visit for a one on one discussion. His opinion of you may go a long way toward minimizing the risk factor in his mind. Don't leave questions unanswered or anything to chance. If you don't, your loan request will most likely be quickly approved.

Substantiating details are essential to those who review your application for the financial decision makers. Such details include statements of your net worth, cash flow, and tax status. The following describes how to collect the information needed to make your financial statements clear and accurate.

Establishing your net worth

To find out what you are worth, all you need to do is list and sum your assets (what you own) and liabilities (what you owe), and then find the difference between them. The result is your net worth, a key indicator of your financial well-being.

Whenever you fill out an application for loans such as home mortgages and large personal loans, including marine financing, you have to detail your assets and liabilities. In order to prepare for such requests, you need to gather all the data now, and prepare an initial personal financial statement. Allow yourself ample time to complete this work, and in that way you will not overlook some important item.

Determining your assets - These are items you own. If you own your own home, it is probably your largest asset. An estimate of its value can be based on the prices of similar homes in your area that have sold recently. Appraisers or real estate agencies can be helpful in providing these estimates. Don't confuse the asset value of your home with the amount of equity in it. Home equity is the result of subtracting any loans on the house from your estimated value of the home. In effect, home equity is a component of your net worth, which is discussed below.

The market value of each automobile and boat you own is determined in a similar way. Look up the resale price of the boat or car in one of the standard industry references (such as the NADA Guide or BUC's Guide to Used Boats), and add these figures to your asset base.

Any business you own has an asset value equal to your percentage ownership of the business' net worth. How much is that net worth? Conservatively, it is the book value of the company's shareholder equity. More aggressively, it is whatever amount for which you think the business could be sold.

Other assets may include monies in the bank or in money market accounts; stocks, bonds, or commodities; real estate (in addition to your home); mortgages owned; notes receivable; tangible investments, such as art or coin collections; and the cash surrender value of life insurance policies. This information is usually contained within the monthly statements provided by each agency servicing your various savings and investment accounts.

At this point, you must identify which assets are the most liquid, i.e., which ones can be quickly converted to cash for a downpayment on a boat. Obviously, the most liquid asset is cash. Next to cash in liquidity are commodity contracts, stocks and mutual funds. Real estate, mortgages, and some bonds are among the most illiquid. While converting assets to cash, strike a balance between giving up a profitable investment and missing a good financial deal on the boat of your dreams.

Since you don't want to short change yourself be sure that you have a reasonable cushion of liquid assets remaining after you pay the upfront monies. In addition to the downpayment there may be loan origination, attorney, and documentation fees, and prepaid interest (points). Points are usually quoted as a number such as "three points". This is equal to 3% of your loan balance.

Preliminary planning such as this is necessary to guarantee that you can pay the initial costs. Your ability to do this within your own resources is important to finance companies. If you need a loan to finance your downpayment, you may disqualify yourself for a loan to finance the balance of the purchase price.

Determining your liabilities - Personal loans, mortgages and outstanding balances on revolving charge accounts or credit cards are liabilities. The loans used to finance the acquisition of the houses, cars and boats you listed as assets are also liabilities, as well as are any refinances of those loans. To find specific loan balances you can contact the holder of your home mortgage, equity loan, car or boat loan and get a current payoff. This will be approximately equal to the current principal debt. An easier, though less accurate, method is to simply construct your own amortization schedule and look at the current payoff value for the number of months you have had the debt.

Other liabilities include broker margin accounts, loans against life insurance policies, and taxes. Contingent liabilities such as a personal loan guarantee for a friend also are important to bankers. Although these do not need to be noted as liabilities on the financial statement, they should be at least footnoted.

Collecting this data may take you several weeks if you haven't done it for awhile. List and total your liabilities. Subtract them from your assets to find your net worth as in Exhibit 2-2.

This net worth tells you, in effect, what you would have left over if you liquidated everything and paid off all your creditors. Obviously, this would not occur in any but the most extreme of situations. Nevertheless, it does indicate the cushion you can fall back on if events having a negative impact do occur.

Exhibit 2-2

Net Worth Report

Assets

Liquid

Checking	$ 1,500.00
Money market fund	5,280.00
Insurance cash value	2,700.00
Securities	
Stocks	15,450.00
Options	10,500.00
Mutual funds	4,350.00

Illiquid

IRA	16,750.00
Real estate	255,250.00
Vehicles	20,375.00
Furnishings	45,000.00
Other assets	1,500.00
Total Assets	**$378,655.00**

Liabilities

Home mortgage	$125,000.00
Personal loan	4,500.00
Car loan	12,575.00
Revolving charges	775.00
Total Liabilities	**$142,850.00**

Net Worth

Assets	$378,655.00
Liabilities	$142,850.00
Total Net Worth	**$235,805.00**

Does your cash flow?

Getting a loan approved and deciding how to make your downpayment is just the beginning. Your finances must also allow you to pay for maintenance, insurance, marina fees, fuel, and other use costs. If you have only $10 left at month's end, you're not going to enjoy boating, and neither will your family. Sooner or later you'll be forced to give it up, so let's figure out how to prevent this from happening. A realistic cash flow plan will do the trick.

A cash flow plan differs from a net worth statement. The latter deals with assets and liabilities while income and expenses make up the cash flow picture. All you need to do is list and total your sources of income, and then subtract your total expenses from them in order to determine your net savings or borrowings.

Cash flow plans may be either annual (Exhibit 2-3a) or monthly (Exhibit 2-3b). The former is more general and lets you see at a glance your major expenditures. It also gives you a starting point for determining how much boat you can afford. The monthly cash flow plan, on the other hand, gives you month by month details on which expenses you can reduce so that you can set aside enough discretionary cash for the boat payments and upkeep. The monthly plan is more controllable and lets you more finely adjust your cash flow according to how you use and maintain your boat.

Exhibit 2-3a

Annual Income And Expenses Before Buying A Boat

Sources of Income	Annual	% Total Income
Salary	$45,000	82.2%
Dividends		
Investments	2,000	3.7%
Other	940	1.7%
Interest		
Savings accounts	500	.9%
Bonds, taxable	750	1.3%
Other	850	1.6%
Capital gains (losses)	4,700	8.6%
TOTAL ANNUAL INCOME	**$54,740**	**100%**

Annual expenditures

Fixed

	Annual	%
Housing (mortgage or rent)	$12,000	21.9%
Utilities and telephone	2,500	4.5%
Food	5,400	9.9%
Clothing and cleaning	600	1.1%
Federal income tax	4,700	8.6%
State income tax	1,700	3.1%
Social security	3,600	6.6%
Property taxes	1,500	2.7%
Transportation	1,200	2.2%
Medical/dental/prescription	2,300	4.2%
Debt repayment	2,000	3.6%
Housing supplies/maintenance.	1,500	2.7%
Life insurance	1,200	2.2%
Property and liability insurance	1,480	2.7%
TOTAL FIXED EXPENDITURES	**$41,680**	**76%**

(continued on next page)

Exhibit 2-3a (continued)

Discretionary

Vacations, travel, etc.	1,200	2.2%
Recreation/entertainment	800	1.5%
Charity	750	1.4%
Household furnishings	800	1.5%
Educational expenses	1,000	1.8%
Investments - stocks	2.000	3.7%
Investments - bonds	1,500	2.8%
Retirement fund - IRA	2,250	4.1%
Other: Boat loan payments	0	0%
Boat upkeep	0	0%
TOTAL DISCRETIONARY EXPENDITURES	**$10,300**	**19%**
TOTAL EXPENDITURES	**$51,980**	**95%**
NET SAVED (BORROWED)	**$2,760**	**5%**

Exhibit Assumptions:

This exhibit assumes that the 1988 tax tables are used with four exemptions, married, filing jointly with deductions itemized. A flat 3.1% state income tax is used.

Exhibit 2-3b

Monthly Income And Expenses Before Buying A Boat

	JANUARY	FEBRUARY	MARCH	APRIL	MAY	JUNE	J
Open balance	1,500.00	1,802.51	2,085.02	2,747.53	1,650.04	2,902.55	3,48
Salary	3,750.00	3,750.00	3,750.00	3,750.00	3,750.00	3,750.00	3,75
Dividends	0.00	0.00	735.00	0.00	0.00	735.00	
Interest	175.00	175.00	175.00	175.00	175.00	175.00	17
Capital gains	1,000.00	300.00	0.00	1,500.00	950.00	0.00	
Total Cash	**6,425.00**	**6,027.51**	**6,745.02**	**8,172.53**	**6,252.04**	**7,262.55**	**7,41**
Food	450.00	450.00	450.00	450.00	450.00	450.00	45
Clothing	50.00	50.00	50.00	50.00	50.00	50.00	5
Mortgage	1,000.00	1,000.00	1,000.00	1,000.00	1,000.00	1,000.00	1,00
Utilities	208.33	208.33	208.33	208.33	208.33	208.33	20
Maintenance	125.00	125.00	125.00	125.00	125.00	125.00	12
Home furnishings	66.67	66.67	66.67	66.67	66.67	66.67	6
Car fuel	60.00	60.00	60.00	60.00	60.00	60.00	6
Car repair	0.00	220.00	0.00	150.00	0.00	0.00	
Charity	62.50	62.50	62.50	62.50	62.50	62.50	6
Vacations	0.00	100.00	0.00	0.00	0.00	0.00	80
Recreation	60.00	60.00	60.00	60.00	60.00	140.00	6
Total Living	**2,082.50**	**2,402.50**	**2,082.50**	**2,232.50**	**2,082.50**	**2,162.50**	**2,88**
Life insurance	100.00	100.00	100.00	100.00	100.00	100.00	10
Home insurance	43.33	43.33	43.33	43.33	43.33	43.33	4
Car insurance	80.00	80.00	80.00	80.00	80.00	80.00	8
Total Insurance	**223.33**	**223.33**	**223.33**	**223.33**	**223.33**	**223.33**	**22**
IRA	**0.00**	**0.00**	**0.00**	**2,250.00**	**0.00**	**0.00**	
Medical expenses	36.00	36.00	36.00	36.00	36.00	36.00	3
Dental expenses	140.00	140.00	140.00	140.00	140.00	140.00	14
Prescriptions	15.67	15.67	15.67	15.67	15.67	15.67	1
Total Health	**191.67**	**191.67**	**191.67**	**191.67**	**191.67**	**191.67**	**19**
Investment - stocks	500.00	0.00	0.00	500.00	0.00	0.00	50
Investment - bonds	0.00	0.00	375.00	0.00	0.00	375.00	
Education expense	500.00	0.00	0.00	0.00	0.00	0.00	
Loan payment	166.67	166.67	166.67	166.67	166.67	166.67	16
Total Financial	**1,166.67**	**166.67**	**541.67**	**666.67**	**166.67**	**541.67**	**66**
State income tax	141.66	141.66	141.66	141.66	141.66	141.66	14
Federal income tax	391.66	391.66	391.66	391.66	391.66	391.66	39
FICA	300.00	300.00	300.00	300.00	300.00	300.00	300
Property tax	125.00	125.00	125.00	125.00	125.00	125.00	12
Total Tax	**958.32**	**958.32**	**958.32**	**958.32**	**958.32**	**958.32**	**95**
Total uses	**4,622.49**	**3,942.49**	**3,997.49**	**6,522.49**	**3,622.49**	**4,077.49**	**4,92**
Residual Cash	**1,802.51**	**2,085.02**	**2,747.53**	**1,650.04**	**2,902.55**	**3,485.06**	**2,48**

Exhibit 2-3b (cont.)

Monthly Income And Expenses Before Buying A Boat

GUST	SEPTEMBER	OCTOBER	NOVEMBER	DECEMBER	TOTAL	SECTION %	TOTAL %
487.57	3,630.12	3,792.63	3,595.18	3,897.69			
750.00	3,750.00	3,750.00	3,750.00	3,750.00	45,000.00	82.81	
0.00	735.00	0.00	0.00	735.00	2,940.00	5.37	
175.00	175.00	175.00	175.00	175.00	2,100.00	3.84	
950.00	0.00	0.00	0.00	0.00	4,700.00	8.59	
362.57	8,290.12	7,717.63	7,520.18	8,557.69	54,740.00	100.00	
450.00	450.00	450.00	450.00	450.00	5,400.00	20.19	
50.00	50.00	50.00	50.00	50.00	600.00	2.24	
000.00	1,000.00	1,000.00	1,000.00	1,000.00	12,000.00	44.86	
208.33	208.33	208.33	208.33	208.37	2,500.00	9.34	
125.00	125.00	125.00	125.00	125.00	1,500.00	5.61	
66.67	66.67	66.67	66.67	66.63	800.00	3.00	
60.00	60.00	60.00	60.00	60.00	720.00	2.70	
110.00	0.00	0.00	0.00	0.00	480.00	1.79	
62.50	62.50	62.50	62.50	62.50	750.00	3.80	
0.00	0.00	0.00	0.00	300.00	1,200.00	4.47	
60.00	60.00	60.00	60.00	60.00	800.00	3.00	
192.50	2,082.50	2,082.50	2,082.50	2,382.50	26,750.00	100.00	51.46
100.00	100.00	100.00	100.00	100.00	1,200.00	44.88	
43.33	43.33	43.33	43.33	43.37	520.00	19.40	
80.00	80.00	80.00	80.00	80.00	960.00	35.81	
223.33	223.33	223.33	223.33	223.37	2,680.00	100.00	5.16
0.00	0.00	0.00	0.00	0.00	2,250.00	100.00	4.34
36.00	36.00	36.00	36.00	36.00	432.00	18.78	
140.00	140.00	140.00	140.00	140.00	1,680.00	73.04	
15.63	15.67	15.67	15.67	15.67	188.00	8.17	
191.63	191.67	191.67	191.67	191.67	2,300.00	100.00	4.51
0.00	0.00	500.00	0.00	0.00	2,000.00	27.28	
0.00	375.00	0.00	0.00	375.00	1,500.00	18.18	
0.00	500.00	0.00	0.00	0.00	1,000.00	18.18	
166.67	166.67	166.63	166.67	166.67	2,000.00	36.36	
166.67	1,041.67	666.63	166.67	541.67	6,500.00	100.00	12.50
141.66	141.66	141.66	141.66	141.66	1,700.00	14.78	
391.66	391.66	391.66	391.66	391.66	4,700.00	40.86	
300.00	300.00	300.00	300.00	300.00	3,600.00	31.30	
125.00	125.00	125.00	125.00	125.00	1,500.00	13.06	
958.32	958.32	958.32	958.32	958.32	11,500.00	100.00	22.12
732.45	4,497.49	4,122.45	3,622.49	4,297.69	51,980.00		100.00
630.12	3,792.63	3,595.18	3,897.69	4,260.00	2,760.00	5.04	

If your salary or other income is seasonal or consists of periodic commissions, and if your boat expenses are seasonal, managing your monthly outlays becomes even more critical. If your income is out of phase with expenses, you need to anticipate this and figure out how to cover expenses. On the other hand, year round operation in southern climates will even out the periodic costs. And no matter where you live or how your cash flows, you must always consider unexpected repairs or expenses. The test of your cash flow plan will be in meeting the unexpected with little or no financial pain.

Finally, you need to look at the effect buying a boat will have on your annual Federal tax liability.

The effect of taxes on cash flow - The purpose of the following is to outline some key tax considerations of which you should be aware as you plan your cash flow. The comments should be checked with your tax advisor to ensure that you are in compliance with current Federal as well as state tax laws.

An important tax planning technique is to consider the after tax affect of your boat loan. If you are in the 28% tax bracket and you deduct interest payments from your adjusted gross income (assuming, of course, that you itemize deductions), the effect is to reduce interest cost by approximately 28%.

For instance, if you buy a boat and the loan amount is $22,000, the monthly payment is $250 (assume an 11% interest rate and 15 year term). The first year's interest which can be deducted is $2,390.00. The interest expense which you can claim on your tax return is $2,390.00. The resulting tax benefit is $669.20 (28% x $2,390.00).

This deduction assumes that your boat qualifies as a second residence, that is, it has sleeping space, a head and a galley. If you already are claiming a summer home as a second residence, the boat interest would be considered "personal interest" which is being phased out over the years 1987 to 1991.

Nevertheless, monthly cash flow can be increased somewhat due to tax deductions to partially cover the new boat loan cost. You can reduce from your paycheck your monthly Federal tax withholding by increasing the number of exemptions you have been claiming on a Form W-4 and submit this to your employer's payroll department. Your objective is to increase your monthly take-home pay by $55.77 ($669.20/12).

Whenever you increase your exemptions as a way to increase your take home pay, the IRS may ask for a justification. They do this by asking for a newly completed W-4 in order to substantiate your claim. On relatively low numbers of exemptions (up to ten) the W-4 suffices. A larger number will require advance permission from the IRS which may be difficult to obtain unless you paid little or no taxes in the prior year. Either way, it is prudent to keep the claimed exemptions reasonable so as not to cause problems with the IRS. They do have the authority to tell your payroll department that you are not allowed the extra exemptions. Careful planning, however, will help you avoid such difficulties.

Determining what you can afford - After listing and adding up your income and expenses, check the results. Is there sufficient margin to cover your expected monthly boat expenses? If not, can you reduce any fixed or discretionary expenses that are particularly high, combine some, and/or eliminate others? Out of this should come enough discretionary income to make loan payments and handle operating and maintenance expenses. You may want to include a 5-10% safety buffer between your projected monthly boat costs and other living expenses to cover contingencies. This way, you can get a new propeller for the boat and new brakes for the car without too much strain.

After evaluating all your income and expenses, the next step is to determine how much you can afford to pay for a boat. Exhibit 2-4 shows how to assess your income and expenses, rearrange your priorities, and decide how much you can afford to spend for your boat, and identify those funds in a specific category on your income and expense plan, based on Exhibit 2-3a.

Exhibit 2-4

Reductions in Selected Expenses

(1) Potential annual reductions in current expenses:

    (i)   Repay debt without penalty to save $2,000 per year in fixed expense.

    (ii)   Reduce other discretionary expenses to yield further savings.

Vacations and travel	$ 600/year
Recreation and entertainment	300/year
Investments - stocks	1,700/year
Investments - bonds	1,300/year
Total	$3,900/year

(2) The result of taking these two steps is to increase your net savings from 5% to 7%.

Sources of Income		Annual	% Total Income
Salary		$45,000	82.2%
Dividends			
	Investments	2,000	3.7%
	Other	940	1.7%
Interest			
	Savings accounts	500	.9%
	Bonds, taxable	750	1.3%
	Other	850	1.6%
Capital gains (losses)		4,700	8.6%
TOTAL ANNUAL INCOME		**$54,740**	**100%**

(continued on next page)

Exhibit 2-4 (continued)

Annual expenditures	Annual	% Total Income
Fixed		
Housing (mortgage or rent)	$12,000	21.9%
Utilities and telephone	2,500	4.5%
Food	5,400	9.8%
Clothing and cleaning	600	1.1%
Federal income tax	4,700	8.6%
State income tax	1,700	3.1%
Social security	3,600	6.6%
Property taxes	1,500	2.7%
Transportation	1,200	2.2%
Medical/dental/prescription	2,300	4.2%
Debt repayment	0	0%
Housing supplies and maintenance	1,500	2.7%
Life insurance	1,200	2.2%
Property and liability insurance	1,480	2.7%
TOTAL FIXED EXPENDITURES	**$39,680**	**72.3%**
Discretionary		
Vacations, travel, etc.	$ 600	1.1%
Recreation/entertainment	500	.9%
Charity	750	1.4%
Household furnishings	800	1.5%
Educational expenses	1,000	1.8%
Investments - stocks	300	.5%
Investments - bonds	200	.4%
Retirement fund - IRA	2,250	4.1%
Other: Boat loan payments	0	0%
Boat upkeep	0	0%
TOTAL DISCRETIONARY EXPENDITURES	**$ 6,400**	**11.7%**
TOTAL EXPENDITURES	**$46,080**	**84%**
NET SAVED (BORROWED)	**$ 8,660**	**16%**

(3) Total net savings are now $8,660. This is adequate to cover $7,500 per year for buying and owning a boat, and still retain 2% net savings as a buffer against unexpected costs.

(continued on next page)

Exhibit 2-4 (continued)

(4) Assume the ratio of loan payments to upkeep is 2:3 (refer to Table 2-3). This splits the allocated $7,500 annual boat costs into $3,000 for loan payments and $4,500 for upkeep.

(5) Assume for a new boat loan that the downpayment is 20%, the term is 15 years and an interest rate equal to 11%.

(6) If the loan payment is $3,000/year, then the monthly payment is $250 and the loan balance is computed to be $22,000 (you can use a handheld calculator with financial functions to make this computation or use payment tables located in Appendix D).

(7) A 20% downpayment ($5,500) means that the purchase price of the boat is $27,500.

(8) From Table 2-1, $27,500 is assumed to purchase a 25 foot powerboat or a 27 foot sailboat.

Table 2-1

Boat Sizes And Price Ranges

Size (feet)	Powerboats Price Range	Size (feet)	Sailboats Price Range
19-22	$7,800 to $27,800	19-24	$7,750 to $6,900
22-24	$14,800 to $35,700	24-28	$14,000 to $29,800
24-26	$16,800 to $42,000	28-32	$32,000 to $61,000
26-30	$20,700 to $72,000	32-36	$32,900 to $85,000
30-35	$22,500 to $112,000	36-40	$73,900 to $56,000
35-40	$78,500 to $243,000	40-50	$89,900 to $200,000
40-50	$100,000 to $411,000	50-76	$150,000 to $825,000
50-90	$189,500 to $1,000,000+		

Courtesy of Motor Boating & Sailing.

These size/price ranges are dependent upon the type of vessel, its accommodations, equipment, design, builder and construction to name only a few of many variables upon which a selling price is determined.

In the previous analysis, the determination of your monthly boat mortgage payment was made by assuming arbitrary loan terms. By selectively choosing the loan terms most advantageous to you, it is possible for you to buy a larger or more fully equipped boat. Such fine tuning of your financial plan is necessary in order to get the most from your boat dollar. In the next section, you will discover the variables that have the greatest effect on mortgage payments.

The effect of loan terms on cash flow

Numerous loan terms are generally available from marine bankers and it is best to understand your options early. You should evaluate different terms so as to understand their effect on your cash flow for the boat you have selected. If you have been assuming that you only qualify for a ten year note, calculate the change in monthly payments on a fifteen year term. Does this produce a more affordable boat by reducing your monthly payments? How about changing the interest rate, the downpayment or the type of loan? There are a number of different combinations that can reduce monthly outlays including new types of mortgages.

As a general rule, consider the loan terms and conditions as changeable. Establish the terms you can live with and explain them to the loan company when you apply. Most boat mortgages have fixed terms ranging from ten to fifteen years but some banks will allow for payment over twenty years. Downpayments typically range from 20-25% and interest rates may be at or near the prime rate. Ask for a change if none of these terms are to your liking.

Of all the variables, loan terms have the greatest influence on your payments. The longer the term, the lower the payments by a significant amount. Table 2-2 shows the result of changing loan parameters.

Table 2-2

Changing Loan Factors

| | ——————— Type Boat ——————— | | | |
	A	B	C	D
Cost of Boat	**$10,000**	**$18,800**	**$33,500**	**$53,500**
Basic Assumptions:				
Loan term	10 years	10 years	10 years	10 years
Down payment %	20%	20%	20%	20%
Down payment $	$2,000	$3,760	$6,700	$10,700
Amount financed	$8,000	$15,040	$26,800	$42,800
Simple interest rate	14%	14%	14%	14%
Monthly payments	$124.24	$233.53	$416.11	$664.54

Alternative 1: Change term from 10 to 15 years

Cost of Boat	**$10,000**	**$18,800**	**$33,500**	**$53,500**
Basic Assumptions:				
Loan term	15 years	15 years	15 years	15 years
Down payment %	20%	20%	20%	20%
Down payment $	$2,000	$3,760	$6,700	$10,700
Amount financed	$8,000	$15,040	$26,800	$42,800
Simple interest rate	14%	14%	14%	14%
Monthly payments	$106.54	$200.29	$356.91	$570.00

Decrease in monthly payments = 14%

(continued on next page)

Table 2-2 (continued)

Alternative 2: Change down payment from 20% to 25%

Cost of Boat	$10,000	$18,800	$33,500	$53,500
Basic Assumptions:				
Loan term	10 years	10 years	10 years	10 years
Down payment %	25%	25%	25%	25%
Down payment $	$2,500	$4,700	$8,750	$13,325
Amount financed	$7,500	$14,100	$25,125	$40,125
Simple interest rate	14%	14%	14%	14%
Monthly payments	$116.45	$218.93	$390.11	$623.01

Decrease in monthly payments = 6%

Alternative 3: Change simple interest rate from 14% to 12.5%

Cost of Boat	$10,000	$18,800	$33,500	$53,500
Basic Assumptions:				
Loan term	10 years	10 years	10 years	10 years
Down payment %	20%	20%	20%	20%
Down payment $	$2,000	$3,760	$6,700	$10,700
Amount financed	$8,000	$15,040	$26,800	$42,800
Simple interest rate	12.5%	12.5%	12.5%	12.5%
Monthly payments	$117.10	$220.15	$392.29	$626.49

Decrease in monthly payments = 5.7%

Alternative 4: Change simple interest rate from 14% to 12.5%, term from 10 to 15 years and downpayment from 20% to 25%.

Cost of Boat	$10,000	$18,800	$33,500	$53,500
Basic Assumptions:				
Loan term	15 years	15 years	15 years	15 years
Down payment %	25%	25%	25%	25%
Down payment $	$2,500	$4,700	$8,750	$13,325
Amount financed	$7,500	$14,100	$25,125	$40,125
Simple interest rates	12.5%	12.5%	12.5%	12.5%
Monthly payments	$92.44	$174.24	$309.67	$494.55

Decrease in monthly payments = 34.4%

Long Range Planning

Exhibit 2-5 is your new annual income and expense plan that shows the effect of boat payments and upkeep. While it is important to understand your current cash flow status when you first purchase a new boat, it is just as important to be able to project your cash flow over the next several years so that your boat remains affordable. Financial projections are not easy even for experts in the field, but with common sense you can assume reasonable projection percentages.

Exhibit 2-5

Cash Flow After Buying Boat

Sources of Income		Annual	% Total Income
Salary		$45,000	82.2%
Dividends			
	Investments	2,000	3.7%
	Other	940	1.7%
Interest			
	Savings accounts	500	.9%
	Bonds, taxable	750	1.3%
	Other	850	1.6%
Capital gains (losses)		4,700	8.6%
TOTAL ANNUAL INCOME		**$54,740**	**100%**

Annual expenditures

Fixed	Annual	% Total Income
Housing (mortgage or rent)	$12,000	21.9%
Utilities and telephone	2,500	4.5%
Food	5,400	9.8%
Clothing and cleaning	600	1.1%
Federal income tax	4,700	8.6%
State income tax	1,700	3.1%
Social security	3,600	6.6%
Property taxes	1,500	2.7%
Transportation	1,200	2.2%
Medical/dental/prescription	2,300	4.2%
Debt repayment	0	0%
Housing supplies/maintenance	1,500	2.7%
Life insurance	1,200	2.2%
Property and liability insurance	1,480	2.7%
TOTAL FIXED EXPENDITURES	**$39,680**	**72.3%**

(continued on next page)

Exhibit 2-5 (continued)

Discretionary	Annual	%Total Income
Vacations, travel, etc.	$ 600	1.1%
Recreation/entertainment	500	.9%
Charity	750	1.4%
Household furnishings	800	1.5%
Educational expenses	1,000	1.8%
Investments - stocks	300	.5%
Investments - bonds	200	.4%
Retirement fund - IRA	2,250	4.2%
Other: Boat loan payments	3,000	5.6%
Boat upkeep	4,500	8.3%
TOTAL DISCRETIONARY EXPENDITURES	$13,900	25.7%
TOTAL EXPENDITURES	$53,580	98%
NET SAVED (BORROWED)	$ 1,160	2%

Exhibit 2-6 is a five year projection of the current year cash flow plan. It assumes that your total income increases 5.2% per year and that the total expenditures increase 4.4% per year. The cash flow projection shows that it is possible to afford a more expensive boat in the fourth year.

Exhibit 2-6

Long Range Cash Flow - I

SOURCES OF INCOME	Assumed Annual Increase	1st	2nd	3rd	4th	5th
Salary	(+5%/yr)	$45,000	$47,250	$49,613	$52,093	$54,698
Dividends						
Investments	(+5%/yr)	2,000	2,100	2,205	2,315	2,431
Other	(+3%/yr)	940	968	997	1,027	1,058
Interest						
Savings	(+4%/yr)	500	520	541	562	585
Bonds	(+6%/yr)	750	795	843	893	947
Other	(+2%/yr)	850	867	884	902	920
Capital gains	(+8%/yr)	4,700	5,076	5,482	5,921	6,394
TOTAL ANNUAL INCREASE	(+5.2%/yr)	$54,740	$57,576	$60,565	$63,714	$67,033

(continued on next page)

45

Exhibit 2-6 (continued)

ANNUAL EXPENDITURES	Assumed Annual Increase	1st	2nd	Years 3rd	4th	5th
FIXED:						
Housing	(+3%/yr)	$12,000	$12,360	$12,731	$13,113	$13,506
Utilities and telephone	(+3%/yr)	2,500	2,575	2,652	2,732	2,834
Food	(+6%/yr)	5,400	5,724	6,067	6,431	6,817
Clothing and clean	(+8%/yr)	600	648	700	756	816
Federal income tax	(+5.2%/yr)	4,700	4,944	5,202	5,472	5,757
State income tax	(+5.2%/yr)	1,700	1,788	1,881	1,979	2,082
Social security	(+3%/yr)	3,600	3,708	3,819	3,934	4,052
Property taxes	(+5%/yr)	1,500	1,575	1,654	1,736	1,823
Transportation	(+8%/yr)	1,200	1,320	14,52	1,597	1,757
Medical and dental, etc.	(+6%/yr)	2,300	2,438	2,584	2,739	2,904
Supplies and maintenance	(+4%/yr)	1,500	1,560	1,622	1,687	1,755
Life insurance	(+2%/yr)	1,200	1,224	1,248	1,273	1,299
Property and liability insurance	(+3%/yr)	1,480	1,524	1,570	1,617	1,666
TOTAL FIXED EXPENDITURES	(+4.4%/yr)	**$34,680**	**$41,389**	**$43,184**	**$45,068**	**$47,068**
DISCRETIONARY:						
Vacations, travel	(+10%/yr)	$600	$660	$726	$799	$878
Recreation/entertainment	(+5%/yr)	500	525	551	579	608
Charity	(+5%/yr)	1,000	1,050	1,103	1,158	1,216
Household furnishings	(+3.4%/yr)	800	827	855	884	914
Educational expenses	(+7%/yr)	1,000	1,070	1,145	1,225	1,311
Investments - stocks	(+15%/yr)	300	345	397	456	525
Investments - bonds	(+10%/yr)	200	220	242	266	293
Retirement fund	(+0%/yr)	2,250	2,250	2,250	2,250	2,250
Boat loan payment	(+20% 4th yr)	3,000	3,000	3,000	**3,600**	3,600
Boat upkeep	(+4%/yr) (+20% 4th yr)	4,500	4,680	4,867	5,841	6,074
TOTAL DISCRETIONARY EXPENDITURES	(+4%/yr)	**$13,900**	**$14,365**	**$14,860**	**$16,768**	**$17,669**
TOTAL EXPENDITURES	(+4.4%/yr)	**$53,580**	**$55,754**	**$58,044**	**$61,836**	**$62,977**
NET SAVED (BORROWED)		**$1,160**	**$1,822**	**$2,521**	**$1,878**	**$2,296**
PERCENT OF INCOME		**2%**	**3%**	**4%**	**3%**	**3%**

The timing of your cash flow as shown in Exhibit 2-6 depends on numerous assumptions you must make about your future income and projected expenses. Answers to the following questions are implicit in your assumptions.

▶ How much will your income grow each year?

▶ Can non-boat expenses be controlled to allow net savings to increase?

▶ Are interest rates expected to be higher or lower four years from now?

▶ Will your future income (from all sources) cover your future costs?

▶ How much risk is involved if you buy the boat now and count on future incomes to cover future expenses?

▶ Will tax brackets be different in four years?

▶ How much will your boating needs change?

The problem you have to solve is how to buy the boat you really want without getting yourself into a financial strait jacket in the future. According to industry sources, the average owner keeps his boat for only 39 months. This is why the boat related expenses were increased in the fourth year in Exhibit 2-6, that is, to assume a trade up to a bigger boat. Shown below are the computations assuming you trade in your first boat on the second one in the beginning of the fourth year. The 20% increase in loan payments equates to a $31,450 boat purchase price. Consider the following:

▶ Loan payments are assumed to increase by 20% ($3600/year = $300/month).

▶ The terms of a new loan are an 11% interest rate and 15 year term. Based on these factors, the new loan principle is $26,400.

▶ Assume that the first boat is traded for the second vessel, and that the trade-in price is $25,000. No downpayment is required.

▶ Your equity in the first boat, $5,050, is the difference of the trade-in price ($25,000) and the mortgage payoff amount ($19,950) at the end of the third year.

▶ The new loan principal plus your equity in the first boat lets you purchase a new boat for up to $31,450.

▶ The new purchase price covers powerboats to 28 foot or sailboats to 30 feet. Both are a move up in size compared to the first boat.

As this analysis shows, boats can be affordable once you understand the financial elements as well as your own financial status. As long as you don't overburden yourself with boat payments you can start off with a boat that meets your family's needs and within a few years move up to a larger vessel as your finances change.

Exhibit 2-7 illustrates a case in which you chose to spend 43% more in the fourth year for boat payments and upkeep. Your net savings are reduced to 0% in the fourth year. This change means you are allocating an additional $3,383 per year for payments and upkeep. Calculations based on the previous assumptions yield a new boat purchase price of $36,550. This equates to a 30 foot powerboat and a 32 foot sailboat.

Exhibit 2-7

Long Range Cash Flow - II

SOURCES OF INCOME	Assumed Annual Increase	1st	2nd	Years 3rd	4th	5th
Salary	(+5%/yr)	$45,000	$47,250	$49,613	$52,093	$54,698
Dividends						
Investments	(+5%/yr)	2,000	2,100	2,205	2,315	2,431
Other	(+3%/yr)	940	968	997	1,027	1,058
Interest						
Savings	(+4%/yr)	500	520	541	562	585
Bonds	(+6%/yr)	750	795	843	893	947
Other	(+2%/yr)	850	867	884	902	920
Capital gains	(+8%/yr)	4,700	5,076	5,482	5,921	6,394
TOTAL ANNUAL INCREASE	(+5.2%/yr)	$54,740	$57,576	$60,565	$63,714	$67,033
ANNUAL EXPENDITURES						
FIXED:						
Housing	(+3%/yr)	$12,000	$12,360	$12,731	$13,113	$13,506
Utilities and telephone	(+3%/yr)	2,500	2,575	2,652	2,732	2,834
Food	(+6%/yr)	5,400	5,724	6,067	6,431	6,817
Clothing and clean	(+8%/yr)	600	648	700	756	816
Federal income tax	(+5.2%/yr)	4,700	4,944	5,202	5,472	5,757
State income tax	(+5.2%/yr)	1,700	1,788	1,881	1,979	2,082
Social security	(+3%/yr)	3,600	3,708	3,819	3,934	4,052
Property taxes	(+5%/yr)	1,500	1,575	1,654	1,736	1,823
Transportation	(+8%/yr)	1,200	1,320	14,52	1,597	1,757
Medical/dental, etc.	(+6%/yr)	2,300	2,438	2,584	2,739	2,904
Supplies and maintenance	(+4%/yr)	1,500	1,560	1,622	1,687	1,755
Life insurance	(+2%/yr)	1,200	1,224	1,248	1,273	1,299
Property and liability insurance	(+3%/yr)	1,480	1,524	1,570	1,617	1,666
TOTAL FIXED EXPENDITURES	(+4.4%/yr)	$39,680	$41,389	$43,184	$45,068	$47,068
DISCRETIONARY:						
Vacations, travel	(+10%/yr)	$600	$660	$726	$799	$878
Recreation/entertainment	(+5%/yr)	500	525	551	579	608
Charity	(+5%/yr)	750	788	827	868	912
Household furnishings	(+3.4%/yr)	800	827	855	884	914
Educational expenses	(+7%/yr)	1,000	1,070	1,145	1,225	1,311

(continued on next page)

Exhibit 2-7 (continued)

DISCRETIONARY:	Assumed Annual Increase	1st	2nd	3rd	4th	5th
Investments - stocks	(+15%/yr)	300	345	397	456	525
Investments - bonds	(+10%/yr)	200	220	242	266	293
Retirement fund	(+0%/yr)	2,250	2,250	2,250	2,250	2,250
Boat loan payment	(+20% 4th yr)	3,000	3,000	3,000	4,408	4,408
Boat upkeep	(+4%/yr) (+20% 4th yr)	4,500	4,680	4,867	6,960	7,238
TOTAL DISCRETIONARY EXPENDITURES	(+4%/yr)	$13,900	$14,365	$14,860	$18,578	$19,337
TOTAL EXPENDITURES	(+4.4%/yr)	$53,580	$55,754	$58,044	$63,645	$66,233
NET SAVED (BORROWED)		$1,160	$1,822	$2,521	$68	$1,010
PERCENT OF INCOME		2%	3%	4%	0%	2%

These computations were completed using a personal computer and an electronic spreadsheet program. The results have been rounded to zero decimal places. If a computer is available either at home or work, you can set up your own annual or monthly cash flow statements as well as five year projections. It also will be worth the effort to use the computer and electronic spreadsheet to prepare your financial statements. However, a pencil, paper, and desktop calculator work ok, too — it just takes longer.

After comparing your cash flow picture with the preceding exhibits you have to be firm and ask yourself, "can I still afford my dream boat?" If not, why not? Can your financial parameters be changed? For example, sell the Cadillac and keep the Chevy (create more liquid assets), pay off an existing loan to improve cash flow (decrease liabilities), or receive a bonus earlier this year (increase income).

Determining Ownership Costs

In order to minimize the unexpected, your ownership costs other than financing must be controlled. This means you need a clear view of these costs. Slip fees, maintenance and repairs, operational costs, insurance, and additional equipment to upgrade your boat are the major items.

The amount of money a boat owner spends on his boat annually is dependent upon a lot of factors — type and construction of his boat, who does the work, how and where the boat is used, the age and condition of the boat, and her size and complexity. Obviously, a small, fiberglass boat maintained by the owner, used in fresh water and stored on land between uses probably means the lowest cost annual upkeep. Conversely, a forty-five foot, turbo-charged, twin gas engined sport fisherman operating in Florida waters, used weekly and maintained by a premium boat yard is going to cost a bundle to keep up and running. Somewhere in between these two extremes is an "average" boat and its associated costs. In order to more clearly understand what costs one can reasonably expect, two boats are compared. One is a 28 foot cruising sailboat, and the other a twin engined, 28 foot sport fisherman. Exhibit 2-8 shows the basic assumptions about each boat, and Table 2-3 lists the estimated annual costs.

Exhibit 2-8

Annual Cost Assumptions

Powerboat

Chris Craft Commander Sport Fish;
twin 260 hp gas inboard engines
modified-V hull;
draft: 2'4"; length: 28'2", beam: 10'0"
displacement: 7,500 lbs.
base price/lb: $5.73
base price: $43,000

Sailboat

O'Day 28; diesel power, sloop rigged
length overall: 28'3"
length water line: 22'1"
beam: 10'3"; draft: 4'8"
displacement: 7,300 lbs.
ballast: 2,550 lbs.
sail area: 370 sq.ft
base price/lb: $4.74, auxiliary
base price: $34,600

Assumptions

▸ Both boats are fiberglass.

▸ Included in financing is the base price, 5% for equipment, and 4.4% sales tax.

▸ Fuel usage: power — 20 gph (100 hours/season)
 sail — 2 gph (30 hours/season, sailing other 70 hours)
 price per gallon — $1.50

▸ Dockage fees are for summer and include 110v AC electricity.

▸ Financing terms: 13% interest rate, 15 year term, 20% downpayment

▸ Transportation not included.

▸ Annual equipment upgrades: 3% original purchase price.

▸ Annual maintenance: 6% original purchase price.

▸ Winter storage on owner's cradle.

▸ Insurance includes hull coverage at purchase price and $300,000 liability.

▸ Assumes five month winter storage.

Table 2-3
Sample Annual Costs

	Sail	Power
Hull type	Displacement	Planing
Purchase price	$44,541.00	$51,626.00
Downpayment	$8,308.00	$10,325.00
Amount financed	$33,233.00	$41,301.00
Monthly payment	$420.47	$522.56
Annual payments	$5,046.00	$6,271.00
Insurance	$537.00	$570.00
Dockage (open slip and electicity)	$1,841.00	$1,841.00
Hauling/launching	$280.00	$280.00
Wash hull	$80.00	$80.00
Winterizing and summerizing: Remove/install frame and cover	$120.00	$120.00
Batteries/electronics, storage and service	$225.00	$225.00
Engine and transmission	$150.00	$175.00
Fresh water system	$75.00	$75.00
Other	$100.00	$100.00
Maintenance and repairs	$2,672.00	$3,000.00
Equipment (new/replace)	$1,336.00	$1,500.00
Fuel	$69.00	$2,300.00
Sail repairs	$100.00	---
Taxes/fees	$25.00	$25.00
Annual operation and maintenance expenses	$12,656.00	$16,562.00
Ratio of loan payments to total expenses	40%	38%

References for calculating annual charges:
1. BOATING COST GUIDE, Godfrey, Robert Sturgis, Ed-in-Ch., Robert Snow Means Company, Inc., Kingston, MA, 1984
2. PRACTICAL BOAT BUYING, ed. Practical Sailor, Englander Communications, Inc., Riverside, CT 1984

In Table 2-3, the financing charges account for almost 40% of the total annual charges, or a 2:3 ratio. This means that two dollars out of every five spent on the boat go into the payments. Another way to look at this ratio is to say that for every dollar of loan payment, you will have to spend another $1.50 just to cover the other costs of ownership.

Areas where you can cut costs lie in maintenance and repairs (perform most of the work yourself), equipment (don't buy as much), and dockage (use a mooring and save $6 to $12 a foot per month). You can save a little more by do-it-yourself winterizing and summerizing along with installing and removing your own frames and covers. This sort of work may save you between 15% and 20% of your annual costs.

Good Relations With Your Yard Man

Your relations with your yard man may largely determine how much you can save on annual storage and maintenance costs. Knowing in advance what you expect them to do as well as your contractual arrangements with them should help divert future problems.

Much like setting up a good relationship with an auto mechanic, family doctor or dentist, or searching for a CPA, your boat needs a boat yard that you can trust and in which you have confidence. Carefully selecting one will provide you the most satisfaction. Unlike an auto mechanic, the yard owners, managers and technicians have a much greater responsibility for the well-being of your expensive possession. Not only do they make your boat better when she's sick, but they give her a home (sometimes with a roof over her head) and treat her with TLC in your absence. At least that is what we hope they do.

Services and facilities

Your best source of information about boatyards is word-of-mouth. Most yard customers are vocal about their experiences at a particular yard, and will share with you their opinion of the yard. The range of services performed by the yard, the advertising it does, its cleanliness and the experience of the owners are all ways to judge the quality of one yard from another. Once you select the yard, the next step is to contract with them for the services you expect. Well equipped boatyards can handle a variety of tasks, such as engine work, rigging and sails, carpentry, fiberglass repair, propeller reconditioning, painting and canvas work. Provisions for storing your boat can either be made on land or in the water with a bubbler system to prevent ice formation around the hull.

Beyond this, a ship's store, grocery and tackle shop are convenient. The more glamorous marinas may have swimming pools, tennis courts, barbeques and similar recreational facilities for their owner's enjoyment. Dock parties are a lot of fun and provide a good chance to mix with the other owners for a good time. The business end of the marina and boatyard operation, however, is specified by a contract between you and the yard. It's a good idea to be sure you understand this contract so you won't be surprised when you receive your next bill. This could throw cold water all over your party.

Contracts

The operations of boatyards are regulated by maritime and state laws, and the primary purpose of the contract is to protect the boatyard. The exposure that a yard has to accidents, lawsuits and bad feelings between yard operator and boat owners is compounded by the wide variation in the people who own boats. There are the inexperienced and old salt, young and old, starry eyed and wisened, honest and questionable, and so forth. Contracts spell out the obvious particularly for those who aren't sure why they bought the boat in the first place. Lastly, boatyards intend to be profitable like other businesses and contracts keep the yard headed toward profitability.

Standard items like docking equipment are specified so that the boats are secure in their slips and are protected from abrasion by fenders. Restrictions governing fuel tanks are largely specified by the yard's insurance policy. Similarly, accidents with ladders, scaffolding, ramps and the use of other equipment which can result in injury are covered by contract disclaimers.

Responsibility for damage that is not caused by the yard is the owner's responsibility. For example, if the boat is damaged when it is being hauled, moved, or worked on, then the responsibility is with the yard. Wind, storm or damage caused by the wrath of Mother Nature is the responsibility of the owner. Water damage caused by improperly serviced through-hull fittings which was done by the yard is their concern. The yard must make good the damage up to certain limits. In this case, it is assumed that some sort of written arrangement was made with the yard to accomplish the work if it is not specifically contained in the base contract. In the case where a boat was hauled in preparation for winterization that had not been completed, and was damaged by a freak freeze in September, then the yard could claim that this occurred as an Act of God. Such a freeze in November could not be construed as such since this would be normal in many northern areas. The yard should have been prepared for it, especially if the owner had previously contracted for winterizing. As a result, many yards include an insurance factor in their winterizing rates to provide a buffer against such a liability.

Fees

Most boatyards have set fees for routine service items like winterizing and summerizing engines, heads, and water systems, stepping and unstepping masts and storing spars, removing batteries, erecting frames and covering, supplying cradles, setting up bubbler systems, etc. Many such fees are flat and others are based on the length of the boat. Surprise bills can be avoided by getting a copy of the rate sheet and understanding exactly what is to be done to your boat. Payment is often "net 30 days" and is subject to a carrying charge or interest if not paid by that date. Charges from yard to yard vary, too. Some include in the contract hauling, washing, storage, and launching. Sanding and bottom painting also may be specified as contract work. Some yards may only include hauling and launching, and charge separately for all the other work. There may be an opportunity for some owners to perform their own maintenance depending on how rigid the terms of the contract. It pays to become familiar with the ins and outs of the formal arrangement that you have with the yard both in money and frustration. In this way, the dock parties will be all that more fun.

Ensuring Success

Before visiting a lender, there are three items that you should consider to increase your chances of success with the lender. These last steps involve comparing your financial picture to that which the lender will view. The three key criteria by which your finances are viewed by the lender are the Three C's of Credit — capacity, credit and collateral.

Capacity is regarded as your ability to comfortably repay the boat loan along with all your other debts and expenses. This requires an assessment of your debt to income (D/I) ratio. If the summation of all your debt is less than 40% of your total income generally this is an acceptable standard by which you are judged. Percentages between forty and fifty are marginal and greater than fifty percent is usually unacceptable unless there is some sort of specific justification for such a high debt to income ratio. Review your cash flow charts to determine your D/I ratio. If you find it may be approaching 40% or is even beyond that threshold make adjustments to your financial plan or prepare adequate justification for the higher D/I ratio level. This work will help to ensure that you clear the first credit hurdle, capacity.

The second hurdle is *Credit*. Do you have a satisfactory rating as reported by a national credit rating firm? While there is little you can do to alter your past credit history you may wish to contact the rating firms for a credit report so as to determine that it properly reflects your history, and to prepare answers to questions it might raise in the boat financier's mind. Generally, a credit report is not an absolute determinent of your loan acceptability. Instead, it serves as a weighting factor in a series of judgements. The credit history points to trends in your ability to qualify for credit and handle loan payments. A recent trend that is favorable is more beneficial to you than one that is headed downward.

Collateral is the third key credit decision component. It is defined as the security pledged for a boat loan. Your boat will be the security that permits the lender to recoup his loan plus accrued interest and expenses in the event that you are no longer able to make payments due to such unforeseen circumstances as a job loss or your inability to work. In such cases the lender may legally repossess the boat and pay off all debts and other costs once the boat is eventually resold.

Lenders expect the boat to cover about 70 to 80 percent of the original purchase price. As you would expect, a new boat has a better collateral value than a used one. Restored wooden character boats may sell at a premium price but have less collateral value to the lender. A resale after repossession may not net enough to cover the outstanding loan and expenses because such boats are not only hard to sell but their beauty is often only in the eye of the beholder. For these reasons, it is difficult to borrow on such boats.

If you can prepare yourself for questions on capacity, credit, and collateral before you visit the lender, you will have a much better chance to close the deal in your favor. Not only that, but such preparation will permit you to more effectively communicate your financial position to the lender. This will save time and effort for both of you. In Chapter 3, we looked more closely at qualifying for credit from a lender's viewpoint.

Twelve Steps To An Affordable Boat

1. Outline your boating objectives.

2. Decide on the type and design of boat to meet these objectives (use Appendix A).

3. Prepare your initial financial statements:
   A. Net worth   (Exhibit 2-2)
      (1) Assets
      (2) Liabilities
   B. Cash flow
      (1) Annual   (Exhibit 2-3a)
      (2) Monthly (Exhibit 2-3b)

4. Determine what you can afford:
   A. Initial costs
      (1) Downpayment (10%, 15%, 20%?)
      (2) Closing costs (estimate by lender)
      (3) Insurance premium (estimate by agent)
      (4) Boat equipment (estimate for pleasure or charter)
   B. Periodic outlays
      (1) Estimate total annual costs and divide into monthly or other periodic outlay
      (2) Assume loan payments are 40% of the total annual costs when determining your maximum affordable outlay

5. Choose a range of boats that are within an affordable range (Table 2-1).

6. Choose loan terms that allows for your maximum affordable payment (Table 2-2).

7. Select a lender:
   A. Prepare the financial sales plan
   B. Prequalify yourself for a loan
   C. Compare your plan with the Three C's of Credit

8. Select a dealer/broker and builder.

9. Negotiate the sale price, terms and conditions with the dealer/broker.

10. Make final loan arrangements with the lender.

11. Choose a settlement date and finalize the sale.

12. Select a marina/boat yard in your boating area.

CHAPTER 3

QUALIFYING FOR CREDIT: The Lender's View

Before you can be confidently armed with the knowledge that the particular loan program you're going to select is just right, you must apply for and gain a loan approval. Sound easy? It is, if you do it right. Most people underestimate their borrowing power as often as they overestimate the difficulty in achieving it. As a result they settle for less boat than they want or apply to a dozen lenders hoping to get a "yes". What a waste of time! Instead, by following a few simple rules you'll be able to view yourself as the average lender does, finding out just how much money you're good for and how to get it quickly and efficiently, usually at the first lender you approach.

In Chapter 2, we looked at all the elements needed to develop your financial sales plan. Here, we put them together in a way that makes it easy for you to borrow money.

The Lender's Job

Two functions characterize every lender's job: First, they must make loans. Second, they must make **good** loans. Almost always these two duties are in conflict, creating a tension lenders live with constantly. The conflict is caused by the need to book lots of loans — without them most financial institutions couldn't justify their existence — when the competition for these loans is fierce; deregulation has seen to that.

At the same time, the loans acquired must be good, in terms of the way they perform once they've had a chance to sit on the books for awhile. Profit margins on loans are very small. It's one example of a business where you truly do "make it up in volume". A lot of unexpected loan losses can put a bank out of business very fast.

The key to applying successfully for a loan lies in eliminating this tension for the lender. Demonstrate the loan will be a good one and keep reminding the bank the business is theirs for the asking. Provide the information asked for and any attendant explanations you feel might be helpful. In many cases, your yacht purchase could represent the largest personal debt you've taken on to date. Treat it with concern; give it a high priority. Credit granting is ultimately a subjective process especially in the larger dollar ranges. You won't always agree with what a lender says. Nevertheless, pay that subjectivity some respect because even though you may feel your lender is not the smartest man or woman alive, he or she does, for the moment, have the money.

Avoid shopping your loan application around too much if you can. We'll give you a technique for gaining approval, 90% of the time, at the **one** bank you apply at. Select your lender by both the program that fits and in accordance with some of the subjective criteria pointed out in the next two chapters, then stick with that lender unless and until you have a good reason to switch. The method by which credit bureaus report inquiries lets every lender running a credit report know where you have applied in the last year or so. If you show a half dozen inquiry entries, you may arouse suspicion or at the very least make it look like you're out to waste somebody's time.

Above all remember once again, Credit Is Subjective. None of what follows is an inviolable rule. Lenders set their own policy and, if they choose, are free to break that policy. The decision makers are ordinary people like you and me, and they must occasionally make close calls on tough loans. Their attitude is important and, consequently, so is yours. If you approach your lender with optimism, confidence, and reasonableness, you stand your best chance.

The Three Cs of Credit

As we touched on in the previous chapter, there's an old rule of thumb regarding credit that somebody years ago decided to coin as the "three Cs of credit". Each "C" stands for one aspect of a credit profile that every lender supposedly evaluates. (Since that time the number has grown to four Cs, and now maybe five. We'll keep it simple and stick to three.)

Capacity

The first C, capacity, refers to an individual's ability to pay back the requested loan along with all other existing loans and normally recurring expenses. In other words, the capacity to comfortably repay. The concept should concern the borrower as well as the lender. What fun is a boat if you have to sacrifice necessities to own it? A lender thinks in a similar fashion.

Capacity analysis requires evaluating your incoming cash flow set off against your current debt service and fixed expenditures, including the requested boat loan. A ratio is obtained (by simple division) that indicates the percentage of your cash flow that is necessary to make required payments.

For example, if your cash flow is determined to be $4,000/month and you have a home mortgage of $500, a car loan of $250 and you wish to buy a boat requiring debt service of $750/month, your (simplified) debt to income (D/I) ratio would be ($500 + $250 + $750) ÷ $4000 or 37.5%. Which is to say that just over a third of your available monthly funds are earmarked for fixed expenditures. What about the rest? The lender assumes it goes towards living expenses, state and federal taxes, savings, whatever.

This is a simple example but it demonstrates the basics. At this juncture, lenders start to diverge on certain points such as:

What constitutes a fixed expenditure? - Some will add an estimate for monthly boat expenses such as insurance, slip fees, haul outs, maintenance and so forth. The amount attributable to boat expenses may range from 3% to 10% of the vessel cost, per year, depending on a lender's beliefs about boat ownership. Generally, their figure will underestimate acutal costs, which were explored in detail in Chapter 2. If the boat is used as a liveaboard, some lenders will add an imputed figure for land based residence under the assumption that certain events can easily force the liveaboard to leave the water. Finally, certain miscellaneous expenditures may be included such as alimony or child support, required payments to a partnership, and lease payments.

What constitutes cash flow? - No uniform answer here, either. The methods of calculating cash flow are as numerous as lenders out there calculating. A very elementary approach is to simply set cash flow equal to income. For a salaried individual with no tax shelter, outside income, or other significant financial dealings, this estimate for actual cash flow is very accurate. Boat buyers generally present a more complex financial profile and it would usually be to their great disadvantage to have a simple income analysis performed.

For this reason most lenders rely on an examination of tax returns (you will invariably be asked for them when applying) to determine cash flow. Tax returns tend to present all the data necessary to work backwards into a fairly accurate cash flow picture. Perhaps you report a very small figure as taxable income on your form 1040. But your lender will notice, for example, the heavy depreciation on Schedule E (Supplemental Income Schedule) or perhaps the pension plan accrual on the form 1120S (Sub-Chapter S Corporation Income Tax return) and perhaps allow a portion of both to be added back to improve the income picture.

Offer to point out other non-cash deductions and losses. If you are self-employed, you will want to indicate which of your business expenses are also supporting part of your personal expenses, such as automobiles or travel and entertainment. Just don't overdo it. It's not enough to say "My company pays for everything" and expect to get approved. Get your CPA involved if you don't feel up to explaining all the intricate tax work for which you paid so much. The objective is to present documented evidence that you possess a reasonable debt to cash flow ratio.

Generally, the more sophisticated the lender (in terms of programs offered, choice of rates, etc.) the more sophisticated their cash flow analysis. For the big boat buyer, the self-employed or the owner of a closely held company, such a lender provides a real advantage.

What is an acceptable debt ratio? - In this area we find a little more uniformity, although since the answers to the first two questions above can be so disparate, one wonders just how similar those D/I ratios **really** are. At any rate, the high end acceptable range for a debt to income ratio with boat lenders seems to be 40%-50% for those evaluating the figure before income taxes, and up to 60% for those including taxes as a fixed expenditure. Below 40% and you won't get called out for debt service capacity. Above 50% or 60% and you should have a good reason ready, although it is still **very** possible to qualify at even higher levels. If you question this keep in mind that yacht lenders seem less structured on this point than real estate lenders, from where you may be drawing your experience. Most real estate lenders try to make credit decisions in conformity with the requirements of the big secondary buyers like the FNMA. Yacht lenders are more used to the high leverage situations frequently encountered with big boat buyers. Also, as personal income grows, discretionary spending usually does not grow proportionatly. So with a very large income, a higher D/I can be comfortably managed.

The work sheet below provides the means to do your own debt and income itemization producing a final D/I ratio that will provide a fairly accurate indication of the maximum loan for which you might qualify. Again, use this only as a guide. Each lender evaluates these figures differently.

Exhibit 3-1

Debt To Income Worksheet

Adjusted Gross Income from 1040 (line 31 in 1988)	_____	Home Mortgage (Including taxes, insurance, homeowners fees)	_____

*Add Back:

Non-cash Deductions Schedule C,E,F depreciation Amortization, depreciation, non-cash accruals on form 1120 and 1065	+_____ +_____	Installment Debt e.g. auto, home improvement	+_____
		Other Term Debt e.g. unsecured loans, partnership debt	+_____
Non-recurring Losses and Expenses Schedule D losses Schedule C,E expenses, improvements	+_____ +_____	Revolving Credit e.g. credit cards, credit lines (use 5% of balance as monthly payment)	+_____
Contribution to IRA or Keogh Other	+_____ +_____	Other Fixed Obligations e.g. child support, alimony	+_____

Deduct:

Non-recurring Gains Schedule D gains Sale of residence gain	−_____ −_____	Boat Payment (monthly)	+_____
		Boat Expense (monthly)	+_____
Interest income on withdrawn funds (such as for vessel downpayments)	−_____		
Other	−_____		

TOTAL CASH FLOW	_____	TOTAL DEBT	_____

$$\frac{\text{TOTAL DEBT}}{\text{TOTAL CASH FLOW}} = \text{DEBT TO INCOME RATIO (D/I)}$$

* Note: Other sources, less commonly noted, may also be included. For example, pension plan contributions from owners of closely held corporations; bad debt accruals and write-offs; goodwill and start-up cost amortizations.

Credit

The second C, credit, means different things to different people. Lenders generally regard it as a combination of the applicant's actual credit history along with a very subjective evaluation of the applicant's character.

The credit record itself is fairly objective. It consists of a report listed by one or more of about five national credit reporting agencies around the country[1]. There is nothing mysterious about a credit agency. For a fee, they provide subscribers (usually banks, finance companies, loan brokers, etc.) with a detailed, computer tracked history of most of an individual's credit record for the past several years as reported by thousands of banks, finance companies and other lenders who input to the system.

Most matters pertaining to the reporting of credit are regulated by a law known as the Fair Credit Reporting Act. Even so, the system is less than perfect. Some lenders don't bother reporting at all. Others make mistakes. At the end of the chapter, we'll look at what to do in the event you feel you've been treated unfairly; for now let's stay with the lender's evaluation of the report.

The credit report lists many transactions from credit card usage to major mortgage and installment loans. Inquiries are also listed so a lender can see how many times, and to whom, you have applied for credit in the past year.

After each entry, a brief history lists account numbers, high credit extended, amounts outstanding and, of course, the number of times the account was late (ranked by 30, 60, or 90 + days) and any sums presently considered past due. In addition, any charge-offs (where the bank wrote off unpaid debt) are recorded. There is usually a section to record tax liens, court judgments, bankruptcies and so forth. But because public record information is researched and included in the report by the agency itself, it may not appear on two competing agency reports servicing the same area. In fact, since few credit agencies are considered strong in all geographic areas, two reports may contain quite different levels of detail.

By law, adverse information is reportable no more than seven years prior to the current date, except bankruptcies, which may go back ten years. Technically, this law does not apply to credit transactions over $50,000; since the credit agency does not know how much a lender is considering in an application, they stick to the seven and ten year rules.

Once the report is obtained, and depending on the size of the credit request or policies of the institution, further verbal or written inquiries will be made to institutions holding deposit and credit accounts of the applicant. The final result is a fairly detailed and accurate picture of the historic borrowing practices for a given applicant. And again, while mistakes are possible, once the full investigation is completed you'll have a hard time convincing the lender there's been a total error if you don't like what comes up. If you suspect you might have a problem, however, take the time to obtain your **own** report in advance. It's fairly easy and any credit bureau is required to do it for you upon demand free of charge if you have been turned down for credit, and about $10 otherwise.

How does a lender use the report? Generally as a negative decision maker. If it looks real bad, you'll probably be turned down, or at least be required to work through a lender specializing in applicants with derogatory credit, usually at a much higher interest rate. If it's spotless, you won't get a lot of extra credit. After all, once you borrow money you're supposed to pay it back in accordance with terms. It is better, of course, to have a steady history of good credit transactions rather than a very few but in general a myth has been popularized that you can't borrow money "without credit". If you have only one or two borrowing relationships, having instead preferred to pay cash for your major purchases, and now want to try for a large yacht loan, explain your conservative borrowing habits to the lender. He'll probably try to talk you into a bigger loan.

Since the credit report and subsequent investigation is also used to develop a more comprehensive picture of your fixed expenses for purposes of the debt analysis, be upfront about those debts. Not listing a debt on the credit application does not mean it won't be found. And if a lender thinks you might be trying to hide something, you might as well forget it and withdraw the application.

Collateral

Our third C, collateral, refers to the very point of this whole endeavor — the boat. Because yacht lending is secured lending, the role of your boat, the collateral, becomes very important.

Your boat will be evaluated in terms of its perceived value with respect to the loan amount. A secured creditor wants to feel confident that, in the unlikely event a default and repossession occurs, enough value exists in the vessel to recover the debt balance outstanding plus accrued interest, expenses, legal fees and numerous other costs.

This helps to also explain why capacity is so important. Many borrowers are confused when lenders look so deeply into their financial situation. They ask in amazement, "Why do you need this? You've got the boat!" The answer is simple. No boat ever made a loan payment and invariably upon repossessing, a lender will lose **some** money, if only in the form of their own valuable time and effort.

The amount borrowed against the vessel as a percentage of the purchase price is often referred to as the "Loan to Value", or LTV, ratio. Most banks and finance companies specializing in marine lending like to maintain this ratio in the 70%-80% range, although as we'll see later, under certain conditions, they may extend 90% or even 100% financing. New boats command the higher LTVs with used vessels coming in at an average 5% less at a given institution. Thus, if one lender has an 80% LTV for new boats chances are the used boat guideline is 75%[2].

New boat collateral value - For new boats the numbers are fairly straight forward. A purchase agreement is presented that indicates the base price, options prices, and certain related costs such as tax, freight and commissioning. Most lenders will allow tax to be included in the purchase price, many exclude commissioning, and freight is a toss up. Obviously, the more items you can get included in the definition of purchase price, the more money you can borrow given a fixed LTV approval. Avoid building up the invoice with equipment "orders" you intend to cancel just before closing; it is extremely irritating to lenders and can easily lead to a declared default of your loan agreement if you are discovered. While some unscrupulous dealers may suggest it to you as a way of getting into a bigger boat for which you haven't got the down payment, it will get you into **very hot** water with most lenders.

Since the markup on new boats varies widely, especially on some of the more recently introduced foreign produced hulls, you may find more lenders applying different LTVs to different makes. If you think their evaluation is unfair, go to the resale market and see what the boat's price performance is over the years. Maybe it **has** depreciated rapidly because of that markup. You might want to consider whether you are paying too much.

Used boat collateral value - Much more difficult to evaluate are used boat values. The purchase price is the best indicator, a point that seems to escape a lot of lenders. They often choose instead to rely on a national price guide known as the BUC International Corporation Used Boat Price Guide, or more commonly, the BUC book. Discrepancies abound because the guide, useful as it is, cannot possibly account for every selling situation nor can it recognize sudden or regional shifts in vessel popularity, model shortages or surpluses, and other factors. As the guide itself says in the introduction,

> "Depreciation of boats also depends on current economic conditions...
> so that depreciation patterns and rates will undoubtedly fluctuate
> almost monthly... Obviously prices of reported boats reflect myriad
> variations due to its location, condition and the amount of optional
> equipment and accessories found on the boat"[3].

Nevertheless, since so many lenders rely on it, should you encounter a major discrepancy, ask your broker why and make sure he is able to explain it to the lender.

Quite often lenders will solicit the opinion of local yacht brokers, especially if they have an existing business relationship with several in the area. Examining current listings for sisterships and similar models is also helpful. In order to bolster your contention that the price you are paying is justified, or conversely that you got a real deal and a higher LTV is called for, put together your own vessel market research package and give it to the bank. After all, you probably went to the trouble to make the analysis anyway. Demonstrate to the lender what a smart shopper you are; it inspires confidence.

This last point about obtaining higher LTVs deserves more attention. Often a boat buyer feels that because of the circumstance of the purchase he or she should qualify for a lower down payment. Perhaps the boat was purchased in distress at a below market price. Maybe you bought a new boat from a friend in the boat business at "dealer cost". Whatever the reason, additional equity exists by virtue of the cost versus market value. But if you ask your lender to waive the down payment requirement, chances are you'll still get a flat no. Creditors like to see a buyer's own hard-earned dollars put into the purchase. They feel, probably with some justification, that it makes it less tempting to walk away from the yacht should a serious problem occur. "Cash means commitment" is the saying bankers like.

Age of the vessel - If you decide to purchase an older vessel, your choice of lenders may become very limited. Quite a few have restrictions on the maximum age of a boat they are willing to finance. Ten to fifteen or twenty years seems to be the cutoff if an age restriction applies. In some cases, you might find a marine lender willing to finance older boats but only at rates considerably higher than normal[4].

This also introduces the role of the survey in the lender evaluation. While you certainly have your own good reasons to request a survey, the lender will almost certainly ask for one also, especially if the boat you plan buying is more than a couple of years old. Policy on the kind of survey required will vary. If the vessel is more than five years old with no previous survey you can bet she'll have to be hauled and carefully looked over. Avoid cutting corners here; most lenders have a good idea of what to look for in a survey and can tell if a so-so job was performed. Their examination of a survey is geared toward 1) analyzing the general condition of the vessel so as to confirm their estimate of market value; 2) identifying structural and cosmetic defects needing repair or replacement prior to closing; and 3) confirming year, make, model, engines, equipment and so forth as stated on the listing and credit application. This last point is very important since so much of the value of a boat can be contained in relatively small components like engines or navigational equipment.

If in the end you don't feel you have received a satisfactory collateral evaluation and consequently are getting a lower LTV than you feel is fair, try asking your lender to come out and look at the boat first hand. While some marine bankers may not know port from starboard, you would be surprised how many, especially from the more established finance companies, are quite knowledgeable on boat valuation. Many are racing yachtsmen, cruising enthusiasts, or come from related fields such as chartering, brokerage and vessel documentation. As a boatman yourself, you should be able to tell after ten minutes of conversation with a lender whether or not he or she knows enough about boats to warrant a physical inspection that would promote your cause.

Construction material - Most boats today are built of fiberglass and related materials, which some say have a seemingly eternal life span. What about other materials a lender must consider in evaluating collateral? The most common are metal (usually steel or aluminum) and wood, with an occasional ferro-cement, or exotic material encountered. Lenders react in similar ways to these other materials. Metal is almost always accepted because it quite often is the material of choice on large ocean motor and sailing yachts which tend to be excellent values. And while you may get turned down for wanting to finance the conversion of a steel barge, it probably won't be for hull material alone.

Wood, on the other hand, causes a much different reaction in lenders. Some have very firm policies against financing wood boats. Often times they are at a loss to explain their policy; perhaps borrowed "wisdom" from another lender's manual. However, wood boats do require substantially greater time and money to maintain than glass boats and are subject to more rapid deterioration. They also have a more limited resale market. This doesn't mean a wooden vessel will necessarily resell for less. Rather, there are simply fewer folks wanting to buy them. This last point matters a great deal to bankers that may someday need to sell a wood boat repossession.

If you are intent on buying a wood boat (and we can't blame you if you are) be aware that you **will** have a problem with financing (not to mention insuring) that friends with glass and metal hulls rarely encounter. The best way to approach the matter is to select a lender by that one criteria alone. Make the first question "Do you finance wood boats?" If you get a "Well, maybe" take that as a yes and be a good salesman on all other counts. The whole point to the "Three Cs" analysis is to score very high on two if you come out somewhat low on the third.

Other Components of Financial Strength

While these so called "three Cs" seem to play a big role in marine credit evaluation, other factors enter the analysis as well. Two very important ones are liquidity and asset/net worth position.

The role of liquidity

We have already examined in detail the concept and use of liquidity in financial planning and structuring your purchase. A banker's view is a bit different. To him, your liquidity is a cushion of cash to fall back on in hard times. Having excess funds to tide you over during a job change or a temporary layoff can mean keeping your boat when you might otherwise lose it. In the worst case, should you have to sell fast, you will find that a boat does not sell easily in a short period, at least not at a price that will likely settle 100% of your debt. While selling at a loss is certainly an unpleasant experience, excess cash can make up the difference and avoid an even worse collection experience with a lender.

Generally, your down payment will absorb a good portion of your liquidity unless a trade boat is involved. In addition to concrete evidence that enough cash on deposit exists to make the down payment, a lender wants to see something extra, although the amount will vary. How much? We know of no rule of thumb employed by lenders but six months worth of payments should be considered near minimum. For example, assume a $100,000 yacht loan at 12% for fifteen years. With a payment of $1,200 we produce a cash requirement, after down payment, of about seven thousand dollars. Sound like a lot in addition to the twenty or thirty put down? It's really not considering the income that someone borrowing $100,000 is likely to enjoy. Most lenders feel this kind of liquidity should be present for someone earning a large income while living within his or her means.

Should you have little cash left after planning your purchase, don't give up. A low debt to income ratio can provide an offset, as can a substantial net worth. If the latter, some lenders can make a 100% advance by further securing themselves with some of your more illiquid assets, thereby preserving your cash. These techniques and others are explored in Chapter 5.

Avoid borrowing money to inflate the appearance of liquidity. A credit investigation can usually identify the time a sum has been on deposit and tax returns do reflect income (or the lack of it) from liquidity. Finally, when you examine your own liquidity and report same to the lender, don't forget to point out certain semi-liquid assets such as IRAs and Keoghs, cash surrender value of life insurance, maybe even take-back mortgages that are marketable. Most lenders do not consider these amounts as immediately accessible liquidity but it does give a better appearance to your financial profile.

Asset/net worth profile

The related concepts of assets and net worth have already been covered in detail. Once again we wish to examine them with the eyes of a lender. While having a huge asset base can be attractive to a banker, it is somewhat less so if offset by an equal mountain of debt. In general, leverage can contribute a great deal to an individual's financial well being but it must rest on a solid net worth foundation.

The two key concepts in asset/net worth evaluation are diversification and growth/stability. Experience has shown that credit worthy individuals typically show a diversity of assets that have exhibited a steady growth over time. The more diversified a person's assets the less influenced that person is by single events affecting a particular group of assets. Show all assets, and include such company sponsored benefits as pension and savings plans, stock options and so forth. You can certainly include the standard "jewelry, household goods, etc." but if the figure appears inflated, it will generally be disregarded by the lender. As a very **general** rule of thumb, most lenders like to see a tangible net worth from 1.5 to two times (or better) the requested loan amount.

Growth/stability is a related concept that demonstrates an individual's willingness to save at a steady pace, which implies a certain amount of stability. Growing net worth through long term ownership of real estate, a residence in particular, is a classic example and one reason lenders like to see long residency periods.

Most bankers also like to see time on a job, or in an occupation. If you have made recent changes, you should let your lender know a little about your financial and employment history; by doing so you could turn a minus into a plus. For example, let's say you just bought a new business but haven't yet filed any tax returns on it. You might describe how you grew your first business from $100,000 in sales to over $3,000,000 before selling last year to buy the new one. Or maybe you've moved three times in five years and just took a new job. Not too promising? Depends how you put it. State that after successfully completing your third relocation in six years, you've landed in a house with over $75,000 in equity and a job that pays three times as much as your first. Presentation can be everything, and your first shot is always your best.

Putting Together A Successful Loan Package

Now comes the moment to tie these principles together. Although all the material in the preceding sections can benefit you even if you decide not to borrow, the point of this chapter is to get you approved for the amount and terms you desire. In order to do so, we'll look at each element of the loan package and point out ways to provide the best presentation.

The application

All lenders require you to complete an application before beginning any loan processing. Applications vary in shapes and sizes but generally ask for the same information. Filling out an application completely and carefully will save more time for you than any other single step in the process. The following deserve particular attention:

1) Provide loan and deposit account numbers, bank names and addresses with telephone numbers where possible. For large accounts, the name of your bank account officer is very helpful. Forget itemizing credit cards and personal loans to others. The former appear on a credit report, the latter are usually disregarded unless fully documented, and both will be noted on your financial statement.

2) Include all information asked about yourself, especially a social security number and home address, and on any co-applicant. Both are necessary to run the credit report.

3) If requested, boat information should be complete regardless of whether you include a purchase order in the loan package. Purchase contracts often don't contain the kind of information needed by lenders such as loan amount requested or trade boat information.

4) Sign the application and any loan information request forms included. While it is not technically illegal to conduct a credit investigation without your signature, few lenders like to do that.

The financial statement - Preparing a financial statement has been well covered in an earlier chapter. If you do it as we've described, your lender should have no problem. You might even discover together you're worth more than you thought. Make sure the statement is less than six months old and be sure to sign it before sending.

Income verification - More problems occur in this area than any other due to the somewhat tricky nature of verifying income. Most people are fairly sensitive about disclosing income especially if it means producing tax returns. Thus, the typical borrower tends to send as few documents as possible to gain approval. Invariably, they under estimate. Hopefully, with the income guidelines presented here, a prospective borrower will know how much income disclosure is necessary to get the nod.

If you are not averse to sending a mountain of documentation, then do so. Keep it organized by year and include a written itemization of what is enclosed. Remember, it is better to err on the side of excess. If you have enjoyed a significant increase in income since your last filed tax return, include also a current paystub to further boost your total income.

If you have other income not reflected on that pay stub, indicate so and provide documentation.

In some cases an individual may claim to make income "off the books" and wants it somehow used to bolster the income analysis. Rarely will lenders consider undocumentable income regardless of the amount. It sort of reflects the old adage that "you can't have your cake and eat it too." When some individuals, for personal reasons, choose not to report income accurately, they gain on the money side but usually lose on the credit side.

The purchase agreement - It's always helpful to send a copy of your purchase agreement, if available. Most lenders will require it as a condition of closing. Buying through a dealer or broker always entails signing some sort of purchase contract. Should you buy in a private sale you or your attorney will need to draw one up.

The cover letter

Here is your chance, maybe your one chance, to say whatever you feel will sell yourself or promote your cause. If you feel there is any question at all that might arise in the course of the evaluation, take the time necessary to adequately explain it. A few hours invested at this point can save you many more down the road.

If you are aware of a credit problem, now is the time to explain it. Your candor will be appreciated and helps to instill confidence. If some fact you wish to emphasize is not readily apparent from the paperwork you have supplied, such as an imminent raise or a yearly bonus, use the letter.

Always present an optimistic and confident attitude. Appear ready and able to make the purchase and take on the loan obligation. You may even want to include your own monthly cash flow and debt analysis to demonstrate that you have already budgeted for the purchase and feel it is within your means.

If you plan to charter, liveaboard, or use the vessel in any other way outside of "normal" usage, indicate so in the letter and explain why you have decided such. Your initial lender shop will have already pre-screened those that don't accept charters, liveaboards or other special conditions. Don't let this fact be hidden until the last minute. It could really put a damper on your closing.

Finally, offer to meet with your lender or supply additional information if requested. If your package was well prepared neither will be necessary. The gesture, however, connotes openness and fosters a better overall character rating on your part.

Below we've written a cover letter of the type just described. It's from a fictional applicant and is included only to give an indication of the kinds of things a cover letter can do. Style is entirely up to the individual but keep in mind: Optimism, Confidence.

Exhibit 3-2

Sample Cover Letter

Mr. John Jones
Loan Officer
First National Bank
Any City, USA

Dear Mr. Jones:

Please accept the enclosed loan application and related materials for consideration in my purchase of a 1978 Hinckley 43 Sloop. I believe the package to be complete, but should you need any additional material, do not hesitate to request it. I have enclosed the following:

1. Signed, completed personal credit application for myself and my wife.

2. Two years 1040 joint tax returns and current pay stub.

3. Two years 1120S tax returns on my corporation, XYZ, Inc.

4. Vessel purchase agreement.

5. Copy of a second mortgage note from Mr. and Mrs. John M. Smith arising from the recent sale of our residence.

I would like to point out the following regarding our income last year:

Our 1988 reported wages of $50,000 is approximately $10,000 less than my wife's current salary. She received a substantial increase in compensation at the end of the year, not fully reflected in that return. We have included a current pay stub to indicate that raise.

XYZ, Inc. is fully owned by myself and all of my income is received from it. The net income of the company as reported on Schedule E, Subchapter S Corporation, was only $2,000 but this figure significantly understates the cash flow available to me from the business' operations.

The 1120S return shows net revenues of $152,000 on sales of $1.2 million against which I deducted operating expenses of $78,000, depreciation of $22,000 and pension plan contributions of $50,000. Thus, estimated cash flow to me for the year is approximately $74,000. With my wife's current salary, we look to earn over $130,000 this year.

Our personal cash position is small, however, the attached schedule of deposits held by banks will verify my Corporation's cash position in excess of $50,000. We would like to retain as much of this cash as possible.

You will discover credit problems in 1982 resulting from effects of the recession on XYZ, Inc.'s business. Our credit profile is extremely important to us and all accounts have been current since 1983. The one charged off loan was paid in full with accrued interest in the same year.

We sold our residence of fourteen years in 1988 and took back a second mortgage for the equity of $175,000. A copy of the note is enclosed, and as you can see, provides payments of $2,000 per month to us. The note is amortized over fifteen years with a balloon payment in three years. We plan to live aboard the vessel but will be reserving sufficient funds should we decide to take up land based residence again.

The vessel we are purchasing is being bought from the Towne Bank, which repossessed it earlier this year. The purchase price is $125,000 which I believe represents a substantial discount from the market value. A recent survey is enclosed and indicates the boat to be in good condition. Sisterships and similar vessels in the area indicate a market value of between $160,000 and $180,000 as noted below:

Vessel	Listed Price	Selling Price
1979 Swan 43	$185,000	$160,000
1979 Hinckley 40	$175,000	not sold
1980 Hinckley 43	$205,000	$180,000

We wish to place $12,000, or approximately 10% of the purchase price down and borrow the remainder for a period of fifteen years at your current five year adjustable interest rate of 12%, to produce a payment of $1,356 per month. In addition, we anticipate monthly maintenance, slip and insurance expenditures of $650 to produce a total of $2,006. This is within our current budget and we feel you will concur.

Should you wish more information on either our credit package or the vessel, I invite the opportunity to meet with you at your office to further discuss our purchase.

Sincerely,

John Q. Borrower

While this letter may be a bit lengthy, the poor fellow did have a few problems. But they were problems of explanation mainly. The loan will probably be a good one.

One nice benefit of the loan packaging approach is the discipline it requires in determining what is realistic. In effect, you pre-qualify yourself with little doubt as to the outcome of the process. We said before this method gives high odds of getting approved. The reason is simple. Although most persons underestimate their borrowing power, the ones that get turned down most often are those that over estimate. Gaining the perspective of the lender allows you to determine what expectations are realistic, while learning to sell yourself brings them home.

What to do if you get turned down

No one likes to be refused credit and everyone feels lousy when it happens. If you've done everything right and really felt you were qualified, by all means go at it with another lender.

Other options are available. Sometimes a lender will allow you an approval at a lower amount on a smaller boat. Maybe a guarantor or co-applicant will help. But if you can see at the outset that your request has a high probability of failure, don't try to "wing it" figuring you'll cut back when turned down. Lenders are often notorious for refusing to change their minds under any terms once they have made a credit decision.

Your rights under Federal law - There are about a half dozen federal acts and Federal Trade Commission rules that regulate credit application, granting, reporting and collecting. Appendix C contains a brief listing of some of the key provisions. The most important are those that apply to a negative decision on your loan request.

Under Federal law, any "adverse action" (that is, a credit denial), must be sent in writing within thirty days of the decision and must contain:

1) a statement of the action taken;

2) the name and address of the creditor;

3) a statement of the anti-discrimination provisions of the Equal Credit Opportunity Act;

4) the name and address of the federal agency that administers compliance of the act for the creditor (which happens to be the Federal Trade Commission at 26 Federal Plaza, N.Y., N.Y.);

5) a statement of the specific reasons for the denial or a disclosure of your right to a statement of specific reasons within thirty days of a request. If any of the reasons had to do with a credit bureau report, the name, address and phone number of the agency providing the report must be given to you. From there, you may contact the agency for detail on the report.

Finally, if you gave it your best shot and really couldn't make it, perhaps you can find out about the impending turn down ahead of time and play for a withdrawal. This simply is a request on your part to withdraw your application to avoid having the credit denial become a part of your credit background for another lender to see another day.

---

(1) The major ones are TRW Information Services, Trans Union Credit Information Co., Associated Credit Services (Pinger), Chilton Credit Reporting System and Credit Bureau Inc.

(2) In apparent acknowledgment of the fact that new boats often depreciate faster than older boats in the first few years, many lenders now go 80% on new and used. In some cases these lenders will also add sales tax financing to the contract which effectively puts the borrower at 85% financing, since sales tax does not really add any value to a boat!

(3) BUC International Corporation Used Boat Price Guide, BUC Research, Ft. Lauderdale, FL 1985, pg. vi, viii

(4) You might be surprised how often a higher rate can get a lender to change their mind on a number of issues.

CHAPTER 4

CREDIT PLANS: Looking At The Numbers

Obviously not everyone buying a yacht will choose to finance it. Some buyers simply opt to pay cash for such purchases. We have tried to point out in Chapter 2 some very good reasons to finance a yacht even if you **can** afford to pay cash. But should you finally decide that the credit method is not for you, read on! Other interesting issues are presented alongside that can stimulate your thinking.

In this chapter we'll introduce a number of topics relating to credit plans currently available for yacht purchases. The information will get fairly technical but plenty of examples will be included to provide insight. You don't need to be a Harvard MBA to follow, but a good financial calculator will help.

Fixed Rate Lending

A near unlimited number of ways exist to lend money and get repaid (hopefully). Generally speaking, loans can be made at a fixed rate of interest (the cost of credit is known beforehand) or a variable rate of interest (the cost of credit is known only after the loan is fully paid and depends on changes in financial markets). In the latter case there are as many ways to make these loans as there are lenders to dream them up. On the fixed rate side, however, one method, simple interest, now predominates[1].

Simple interest

Most homeowners are familiar with simple interest lending; it's the traditional loan arrangement for most fixed rate home mortgages. The monthly payment is always calculated to provide for both (1) one month's interest earnings to the lender; and (2) regular principal repayment, known as "loan amortization", applied against the loan balance. Out of the monthly payment there will be a steadily increasing contribution to principal repayment and a steadily decreasing amount of interest paid to compensate the lender.

The Annual Percentage Rate (the APR) on a simple interest loan is constant, regardless of when you pay it off, so long as no points are charged (more on this later). Don't try to tie this rate in with the finance charge payable over the life of the loan through some tricky manipulation of rate, term, principal or whatever using simple arithmetic; it can't be done. Why? The simple interest name is a bit of a misnomer. The calculations involved all use compounding formulas. Without the use of an electronic calculator, or at the very least, a table listing rates, terms, etc. (which was prepared using some sort of electronic calculator) you won't be able to calculate an exact interest cost for your loan.

If you don't have an electronic calculator at hand and want to do a rough pencil sketch of your total interest cost, the table below will help:

Exhibit 4-1

Total Interest Cost for $1,000 Simple Interest Loan
(for other loan amounts, multiply by loan amount in thousands)

Annual Percentage Rate	Term in Years			
	10	12	15	20
8%	$455.93	$558.73	$720.17	$1,007.46
9%	520.11	638.76	825.68	1,159.34
10%	585.81	720.91	934.29	1,316.05
11%	653.00	805.12	1,045.87	1,477.25
12%	721.65	891.32	1,160.30	1,642.61
13%	791.73	979.46	1,277.44	1,811.78
14%	863.20	1,069.46	1,397.13	1,984.45

You can see from the shaded portion of the table what rate/term combinations produce interest charges that are greater than the amount borrowed. The total finance charge on a simple interest loan is useful to know for cost comparison purposes, although if the loan is paid early only a portion of the total charge will be paid.

Computing a payment is a little easier and can be obtained from the following formula (a calculator will make this one easier):

$$\text{payment} = \frac{PV}{\left[\dfrac{1-(1+i)^{-n}}{i}\right]}$$

where PV = the loan amount
  i = the interest rate
  n = the term in months

If you get this far, then the finance charge can be backed into using the formula:

$$(\text{payment} \times n) - PV = \text{finance charge}$$

This is still an approximate, and depends on whether your loan is a "per diem" type or "pre-computed".

Per diem interest - Loans that charge interest for the exact number of days between payments are known as per diem, or daily accural, loans.

The example below shows how a per diem simple interest loan payment is divided into principal and interest:

Exhibit 4-2

Principle = $100,000
Term = 15 Years
Rate = 12%

Payment = $1,200.17 (from tables)

Total Note = $1,200.17 x 180 = $216,030.60

1st Month Interest = 12% / 365 x 31 days x $100,000 = $1019.18

Principle Reduction = $1,200.17 – $1,019.18 = $180.99

Balance after 1st Month = $100,000 – $180.99 = $99,819.01

In this example we have assumed a payment of $1,200.17 on a $100,000, fifteen year loan. The interest rate is twelve percent, which gives a "per diem", or daily, rate of 12% / 365 days or .00032877. Let's say your first payment arrives at the bank exactly 31 days after you close the loan. Thirty-one "per diems" are deducted from your payment, or 31 x .00032877 x $100,000 = $1,019.18. The balance of your payment, $180.99, goes to reduce your loan to $99,819.01 and the next monthly interest charge is calculated using this new figure as the base.

Precomputed interest - Another simple interest system, known as "precomputed" simple interest, operates in almost the exact same way, but without regard to the payment receipt date. A precomputed and steadily decreasing interest charge is deducted from each payment; a late arriving payment requires a late charge to further compensate the lender. A precomputed simple interest loan will usually allow a grace period (typically fifteen days) before the late fee is assessed.

Pros and cons - What are the relative advantages and disadvantages of per diem and precomputed interest? The per diem format is generally the fairest in that interest is charged at the agreed rate for exactly the time a particular balance is outstanding. As this is the case, it becomes crucial to get payments in by the contractual due date. Late arriving payments have a greater amount of interest deducted; if the payment is sufficiently late, perhaps no principal will be credited resulting in a situation known as "interest short". Exhibit 4-2, above, has been modified slightly below to demonstrate this effect.

Exhibit 4-3

Principle = $100,000
Term = 15 Years
Rate = 12%
Payment = $1,200.17

1st Month Interest = 12% / 365 x 40 days x $100,000 = $1,315.07

Principle Reduction = $1,200.17 – $1,315.07 = –$114.90

Interest Short after 1st Payment = –$114.90

For those who tend to fudge it and drop their payment in the mail the day it is due at the bank, they may be surprised to find a smaller pay down of the loan than expected five years later when they attempt to retire the remaining balance. This situation does not occur on precomputed loans because a standard late fee is assessed which is either a percentage of the payment or a flat dollar amount depending on the type of loan contract used and the state where the transaction took place.

Per diem loans, may, however, allow for more flexibility in partial pay downs. Since payments are applied first to interest then to principal, a large payment will result in a large pay down of principal which reduces the future interest charges and thus allows the loan to pay off faster. A per diem loan might be attractive for an individual accustomed to receiving large yearly bonuses in lieu of substantial monthly income, or for a borrower who wants to double up on payments, or make biweekly installments to achieve the same effect.

Amortization schedules

Prior to establishing your loan, you may wish to ask for an "amortization schedule" that splits each monthly payment into interest and principal. The schedule is useful for tax planning and budgeting, not to mention keeping your lender honest. You can also run one yourself on a calculator or computer, or obtain it from a number of finance reference books. The following table is a partial amortization schedule for the simple interest loan above.

Exhibit 4-4

Principle = $100,000
Term = 15 Years
Rate = 12%
Payment = $1,200.17

Year	Interest	Principle	End of Year Payoff
1	$11,861	$2,539	$97,461
2	11,540	2,860	94,601
3	11,177	3,223	91,378
4	10,768	3,632	87,746
5	10.307	4,093	83,653
6-10	42,311	29,699	53,954
11-15	18,056	53,954	—0—

It is interesting to note that over 80% of the loan in this example pays back after the sixth year.

Fixed rate options

The mathematical uniqueness of simple interest lending allows for a great deal of variation and flexibility. As a result of increased competition, higher rates and greater lender willingness to truly accommodate the needs of borrowers, several new options have been made available in the last few years.

Term options - When marine lending first became a true specialty back in the early seventies, most yacht loans were written for an average seven to ten year term. As prices began to ratchet up, buyers and sellers demanded longer loans from bankers, and terms began to stretch, first to twelve years, then to fifteen and now out to twenty and in some cases thirty years!

Lengthening the term of a simple interest loan accomplishes several things. First, it tends to bring the payment down. As dollar requirements and interest rates have been driven up during periods of high inflation, term has often been the compensating agent. Yet there is limit to this as the example below demonstrates:

Exhibit 4-5

Loan Amount = $100,000

Rate = 12%	Term in Years			
	10	15	20	30
Payment	$1,434.71	$1,200.17	$1,101.09	$1,028.61

In the example, the difference between the first five years of additional term (from ten to fifteen) is $234.54/month, for the last ten years (from twenty to thirty) it is only $72.48/month. The limit to the decrease in payment is $1,000/month, which is interest only, and is computed by dividing the yearly rate by twelve and multiplying by the loan amount.

Extending the term also raises the relative interest component of each payment significantly, especially in the early years of the loan. Many borrowers view an extended term as an attractive way to develop additional tax deductions under the second home rule, reasoning that the money that is not being paid toward (nondeductible) principal can be better invested or spent elsewhere. They know that monthly loan amortization and monthly interest are inversely related to each other and directly related to the loan term. The following table illustrates:

Exhibit 4-6

Rate = 12%		Term in Years			
		10	15	20	30
% of payments in first year that go toward:	Interest	68%	82%	90%	97%
	Principle	32%	18%	10%	3%

From this example, we could assume an individual with a constant earnings stream in a high tax bracket might find attractive a twenty year extended term fixed rate loan. Such a loan provides payment certainty with high interest deductions relative to payment amount. In this case the interest write-off in the first 12 months is 90% of payments, as opposed to 82% for a conventional fifteen year loan. A thirty year amortization provides 97% payment deductibility in the same period. Of course, future tax law changes could eliminate this feature.

Long term financing can be a two edged sword however. The interest deduction feature so many desire can also be detrimental if the loan is written on a per diem basis (as are almost all twenty and thirty year loans). For the first several months payments are almost all interest so early payments that arrive even a few days late may not amortize any principal at all. When our previous example is further modified to include thirty year financing something interesting happens.

Exhibit 4-7

Principle = $100,000
Term = 30 Years
Rate = 12%
Payment = $1,028.61

1st Month Interest = 12% / 365 x 31 days x $100,000 = $1,091.18

Principle Reduction = $1,028.61 − $1,019.18 = $9.43

One day's interest = 12% / 365 x $100,000 = $32.88

Even a one day delay produces an interest shortfall!

Finally, since longer terms amortize more slowly, one should consider potential difficulties encountered at the time the boat is sold and the loan paid off. In the early eighties, the prices of new boats rose rapidly, tending to make for a strong resale market where used boat prices held their own and in some cases even appreciated in value. As inflation moderated and production caught up with demand, owners contemplating a trade up encountered problems with loans not sufficiently amortized to allow for possible depreciation of the trade vessel, especially if the original financing required less than standard down payment amounts. In this instance, insufficient equity (perhaps none at all) may prevent a move to a bigger boat.

A balance must be struck between the need for a payment that fits the budget, the desire for interest deductions and the possible resale value of a particular boat. The table below demonstrates this interplay by using historical data to illustrate several term/resale combinations:

Exhibit 4-8

Year	Boat	Boat purchase price	Loan equal to 80% of price plus tax @ 5%	Pay off Dec., 1988	Value* 1988
1984	36' Cruiser 350 hp gas (twin)	$102,995	$86,516	$79,373 (1) $72,369 (2)	$78,000
1984	32' Performance Sloop	$88,750	$74,550	$68,395 (1) $62,363 (2)	$74,200
1984	38' Cruising Cutter	$198,530	$166,765	$152,997 (1) $139,502 (2)	$143,000

(continued on next page)

Exhibit 4-8 (continued)

Year	Boat	Boat purchase price	Loan equal to 80% of price plus tax @ 5%	Pay off Dec., 1988	Value* 1988
1985	33' Flybridge Sportfish 320 hp gas (twin)	$111,700	$93,828	$88,021 (1) $82,329 (2)	$103,500
1986	25' Performance Runabout 260 hp gas (single)	$43,995	$36,956	$35,346 (1) $33,769 (2)	$33,200
1986	40' Cruising Sloop	$81,250	$68,250	$65,278 (1) $62,364 (2)	$62,800
1987	34' Sunbridge Cruiser 330 hp gas (twin)	$79,995	$67,196	$65,364 (1) $63,568 (2)	$62,800

*1988 Summer/Fall BUC Used Boat Price Guide: "Low BUC" value is used since original purchase price listed is for base boat (factory delivered) without dealer installed options. Example assumes boat purchased in January of model year and financed at 12% simple interest for the term stated: (1) 20 year term; (2) 15 year term.

Adjustables and balloons - Related to term options are "adjustables" and "balloons". Both limit the period over which a rate is fixed, but not the term of the amortization. By limiting the period that the lender commits to a specified rate, a lower rate is usually obtainable. This follows from an economic model known as the "yield curve" which depicts the relative yields of debt instruments with differing maturities. During most times, this curve assumes a "normal" shape, illustrated below, indicating that debt instruments of longer maturities carry higher yields, a reflection of the greater uncertainty in predicting interest rates farther in the future.

Exhibit 4-9

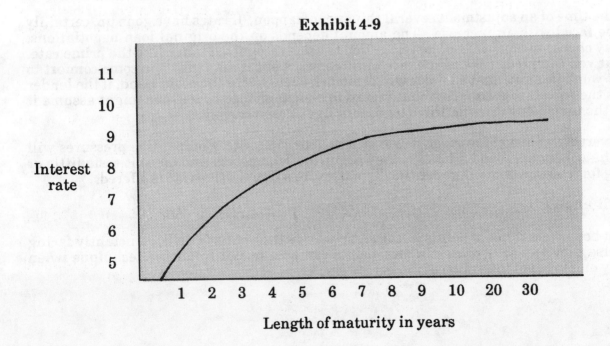

Length of maturity in years

What this means for the boat buyer is far more simple, namely, if one is willing to shorten up on the period over which a rate is fixed, some concession in that rate will be granted, all other things being equal. The result is a semi-fixed rate loan(2). The fixed rate period typically ranges from one to five years; anything longer usually carries the same rate as a full term fixed rate loan because the yield curve varies most in the shorter maturities.

While both adjustables and balloons provide a lower rate in return for a shorter rate commitment, the similarity ends there. A balloon loan is characterized by a long amortization and a short maturity, marked by a single, large final installment; no implicit right to continue the loan at any rate exists. For this reason, it pays to check for the balloon and attempt to stay away from it. Adjustables, on the other hand, give a contractual option to the lender to make periodic adjustments of the rate by giving proper notice to the borrower some time (usually sixty days) prior to the expiration of the adjustment period. The borrower then has the option to accept the new rate, refinance elsewhere, or pay the loan off. The note cannot be called without a new rate first being offered.

Why take an adjustable loan? Quite simply, you can use it to get something for nothing. Yacht loans, taken as a group and regardless of the original terms of the loans, pay off in an average of less than five years from inception. Thus for the average borrower, a lower rate of interest can be gained on a loan that will probably pay off before the end of the first adjustment period.

It is possible, of course, that the adjustment period may be less than the period you feel you'll actually hold the loan. Yet the lower interest rate is attractive. What do you do? It may be possible that the decrease in rate is significant enough to justify taking the loan even if you do expect rates to increase at the time of adjustment. As an example, assume you could get a three year adjustable at a .5% lower rate - a realistic expectation. Over that period the savings on, say, a 13.00%, 20 year contract amount to $1,516 for $100,000 borrowed. At the end of three years, on the reduced balance of $95,900, the rate would have to jump to 13.75% for two more years before that savings is eliminated. Should rates not increase (or better still, should they decrease) you come out a winner.

At the time of an adjustment several things can happen. If rates have gone up, certainly you'll be faced with an increase. The amount depends on the original loan negotiations. You may choose to have your adjustment tied to some recognized index like the prime rate. Not that you can predict the prime rate in three years but it may give you some comfort to know it won't be a rate that a lender will arbitrarily select. On the other hand, if the lender chooses the rate at that time, without regard to an established index, one might assume it will be the then going price for three (or four or five ...) year money.

Conversely, if market rates go down, so will your loan rate. Competitive pressures will see to that. Lenders spend a lot of money acquiring loan assets and since it costs little or nothing for a borrower to refinance they'll make sure a competitive rate is offered.

Point financing

Most borrowers think of points in the same way as the dentist's drill, reluctantly facing it because they feel they must. In fact, points can be a useful financing technique when properly employed at the option of the borrower.

Cost vs. buydown - The term "point" refers to a charge equal to one percent of the base loan amount. Thus, a $100,000 loan with three points would include a $3,000 charge. This charge is added to accomplish one of two things. First, a fee is sometimes included to pay for certain costs of putting the loan together. While the loan interest rate supposedly compensates the lender for its funds procurement, overhead, and profit, some banks are often tempted to increase the return by adding a "no choice" fee. Perhaps it is described as a "closing fee" out of which vessel documentation and registration costs are paid along with a charge to provide loan contracts, close the loan and so forth. Whatever the reason, if a similar loan format without points is not available you're probably paying for costs.

The second use of points involves "buy downs" — a term which has come to mean "a specific reduction in a given note rate made in exchange for a predetermined and fixed charge **at the option of the borrower.**"

The technique is not complicated. In exchange for the points, the lender agrees to reduce the rate by a certain amount. As a practical matter, usually a limited set of point/rate combinations is offered. For example, a lender might offer a no-point rate of 13.5% and an alternate rate of 12.5% plus three points. Should you wish to use the buydown but need a smaller point charge you may be able to negotiate a compromise combination, say 13.00% plus 1 1/2 points. Conversely, a deeper rate reduction may be desired. Maybe 11.5% plus five points can be obtained. Whatever the combination, the lender knows there is a mathematical trade off between rate and points. The pricing sheet they use may limit the offerings but the more clever among them realize a near infinite set of combinations exist that will achieve essentially their requisite pricing.

How then do you, the borrower, decide what is the right combination? More importantly, why should you elect to take a buydown in the first place? The answer to both questions turns out to be the same.

A buydown should be used when you can calculate a lower effective APR than the going no point rate given a certain loan holding period assumption. For the plan to work, the period of loan holding must be longer than the three to five year assumption lenders use. Since the point charge is fixed, the longer you hold the loan the longer you are theoretically spreading the cost of that charge. If you feel confident you'll keep the boat and the boat loan for, say, four years before trading up, you may find that the four year APR on a point loan is less than the corresponding no-point rate. This analysis also holds the key for determining the best point/rate combination. The way most marine lenders price, the longer you hold the loan, the more advantage you receive by using a deep buy down. Thus, even though the APR on a point loan is always greater than the note rate itself, it may make sense to take it.

Why is the APR on a point loan higher? As we will see later, just because you finance $100,000 doesn't mean you'll get $100,000 worth of boat money. After points or other charges are deducted, the actual funds applied against the purchase price can be significantly reduced. When this occurs, the APR is driven up to maintain a basic equivalence between money actually **received** and the future payments, which are based on the amount actually **financed.**

If this sounds confusing, don't worry. The subject of APRs and loan comparisons will be fully addressed in the next chapter. For now let's examine some actual point loans that illustrate the differences among them.

Exhibit 4-10

Effective APR, various point/payoff combinations
Note: Assumes points are paid at time of closing and not financed in the loan.

15 Year Loan
Rate = 11%

Payoff End of Year:	Points			
	1	2	3	4
1	12.26%	13.35%	14.46%	15.58%
3	11.41%	11.83%	12.25%	12.68%
5	11.28%	11.57%	11.86%	12.15%
15	11.18%	11.37%	11.56%	11.75%

As a final word on the subject, two critical items must be stressed. First, make sure you are dealing with a buydown. The best proof of this is to check the lender's no-point rate. If it doesn't exist, you don't have a buydown. In that case ask for a detailed itemization of the costs making up the charge. If you can't get it, shop elsewhere. As we will see shortly, this issue could have significant tax implications as well.

Second, remember the importance of the holding period assumption. We know borrowers who swore they would own their boats for at least five years and then traded (or refinanced) three times during that period using a buydown each time. The final rate was low alright, but all the interim points wiped out the advantage. If you are not sure, go for a straight rate. But if you are sure, don't be afraid to support a little risk that your situation could change.

Paying for points - Let's go back to our earlier example using a three point, $100,000 loan to get a better idea of how points are typically paid. The $3,000 charge could be financed, producing a final loan amount of $103,000 against which interest is then computed. On the other hand, you might choose to pay the charge "up front", or outside the loan contract, in which case while you receive loan proceeds of $100,000 to pay for the yacht, you must also make an out-of-pocket expenditure of $3,000 leaving a net advance of $97,000. As you can see, the final result is very much the same. Either finance $103,000 and get $100,000 or finance $100,000 and get $97,000; you are effectively borrowing a lower amount and repaying a higher. This produces an interesting little paradox. Even though interest is paid on a greater balance when the points are financed, the effective APR, the adjusted yield of the loan that accounts for the point charge, is actually slightly less compared with prepaying the points. Why? Because $3,000 is really only 2.91 points out of $103,000 whereas $3,000 is 3.00 points out of $100,000. You see, unlike most real estate lenders, marine lenders add points to balances instead of creating higher balances and then deducting points. Maybe it's just tradition but it does make point financing more attractive.

If you decide to use points, contact a good CPA or tax attorney to discuss their tax treatment, if you have a strong tax orientation in structuring your loan. At this writing, it appears as if current tax statutes may allow for the deduction of points on a qualifying first or second residence purchase, regardless of whether they are financed, as long as the points somehow represent a prepaid interest charge. This implies that they are okay as a buydown but not as a general loan or origination fee. Confusion could abound here. Detailed disclosure requirements do not apply to consumer boat loans above $25,000, so an accurate description of the point charge may not be found in your loan documents. It is entirely appropriate to ask your lender how the points are used or what they are considered.

Variable Rate Lending

Originally intended to provide lenders with some protection against volatile interest rates, variable rate loans were heavily marketed by commercial bankers in the early 70s. The consumer side was slower to react, mainly because of legal, regulatory and operational problems.

Variable rate loans represent an effort by lenders to do two things. First, by more closely matching the kind of money that banks and other financial institutions have available, variable rate loans make it easier for lenders to provide more money to the boat buying public. Second, because these loans generally are tied to some sort of short term market rate, they allow borrowers who perceive a near term decline in rates to take advantage of that decline either through a decreasing payment or faster principal amortization of their loan.

At first, this trend met with resistance from the boat buying community. Floating rate loans were unfamiliar and often not well explained (nor sometimes understood) by consumer lenders. However, as bank deregulation has created more investment vehicles that themselves generate income on a variable rate basis, more buyers seem interested in matching **their** asset returns and borrowing costs.

As an added bonus, variable rates (which are based on short term market rates) are often substantially lower than fixed (long term) rates, a point noted earlier in the discussion of the yield curve. Combine this with the ease of refinancing a yacht, and we can see another reason variable rate loans are popular: They can be easily refinance at fixed rates if the borrower detects a rise in short term borrowing costs.

Although there are many ways to structure variable rate loans, they all exhibit two common characteristics. The amount paid towards interest is dependent, at least to a degree, on changes in some area of interest rate markets. Thus, there is absolutely no way to determine before the fact the interest you will pay or your total cost of credit. Also, variable rate loans are, with very few exceptions, structured on a per diem simple interest basis. They almost have to be. Since the amount applied to interest varies with some index, there is no way to precompute a specific monthly accrual, unless the payment moves each and every time the index moves.

The role of an index

As more variable rate loans are offered, the choice of "pegs", or market indices available has grown. There are yacht loans tied to the prime rate, various certificate of deposit (CD) and treasury rates, even certain Federal Home Loan Bank Board member borrowing rates. Probably because of its wide use in many bank functions, the prime rate is the current index of choice by lenders. Unfortunately, as the result of the media's preoccupation with the prime, general opinion holds prime as the rate. In fact, it is only one rate of many and a rather artificial one at that. Traditionally defined as "the ninety day unsecured rate that a bank charges its best corporate customers,"(3) a bank's prime rate is usually set by senior management at weekly or monthly meetings. The pricing of prime will often be based on other short term rates such as CDs, treasury bills, or federal funds.

The simple fact that your loan is tied to some identifiable index does not in itself indicate whether a loan is variable. Although it may just be semantics, variable rate loans are usually defined as having a period of rate certainty less than one year. The fixed/adjustable loans mentioned previously constitute a class of hybrid loans and some have adjustments at two or even one year. These very short term adjustables are often tied to corresponding Treasury note rates or similar indices. In a sense, any loan with a provision to adjust at some point could be declared a variable rate loan. It is probably more accurate however, to continue referring to loans with adjustments longer than one year as "semi-fixed" or, as defined earlier, adjustable rate loans.

Many states now have consumer lending laws requiring easy identification of rate pegged indices. Yet even though the rate is easily identified, actually finding a number the bank uses could be difficult. Check this carefully. A phrase like "the one year treasury rate" could imply several different rates, depending on whether, in this example, treasury bills or notes are used. Sometimes a composite rate index is used, which usually is not published in any business news media. The index may also carry an alternate index in case the primary is discontinued. Most prime pegged notes contain such wording.

Once the index is selected and the loan closed, interest charges are computed by adding a fixed additional percentage increase to the index value. This percentage increase is referred to as the "spread" and remains constant for the life of the loan.

Variable rate payment plans

In the previous section we saw that the trick to variable plans lies in the determination of an interest rate. Once set, the simple interest method takes over providing easily determinable interest costs and loan amortization. Of course, to obtain the amortization we must also know the payment. Is it fixed or will it vary? How can a payment plan be structured to fit your needs?

Lenders don't often provide a choice of payment plan for a given variable rate program. The computer support necessary to manage a variable rate program is sufficiently complicated to wring out most of the flexibility in the system. You may find that the ideal rate structure carries a payment plan that is absolutely unacceptable and therefore you must shop elsewhere, possibly accepting a rate that is slightly less attractive. If you do look around you'll find essentially three types of payment plans.

Fixed payment - The first is a fixed payment/variable amortization often used by lenders not wanting to redesign their basic simple interest loan systems. A fixed payment is calculated using a rate equal to the initial index value plus the spread. The fixed period typically lasts three years or longer and once established remains independent of the index selected. Shorter term fixed payments are, of course, available but are likely to change whenever the rate changes. Such payment plans are discussed later.

Once the fixed payment is established, interest begins to accrue in accordance with the initial note rate i.e., the index plus the spread. As we just saw, this rate is free to move at those times specified in the loan contract, subject to any rate "floors" and "ceilings" or maximum annual rate adjustments specified in the note. Should the rate move downward, a decreasing portion of the payment goes toward interest leaving more to amortize the loan. In this case the loan will pay off faster than the original contract term unless a provision exists for adjusting future payments to maintain the original term.

Problems arise should the rate go up. Then, the interest earned by the lender may not be adequately covered by the payment. Should this happen, an interest shortage occurs

CREDIT PLANS: Looking At The Numbers

which either increases the balance of the loan or requires payment at either the end of the fixed payment period, annually or perhaps as a balloon at the termination of the loan.

This situation is all the more likely if the original loan term was long, say fifteen years or greater, or if the index increases soon after the loan is closed. It won't take much of an increase to create this "negative amortization". Recall the discussion on extended term financing. Your principal "cushion" on a long term loan in the early years is very thin indeed!

Variable payment - You can solve this problem by utilizing a second payment plan which we'll call variable payment/fixed amortization. With this approach, the lender calculates monthly interest in the same manner as before but also adds a prescheduled principal component. Since the full amount of interest due will be collected regardless of the rate itself, this plan will always call for a monthly bill instead of the more traditional fixed payment coupon book. Some banks will alternately set up a direct debit of a checking account, but the accounting remains the same. Should rates go up, so will your bill (or debit) but if rates decrease, your payment decreases also. Of course, once you receive the bill, should you send the payment in after the due date, a greater amount of interest will be deducted than specified. Remember, the principal component, while it is prescheduled, is not guaranteed. On any per diem simple interest loan, payments are applied first to interest, then to principal.

A billed system is ideal if you like to keep track of your finances as well as see some pay down of the loan. Every month a full accounting of the loan is provided including the current balance, interest paid and next payment amount. The problem of interest short is rarely encountered as long as payments are made on time. A note of caution however. Because the principal is prescheduled, you may want to take a close look at the method of principal repayment. Some lenders still amortize such loans on a "straight line" basis, meaning equal amounts are charge to amortize the loan each month. Sound fair? Maybe, but because the interest is much higher in the beginning (when most of the principal is still outstanding), the early payments can be as much as 50% higher than graduated principal programs!

Fixed/variable payment - A hybrid of these payment plans is the fixed/variable plan. Sharing more in common with a true variable plan, it allows for fixing of the payment for short periods, usually up to one year in a manner that corresponds to the index period. Thus, if the loan is priced off the six month CD rate, a six month payment will be established. Once those six equal payments are made, a new rate and payment are established for another six months. Amortization is guaranteed (subject to timely payments) and interest is computed on either a per diem or precomputed basis.

Summing It Up

From the preceding, it may look as if credit plans are all a numbers game, although really it's not. For the numbers to make any sense, you've got to look at them in the real world. Am I building enough equity to trade up on? Do I have enough cash left to weather unforeseen problems or repairs? What happens if interest rates take a really unexpected turn for the worse (or better)? Unfortunately, most borrowers never get into the level of analysis undertaken here, so often the payment and interest rate alone are the basis for comparison.

The attempt in this chapter is to make the buyer who borrows money for the purchase of a boat aware of the interplay of rate, term, interest rate market risk, equity building and payment, especially in the context of the personal financial planning discussed in Chapter 2. Once this interplay is well understood, you can line up all of your financing options and eliminate those that fail to meet your objectives.

In the next chapter, a more comprehensive **comparison** of credit plans is undertaken with an eye to selecting the best plan for you on the boat you have chosen.

---

(1)   A second method of fixed rate lending known as the "Rule of the 78ths" is on the decline as a popular consumer lending method. Although in widespread use for over 70 years, it now is employed mainly for small, short term boat financing as well as other small consumer loans. Recent legislation and tax reform are the primary reasons for the decline in usage although a number of boat owners still **hold** 78ths loans.

The essence of the Rule of 78ths method is contained in two simple mathematical concepts: "Add-on interest" and "sum-of-the-digits". To the lender, Rule of 78ths rates are expressed in terms of a percentage known as the add-on factor. The add-on factor gives rise to a "pre-computed finance charge" which is merely the product of the factor, term, and principal. Obviously then, this finance charge may be more than the principal borrowed.

For example, if you wished to borrow $50,000 for ten years, and the add-on factor was 11%, the total finance charge payable over the ten years in addition to the principal is 10 x 11% x $50,000 or $55,000. The monthly payment follows by adding finance charge to principal borrowed and dividing by the term in months: ($55,000 + $50,000) / 120, or $875.00.

Under the Rule of 78ths, the Annual Percentage Rate (the APR) you are quoted is valid only for a loan that does not pay off early. A prepayment on a 78ths loan raises the APR because the interest calculated each month by the lender is "front loaded" during the early years of the loan.

The lender charges (earns) each month that portion of the finance charge equal to **the number of months remaining on the loan** divided by the **"sum-of-the-digits" representing the total term in months.** For example, a twelve month loan has a sum-of-the-digits equal to $12+11+10+9+8+7+6+5+4+3+2+1$ or 78 (thus the Rule of 78ths name). During month one of our twelve month loan the interest earnings are equal to:

$$\frac{\text{months remaining}}{\text{sum-of-the-digits}} \times \text{finance charge}$$

or;

$$\frac{12}{78\text{ths}} \times \text{finance charge}$$

During month two, the interest earnings are 11/78ths of the finance charge, 10/78ths for month three, and so on. Eventually the last month is reached when the final 1/78th of the finance charge becomes earned. The sum of all these monthly earnings is exactly 78/78ths of the finance charge.

Principal amortization, or the reductions in the loan balance itself, consist of whatever is left over after the earnings are deducted each month from the fixed payment. Since the interest charges have been steadily decreasing, you might correctly guess that the principal repayment has been steadily increasing at the same rate. A prepayment of the note requires the borrower to settle up at whatever principal remains.

A chief advantage of the Rule of 78ths was its generally lower payment compared to other loan formats. The offset to this was the higher early payoff values, including the extreme case of a payoff value that was greater than the sum originally borrowed. In such cases the Rule of 78ths generates an interest only situation where not even all the interest is collected!

(2) Real estate lenders call them ARMs for "adjustable rate mortgage" but the principle is very similar.

(3) Recent attacks by disgruntled customers on the Prime Rate as a borrowing index have diminished its popularity with many banks.

CHAPTER 5
LENDERS AND LOANS: Making a Decision

Shopping for money can be a long and arduous process and some buyers choose not to go through it, instead relying on the advice of friends, a dealer or broker, or perhaps the reputation of a lender. If you decide you really want to get involved with the financial arrangements in order to make a truly informed decision, accumulate the proper information on a series of loan programs as outlined in Chapter 4 and use this chapter to develop a means to compare them.

Comparing credit plans has a lot to do with your basic goals and assumptions that were discussed earlier. While we will look at some fairly objective ways to make comparisons, quite often one or two very subjective factors will swing the decision. Some borrowers knowingly take a higher rate program, for instance, because they feel comfortable with the lender and that comfort apparently has a measurable price tag. As you make your own comparisons always pay attention to these subjective aspects, since there may be intangibles with a value not easily recognizable.

Comparing Credit Plans

There are essentially three dimensions along which one can effectively compare credit plans, namely (1) features and benefits, (2) dollar costs and (3) Annual Percentage Rates (APRs). Depending on your needs and objectives, one or more of these criteria will appear appropriate for making comparisons. Don't let a lender, broker, or even your best friend tell you which criterion is most important. You decide.

Features and benefits

This term refers to the non-numerical aspects of loan comparison and is probably the most easily overlooked. Just as a cruising yacht has certain features and benefits in addition to the price, so too does a yacht loan. Yet so often we become conditioned to thinking of borrowing in terms of that one question, "What's the rate", that all else is forgotten. The old saw that "money is money" or "it's all the same color" does not adequately address the issue at hand, which is not money, but a credit plan.

In fact, it may matter very little what the costs are if a key feature you need is absent. As we will see in the next section, yacht financing is oriented toward flexible, creative programs but not all lenders exhibit the same level of creativity and flexibility. For example, let's say you decide that nothing other than an interest only loan will do. Since few lenders offer this particular option your choices on rate, term and so forth will be necessarily limited. But if the feature is important enough, it becomes the primary focus of comparison. Other features might include bridge financing on an existing boat to obtain a downpayment, or perhaps a deferred payment plan for a wintertime purchase.

A feature, then, is some aspect of the credit arrangement that provides a specific benefit, solves a problem or satisfies a need, and one of the nice things about yacht financing is the abundance of features. There are lenders who can provide 100% financing (no down payment), foreign boat import financing, yacht construction financing, charter boat loans, liveaboard financing and much more. To make the correct decision, it takes full understanding of the non-price features needed; some of them will be detailed later. Make yourself aware of all facets of the purchase. Probe the dealer for even minor details by asking "Will I need this?" or "How do I get that?" Too often buyers shopping for rate alone wind up wasting time because the one key feature they desired was not offered by the lender they selected.

Interest costs

Once outside the realm of features, a fairly straight forward comparison can be made in terms of cost. In the most basic sense this means looking at the amount of interest paid under differing pricing assumptions. In Chapter 4, a table was presented that allowed you to roughly estimate total interest costs. However, given the wide variety of pricing formats, this could end up being a bit simplistic.

We can widen the analysis and therefore its validity by pointing out that, from a cost standpoint, any loan can be examined in terms of five dimensions: amount borrowed, term, monthly payment, early payoff value and APR. The APR, since it ties the other four together, will be discussed separately below. In order to make objective loan comparisons we'll need to employ a little math. The appendices at the end of the book will prove helpful although nothing beats a good financial calculator.

The manipulation of these five dimensions can produce amounts paid toward interest, principal and so forth for any required period in any loan format as well as the amount payable for early retirement of the loan. We've already developed some of these figures in the review of lending methods. Sometimes the most effective way to make the comparison is to simply perform a side by side analysis of the relevant figures. The following example will present a number of the variables outlined in Chapter 4.

Exhibit 5-1

Simple Interest Loan Comparison
15 yrs. vs. 20 yrs.
Loan Amount = $100,000

LOAN I				LOAN II				
15 yrs. @ 12%				**20 yrs. @ 11% with 3 points**				
				5 year rate adjustment				
Payment = $1,200/month				**Payment = $1,063/month**				
Year	Payments	Interest	Principal	Payoff	Payments	Interest	Principal	Payoff	Effective APR
1	$14,400	$11,681	$2,539	$97,461	$12,756	$11,254	$1,502	$101,498	14.16%
2	14,400	11,540	2,860	94,601	12,756	11,080	1,676	99,822	12.68%
3	14,400	11,177	3,223	91,378	12,756	10,886	1,870	97,952	12.19%
4	14,400	10,768	3,632	87,746	12,756	10,670	2,086	95,866	11.95%
5	14,400	10,307	4,093	83,653	12,756	10,428	2,328	93,538	11.80%
	$72,000	$55,653	$16,347		$63,780	$57,318	$6,462		

– – – – – – Cumulative totals through year five – – – – – –

6	$14,400	$9,788	$4,612	$79,040	Unknown - rate subject to adjustment				

If the example is carried through in a high rate environment, a different picture emerges.

15 yrs. @ 16%				**20 yrs. @ 15% with 3 points**				
				5 year rate adjustment				
Payment = $1,469/month				**Payment = $1,356/month**				
Year	Payments	Interest	Principal	Payoff	Payments	Interest	Principal	Payoff	Effective APR
1	$17,628	$15,879	$1,749	$98,251	$16,276	$15,391	$885	$102,115	18.22%
2	17,628	15,578	2,050	96,201	16,276	15,249	1,027	101,088	16.74%
3	17,628	15,224	2,104	93,797	16,276	15,084	1,192	99,896	16.25%
4	17,628	14,811	2,817	90,980	16,276	14,893	1,383	98,513	16.01%
5	17,628	14,325	3,303	87,677	16,276	14,670	1,606	96,907	15.87%
	$88,140	$75,817	$12,323		$81,380	$75,287	$6,093		

– – – – – – Cumulative totals through year five – – – – – – –

This example illustrates two loans one might consider, within two separate sets of interest rates. The left side loans are no-point, fifteen year fixed rates. The right side loans show a three point, twenty year format. While current rates might differ from these at the time you buy, the two examples in each set of loan pricings would be considered approximately equal by lenders offering buydowns and adjustables[1].

In the example, interest costs and payoffs at the end of each year for five years are considered, as well as total monthly payments for each year. The interest rate, term, loan payment and payoff values are all different; how does one decide?

That answer is determined by your own internal priorities. Maybe your budget will only accommodate the one payment, and the longer term is required just to get you there. Of course, the offset to a lower payment is less amortization of the loan in the short run. Perhaps you might negotiate a buydown on the fifteen year option; that should not be too difficult. Then, you receive both the benefit of a lower rate with increased equity building.

Equity accumulation should be a concern to any boat owner who intends to trade up in the future. As we saw in Exhibit 4-8, too little amortization of your loan may make it impossible to sell at a price sufficient to clear the note, after taking into account expenses of sale such as commissions, survey, etc. For most, this means dipping into savings — savings that might have been viewed as a new downpayment source. For a few, it could mean creating a charge-off with a lender and a very bad mark against the credit record. Many a purchase has been cancelled when after months of planning for the **new** boat, an owner discovered the **old** one was the problem. It's a good practice then, to obtain a loan amortization schedule up front, or else periodically check your current loan balance against the current resale price of the boat. More on this last point in Chapter 9, **Selling Your Boat**.

Another means of evaluation is through direct cost and cash flow comparisons: At a specific point in the loan term, figures for interest, loan amortization, APR and loan payoff are calculated and analyzed. In Exhibit 5-1, Loan II "costs" $1,665 more than Loan I in terms of interest, yet Loan II will require $8,220 less in cash flow than Loan I. The difference is found in the obviously smaller principal reduction of Loan II; the difference of $9,885 is equal to the total-of-payments difference plus the interest cost difference.

Since the boat will sell for the same price regardless of the original loan format, does this mean that loans should be evaluated solely in terms of interest costs? Not necessarily. One must first consider the effect of that $1,664 difference in yearly payments ($14,440 - $12,756). If that money were reinvested at say, 12% per year, it would be worth a total of $11,188 after five years instead of the original payments difference of $8,220; a $1,665 interest **cost** has now become a $1,303 interest **savings**.

Usually, the choices you've likely given yourself are not as dissimilar as the example above. You first narrow the options and then make a decision between related aspects of the loan. For example, after looking at your expected holding period and desired payment, you could decide between a buy down or a straight rate. The appendices at the end of the book will help establish the breakeven point, that is, the holding period where a point loan has the same APR as a no point loan. Then, depending on where you thought interest rates were headed, or depending on what term assets you were invested in, you could decide whether to take an adjustable rate loan at a slightly lower rate than a full term fixed rate loan.

A side by side comparison produces numbers and costs that sway you one way or the other by providing numerical references points at various times during the loan holding period. These can then be included in your current budgeting and long term financial plan.

Fixed or variable? - An exception to this method lies in the choice many buyers face between fixed and variable rate loans. And the decision is doubly difficult because, with respect to the variable loan, a cost cannot be determined up front. The fixed versus variable decision separates more borrowers than any other and many seem to react emotionally to the choice. "What?! The rate can go all the way to 18%! Not for me!" or "The fixed rate is two percent higher than the floating and you expect me to take it?!" People seem to have an orientation to one or the other. Let that orientation be guided by logic and your basic assumptions.

Assumption I: Where do you expect interest rates to go and how long will they stay there? Most borrowers prefer to avoid the question but if you are optimistic about the current state of the economy, especially if rates are already trending downward, a variable rate loan may be right for you.

Assumption II: How long will you hold the loan? If anticipating a quick payoff, the odds are obviously much less that a variable rate loan will show significant increases.

Variable rates almost always carry lesser rates of interest than fixed rates, because of the normal shape of the yield curve examined earlier. You pay a premium for eliminating risk when you choose a fixed rate. Of course, should the index increase at some point after closing, whatever differential you enjoyed might be wiped out and the cost could exceed the cost of the alternate fixed rate.

Even though you can't perform a direct cost comparison between fixed and variable rate loans, you can quite easily determine the break-even point between the two by doing a side-by-side interest cost analysis using your estimate of likely interest rate movements. Let's assume two programs are available, a 12.5% fixed and a one year variable indexed to the one year Treasury Constant Maturities index (TCM)[2] with a three and one half percent spread. We will amortize both loans over fifteen years. Assume the TCM at time of closing is seven percent.

Exhibit 5-2

Fixed Rate vs. Variable Rate
Simple Interest Loan Comparison

Loan Amount = $100,000
15 Year Term

LOAN I				LOAN II				
12.50%, Fixed Rate				TCM + 3½%, Variable Rate				
				Initial TCM = 7%, Loan Rate = 10.5%				

Year	Payments	Interest	Principal	Payoff	Payments	Interest	Principal	Payoff	Cash Savings
1	$14,790	$12,364	$2,426	$97,574	$13,265	$10,363	$2,902	$97,098	$1,525
2	14,790	12,043	2,747	94,827	13,982	11,013	2,969	94,129	808
					TCM = 8%		Rate = 11½%		
3	14,790	11,680	3,110	91,717	14,681	11,593	3,088	91,041	109
					TCM = 9%		Rate = 12½%		
4	14,790	11,267	3,523	88,194	15,357	12,093	3,264	87,777	−567
					TCM = 10%		Rate = 13½%		
5	14,790	10,800	3,990	84,204	15,357	11,625	3,732	84,045	−567
					TCM = 10%		Rate = 13½%		
	$73,950	$58,154	$15,796		$72,620	$56,687	$15,955		

– – – – – – Cumulative totals through year five – – – – – –

*Note: Not all institutions will compute payments, interest, etc. as in this example. Figures do not always total due to rounding.

Even if the TCM rate goes up by three full percentage points evenly over three years before stabilizing, a borrower would be worse off by originally taking the fixed rate. Considering the lower payments in the early years and the near equal payoff value at five years, one must conclude the variable program was over all the better deal.

The catch, of course, is that this example is hypothetical; rates could go up much higher, faster (or lower, slower...). But the interest differential of $1,467 is tempting, especially considering the savings are in the early years when, as we'll see below, they are worth more.

With a continued rise in interest rates the variable program looks less attractive. If the TCM rate increases another percentage point in the final year, the interest differential becomes only $592. Further increases (or earlier increases) could really put you in the hole, but such increases might be subject to rate "ceilings" and maximum annual rate changes that limit your upward exposure. In that case you have effectively hedged against too rapid a rise in interest rates. But if a loan has a ceiling, you can bet it will also have a "floor", limiting downward rate movement. Such floors and ceilings are often included in variable rate loans and may make the difference in your purchase decision if you are not all that confident in the interest rate outlook. This being the case, you may want to stay away from them altogether.

You might take a variable rate loan on the assumption you could move out to a fixed rate if interest rates rose. While this is fine in theory, it could lull you into a false sense of security. In a rising rate environment long term rates also get dragged up, albeit not as quickly as short term rates, so you will have to refinance at higher than the initial available fixed rate. Once you make your initial decision, should rates go up, you can change only at a price.

On the other hand, should rates rocket up, you should definitely fix — if such rates are available in a rapidly increasing market. You never know when 20% short term rates will be encountered again, as they were in 1981.

Examining an APR

"What exactly is an APR?" We've heard the question asked numerous times, usually from borrowers who, after being told their rate was one figure, noticed in their loan agreement an APR that appeared substantially higher. The reason is simple. An APR is the result of a mathematical equation that produces an equivalence between the initial amount of loan value received[3] and all subsequent payments to be delivered. This includes the final payment which in the event of a early payoff is referred to as a balloon, or prepayment. The APR makes the two sides of the equation (initial value received, subsequent payments made) equal giving full consideration to the timing of the actual payments themselves[4]. After all, a dollar received today is worth more to the lender than a dollar received next year; it can be reinvested in more loans. Thus, while Exhibit 5-1 presented loans that had differing yearly cash requirements and resulting payoffs, the APR figures adjusted for the differences by assuming payment savings are earning a rate equal to the effective APR.

The APR then, most directly compares the true yield of various loan formats; any loan can be compared in terms of an APR. However, when repayment terms are very dissimilar between loan structures, the APR looks fairly hollow; other comparison criteria become more important. For instance, Exhibit 5-2 above represents a comparison that probably needs to be looked at in terms other than APR.

For loans of very similar structure the APR can be quite useful for determining the best deal. Can you tell from looking which of the following loans is the more economical?

Exhibit 5-3

Loan amount = $100,000
15 year term

	LOAN I	LOAN II
Monthly Payment	$1,000	$1,200
Month of Payoff	48 months	48 months
Payoff Amount	$102,578	$86,915
Points Paid at Closing	0	2 points
APR	12.50%	12.50%

Both APRs are 12.5%, even though the loan terms are very different. Unless the payment amount and payoff value differences in this case are important to you, neither loan produces an economic advantage. This technique can cause you to rethink whether you're really getting a good deal.

Appendix D shows payoff values at various rate/term combinations while Appendix E provides a handy chart that can be used to make basic APR estimates. A more direct way to obtain these these figures is through your lender. Just make sure the APR given is for the expected term that you'll hold the loan. And remember that on any simple interest loan with no points or charges, the rate on the note is **exactly** equal to the APR.

Selecting a Lender

Like many other areas of consumer lending, a number of financial institutions are in the business of marine financing as a specialty. Either providing this service as a sole function or committing a group or department to the effort, marine lenders developed the special knowledge and techniques along with the required legal, regulatory, operational, and marketing support vital to the proper execution of this rapidly growing business.

"Why use a specialty marine lender?" you may ask. After all, any one well off enough to buy a yacht probably already has several good banking contacts. For many borrowers though, this may not be true. Even if it is, you are more likely to get better terms from a marine lender than your own bank. Secured lending arrangements are predicated on in-depth knowledge of the security offered. The more a lender knows, the more likely you are to get flexible terms and a wide variety of program choices. Beyond this, there may also be good sense in expanding your lending relationships by including a new marine lender, an especially good point to bear in mind if your current banker shows conservative tendencies and you wish to keep your boat purchase a private matter.

The selection of a lender can be much more important than one might think at first glance. A great range of lending practices, policies and programs characterize marine finance. Quite often, depending on the plan you need, only a small number of lenders might exist to satisfy that need. A good yacht broker can help point you in the right direction. Part of their job consists of knowing **who** offers **what** in the credit community. Of course, before they can help, **you** must know what you need.

Special requirements?

About one out of four yacht purchases have what we'll call "special requirements". Some lenders are equipped to handle these requirements, others are not. A few examples follow.

Liveaboard boats - Many more persons are taking to the water as a primary residence, partly to offset the high cost of land based residence in coastal areas, and partly out of love of the life style.

Not all lenders will finance a boat used as a primary residence. Loan documentation, disclosures and mandatory recession rights (the latter on refinances of liveaboards) make it sufficiently complicated to not warrant the effort. So if you are planning to buy a boat to live on, or are refinancing a liveaboard, make that your first line of inquiry. You may be surprised to find it costs a little more.

Charter boats - If your boat will be in active charter service, either as a bareboat, crewed or in a sailing club, you are probably stuck with a limited lender market, no matter where the boat will be employed. Loan terms may be more restrictive as well. Most large charter operators have key lenders that will enable buyers to obtain financing for boats in the fleet. Again, make that the first question and then shop for other features and terms.

Buying out-of-state - If your plans include buying a boat for delivery to a state other than where you reside, you may limit your choice of lenders although there still are a good many marine lenders that operate on a regional or national level and can handle out-of-state ownership. If you plan on keeping the boat out of the country, perhaps at a vacation spot in Mexico or the Caribbean, then even these lenders may be faced with restrictions. Check this out in advance, since some banks have outright default clauses in their loan contracts that prohibit moving the boat to or from certain locations.

Similar restrictions may be encountered if you plan on buying a boat out-of-state and shipping it to your area. In many cses, the sale requires full payment before the boat can be trucked out, yet many lenders will not pay until delivery is completed. Find out in advance what your lender's policy is since it could irretrievably hang up your deal.

Buying foreign boats - Within the last several years the quality of foreign produced boats entering the U.S. has dramatically improved at the same time that the quantity has greatly increased, particularly in the case of Taiwanese vessels, where major efforts in quality control have created a much wider market in the U.S. A strong dollar was initially responsible in 1985, making foreign goods, including boats, appear attractively priced. Since then, the dollar has fallen back, but the marketing and distribution infrastructure of these foreign builders remains.

If you are contemplating financing the purchase of a foreign boat from an importer, distributor or dealer, you may quickly discover that the sale usually involves more than setting up a standard yacht loan commitment. With occasional exceptions, the builder of the yacht will require an import Letter of Credit (LC) before shipping the boat, or in some cases, before beginning production of the hull.

What is an LC? Simply a form of bank guarantee designed to facilitate foreign trade, the content of which is defined by international convention. The LC provides for payment to the builder (or whomever is designated as the "beneficiary") at the time certain terms of the LC are met. These terms usually include completion and shipment of the vessel in accordance with buyer specifications, transfer of title, delivery of certain shipping documents and so forth. The effectiveness of an LC as a trade instrument lies in its utter reliability. If a boat is produced and shipped according to terms, the builder is absolutely guaranteed of payment. The buyer, on the other hand, can rest assured that if for whatever reason the boat is not produced, no money will pass hands and the LC will expire uncollected.

The burden of producing an LC always falls to the importer, who in turn usually attempts to pass it on to the dealer (if there is one between importer and buyer). Producing an LC presents a problem for most due to the fact that any bank issuing one will want some kind of coverage for itself once the LC pays. This coverage may consist of an established line of credit but more likely will be actual cash deposits which are held pending settlement of the LC payment. For this reason most importers and dealers like to pass on the responsibility for procuring an LC to the customer. A few of the better capitalized sellers have the financial strength to have a number of their own LCs issued at any one time but you won't encounter this too often.

So, it comes down to you, the buyer, having to come up with the money you thought you were going to borrow in order to get the LC. Fortunately for you, there are lenders who are willing to issue LCs to you once you have met their credit guidelines and receive an approval. That approval serves as your "cash in the bank" because, though the loan does not yet exist, your credit line now serves as the backup for the LC. Once your boat arrives this credit line becomes a standard long term yacht loan thereby clearing the LC payment.

The cost for issuing a letter of credit varies from about 1/4% to as much as 1%, the difference usually depending on whether deposits or a credit line back the LC. As far as where to go, the importer or dealer will almost certainly know what lender can handle the loan. A good part of their work day involves managing trade and finance.

Construction contracts - Some of the highest quality custom yachts in the U.S. and most of the large ones (over 65') worldwide are built on a "construction contract" basis. This type of contract between buyer and seller details the design, rigging, equipping and cost of the vessel as well as the manner in which payment will be made. The contract usually calls for a certain initial deposit with subsequent interim payments made at various points in the production cycle. For instance, a 20% order deposit is followed by additional 20% payments due upon hull completion, decking, and final completion with the final 20% paid at delivery.

The reasons such payments are required is twofold. First, because the work is custom oriented, the boat yard wants to know it won't be stuck unpaid for a yacht that might be unsuitable for another buyer's taste. Second, most boat yards do not have sufficient working capital to pay the enormous bills for materials needed to produce extremely large yachts. But that leaves the buyer in a position of either making a cash purchase or foregoing the boat of his dreams.

The solution lies in finding a lender willing to work with you and the builder to develop a plan to finance the construction payments. A few lenders already have established programs with certain builders and those builders will always alert you to program availability. Where an established program does not exist, you and your lender may have to get creative and provide a plan to the builder. Most boat yards don't possess a lot of experience in this area and are used to dealing in cash, but with a sale at stake you may successfully sell them on an idea.

One way to approach the problem is via the Letter of Credit routine just reviewed. This time however, the LC is made to a domestic builder who then obtains loan advances against it at its own bank. You may be required to pay interim interest costs but you would in effect be paying them anyway should you use your own money, since it would no longer be available for investment.

Certain lenders will also make advances against your yacht line of credit established earlier with some sort of interim security such as a portfolio of investment grade securities or real estate. You may have certain investments you are sure will remain intact for a given period (in order to gain, say, preferable capital gains treatment). Use that to increase your borrowing power by pledging them against advances that are paid off by a long term yacht loan when the boat is delivered. You could use the same technique with your investment broker on a margin line of credit, but you will almost certainly receive a greater loan per dollar pledged from a yacht lender due to current margin account restrictions.

Large loan requirements - How large is large when it comes to borrowing money for a boat? If you are a first time buyer any amount seems like a great deal. Lenders have an entirely different perception of average and large and it varies from bank to bank.

The average loan made on a documentable yacht (see Chapter 7 for an explanation of documentation) runs between sixty and eighty thousand dollars. Most marine lenders can easily accommodate borrowing needs up to $150,000 and a good number will quickly climb to $300,000. After that a strange thing begins to happens. Loan committees, higher approval authorities, and other bank departments begin to get involved. Most often these other functions are not nearly as well informed as the people "on the line" developing the business and communicating with the marine market. For that reason, delays set in, unusual requests for information are made and the borrower begins to feel his application may be in jeopardy.

Handling very large requests of $500,000 and over seems to be a specialty that only a handful of marine lenders perform very well and the number capable of quickly and efficiently processing $1,000,000+ requests is perhaps no more than three or four. Of course, many banks are quite willing to lend large amounts to their very well heeled customers, but that always takes place inside of a well established banking relation. For a stranger to go to a new lender and quickly qualify for a $1,500,000 loan with only a yacht as collateral is unusual indeed!

Your broker again can be most helpful in steering you to the right lender for a large loan. The brokerage houses that specialize in these extremely large (and expensive!) yachts are expert in putting the deal **and** the money together and often enjoy the best and most influential lender relationships. Use that relationship to negotiate the most favorable loan structure possible.

Large loan requests imply large personal finances so everything mentioned in **Qualifying For Credit** (Chapter 3) goes double. Send the entire mountain of business and personal statements over to the bank and don't forget to include your CPA's name and phone number.

The differences between lenders

Marine finance institutions fall into three general categories: Indirect lenders, direct lenders and bank service companies. Where and what type of boat you buy, the type program you need and the service level you expect should point you to one of these.

Indirect lenders work strictly through a new boat dealership, generally financing smaller cruisers and trailerable boats. The dealer makes all the financing arrangements and later sells the loan contract to the lender. Since as a buyer you never meet or talk directly with the lender, we will exclude them from our discussion.

The two remaining groups both possess advantages and disadvantages which are outlined below.

Direct lenders - Generally banks and finance companies, they have the money. Direct lenders generate funds in various deposit, capital and money markets and re-lend it to the end boat buyer at a spread sufficient to cover the costs of their overhead and a reasonable profit. This overhead consists primarily of the expense needed to originate the loans including advertising, promotions and sales calling, along with the cost of processing applications and servicing loans once they are approved and closed.

Bank service companies - Also known as a lender service company, these firms work directly with buyers to generate loans which they then package and sell to other financial institutions for a fee. The fee is usually deducted from the future interest that the buying bank will receive although occasionally it is paid in the form of points charged directly to the customer. A bank service company bears the costs of marketing, loan processing and packaging, which are covered by the fee. After originating a loan application the service company sends it along with certain accompanying documents to one or more lenders depending on its own feeling for how difficult the approval will be or what kind of pricing options are available.

Pros and cons - Direct lenders have autonomous credit authority at some level in the organization and are free to set their own policy in accordance with management and shareholder objectives. This does tend to restrict them to that one policy set. A service company usually has a stable of purchasing institutions and so can direct applications to the lender(s) having terms or policies most accommodating to the applicant. This dependency on other lenders can also be a disadvantage to the applicant if a sudden shift in a key lender's policy leaves the customer in the cold.

After closing, loan servicing is rarely handled by a service company. If you work through one, your note will be sold to another institution, and your relationship with the service company pretty much ends there, until such time as you decide to refinance or buy a new boat. Direct lenders service their own accounts although they too, at times will sell loans in the open market. If they do, the servicing is usually kept within their own organization.

Creative financing

The nature of yacht lending is to try out new ideas all the time, and already quite a few creative programs have been covered in some detail. But the term creative financing has become somewhat overused. In an effort to differentiate themselves, some lenders are adding window dressing to basic programs and touting them as creative.

Creativity in yacht financing is more a lender attitude than a particular program. It means possessing the willingness and the ability to structure a loan that best accommodates your needs while still producing the necessary profit to stay in business. **Negotiation** is a key term in the process of creative financing. Find a financier who will do that and you have found the rare lender that always looks for a way to make the loan instead of a reason to turn it down.

Here is a short list of ideas to provide your banker should you wish to explore them. At present, all can be handled by at least several major outfits.

1) 100% financing. At some point, every borrower thinks about putting zero down (Why not?) and some lenders will make 100% loans for a boat purchase "on approved

credit". But even if you do not meet the necessarily high credit standard, 100% financing is still available using either (a) additional side collateral such as real estate, securities or even another boat to cover the imputed down payment or (b) lease financing(5). If you do decide to obtain maximum leverage from your purchase, just be aware that upon selling your boat, after allowing for depreciation, commissions and selling expenses, the sale proceeds may not be sufficient to retire the then outstanding principal balance. This could make trading up to a bigger boat a decidedly unpleasant experience.

2) Interest rate commitments on a future boat delivery based on current rates. The cost is nominal to buy rate protection that protects you against any increase in market rates while you wait for your yacht to be built or delivered. This can be especially useful when you feel a rising interest rate environment lurks ahead.

3) Interest only financing with an option to pay principal within certain guidelines whenever you choose. A very useful program if your income is based on commissions or large periodic bonuses.

4) Deferred payments over a period of non-use, such as wintertime in the Northeast. The skipped payments are refigured into the loan once payments start and are amortized over the remaining term.

5) Floating/fixed convertible loans. If rates are high and likely to fall, these loans allow you to close on a variable rate, enjoy subsequent decreases in payment, with an option to convert to a fixed rate at a later date.

The list goes on, but the theme is simple. When you are borrowing a lot of money, you have the right and the ability to structure the loan in a manner that makes sense to you as well as the bank.

What you should expect...no, demand, from your lender

There are lots of marine lenders out there. At last count, each of the major market areas had at least twenty firms willing to provide yacht loans. In 1988, the National Marine Bankers Association counted 155 member institutions nationwide holding $16 billion in boat loans. With all those choices, you should never be content to simply buy what some lender has; rather, buy what you need. It may require a little shopping but for the money you'll pay in interest and the term you'll be paying it, it's worth the effort. If the broker has steered you to a particular firm and you're not happy with his choice, go elsewhere. Often times a dealer or broker is getting some kind of referral fee or contest prize for sending customers to a particular lender. While that may help his pocketbook it is not necessarily good for you if your needs are not being met.

Once you have selected your loan program, review it carefully with the lender to make sure there are no hidden features like prepayment penalties or boat usage restrictions. You may also want to query your lender on whether your loan can be easily and inexpensively refinanced should interest rates go lower in the future. Will you be contacted or is it up to you to keep checking?

Any question you ask deserves an answer. Be suspicious of a lender who says too often "I'll have to check on that one and get back to you." Quick, confident and correct answers to your questions indicates a lender who knows his stuff and that can save you lots of headaches as you proceed.

A good lender will know essentially all that this book covers. That's their job. Use that expertise to help structure your own loan and don't shy away from really making him work overtime if you have a particularly difficult transaction to pull off. After all, getting to know your banker makes it all that much easier when it comes time to trade up.

---

(1) Note that as rates move upward, the break even APR between the point/no-point loans moves slightly farther out in time. The reason? Simply that at higher rates, a given "amount" of rate that you are buying down becomes a smaller proportion of the overall rate. For this reason, at higher rates you may be able to negotiate a **larger** increase in your buydown for a set amount of points.

(2) Many lenders, who set rates in accordance with the "one year Treasury", the "three year Treasury", and so forth, are actually using the so called Treasury Constant Maturities, an index compiled and published by the Federal Reserve Bank each Monday in Statistical Release H.15. The index is described in that release as follows:

> *Yields on Treasury securities at constant maturity are estimated from the Treasury's daily yield curve. This curve, which relates the yield on a security to its time to maturity, is based on the closing market bid yields on actively traded Treasury securities in the over-the-counter market. These market yields are calculated from composites of quotations reported by five leading U.S. Government securities dealers to the Federal Reserve Bank of New York. The constant yield values are read from the yield curve at fixed maturities, currently 1, 2, 3, 5, 7, 10 and 30 years. This method permits estimation of the yield for a 10-year maturity, for example, even if no outstanding security has exactly 10 years remaining to maturity.*

(3) This is not necessarily the amount **borrowed**. Refer back to the discussion on Paying for Points in Chapter 4.

(4) Mathematically, the APR is equivalent to the Internal Rate of Return for any cash flow sequence of equal and even periods and payments.

(5) Provided, of course, there are no big cancellation fees.

CHAPTER 6

MARINE INSURANCE: Policies and Practices

A friend of ours in the insurance business, attempting to induce a boat owner into buying a liability policy that was more than the owner felt necessary, said "you don't have to be a millionaire to get sued like one." Most likely that cute little phrase is the first thing all insurance salesmen learn to say, but it worked. The yachtsman doubled his coverage on the spot.

Regrettably, many of us have come to view insurance of any kind as a necessary evil at best, a useless expense at worst. Without insurance, however, many normal business transactions, consumer purchases and other routine commitments would be impossible. Insurance is the great equalizer, spreading risk amongst numerous parties to create benefits for the individual. Insurance, in effect, asks all of us to support the cost of a statistically predetermined number of events, or accidents, requiring expenditures to correct, that none of us is willing (or perhaps able) to handle alone.

Marine insurance constitutes a very small portion of this $120 billion a year total market, but it nonetheless has its own unique set of product features and underwriting guidelines. Understanding these features and guidelines allows the informed buyer to structure an insurance program that conforms best to overall objectives. Sometimes these objectives encompass other elements of the purchase such as financing, registration, and charter.

Who Provides Insurance?

Although numerous property-casualty insurance companies will insure boats today, a limited number of underwriters, or carriers, will write a true "Yacht Policy"; they therefore supply the majority of the market needs. The top six or eight marine insurance underwriters now supply approximately 80% of the nation's marine coverage. These companies include Reliance, Cigna, MOAC, Lloyds, Fireman's Fund, and Commercial Union.

A Yacht Policy generally applies to boats of 26' to 30' feet in length and up. Smaller boats are more typically covered on a "Watercraft Policy" or as an endorsement to one's homeowners policy. Companies such as State Farm and Allstate are the major players to small boat insurance.

Because the marine market is small (compared to other insurance markets) and owing to the specialized knowledge and service needs of the marine industry, most of this coverage is placed through independent licensed insurance agents, and each agent may represent several marine underwriters, in addition to other carriers specializing in other insurance lines. These agents play a key role in understanding underwriter concerns and requirements, and are therefore in the best position to obtain the right policy.

Picking the right agent/underwriter team can be a very important first step in obtaining coverage. Just as you want to feel comfortable with your boat broker and marine lender, so should it be with your insurance agency and the company they represent. In the event of a future claim, the agent is your first call in the process of obtaining a final settlement from the insurance carrier that wrote the policy. Get to know both of them at the outset.

Selecting an agent

Although it seems like stating the obvious, it is extremely important to pick an agent who specializes in marine insurance. If you approach the agent who placed your homeowners or auto insurance, you may get a quote that appears reasonable. But the policy itself may include exclusions or coverage you can ill afford, or it may not be a Yacht Policy at all! This is particularly true with respect to liability coverage, addressed later on.

To start, you'll probably want an agent who can place with several sources. Rates and coverage don't vary much from agent to agent within a particular insurance company's program. There may exist, however, an additional 10-15% discretionary credit available for especially good business to agencies designated by the carrier as a Managing General Agent or "Professional Yacht Agent".

From carrier to carrier quotes may vary by 30% in the "standard" market and even more in the excess and surplus markets such as Lloyds. Later on, we'll see what criteria affects insurance quotes; a good agent can direct your business to the source that best fits your needs and experience. Most good marine insurance agents use at least three (five preferably) insurance companies to fully cover the spectrum of possible programs.

Next, examine the agent's operating history. Have they been doing business in your area for an extended period of time? Geography plays a significant role in establishing rates so you'll want to know your agent has experience in placing business from your area. For example, some carriers will no longer write coverage on boats in key locations such as Dade and Broward counties in south Florida, certain areas around New York City, and the Gulf of Mexico.

Also advisable is asking around with other boatmen as to the agent's service record on claims. If you are dealing with an established insurance agency, you'll certainly find someone at the marina or yacht club who has a policy with the company. Such referrals are a valuable source of information that should go into your decision. Two important questions to ask: How fast did the agent respond to a claims request? How easy was it to obtain special endorsements or change coverage?

Look also at the length of time the agent has been working with the intended underwriter. A long term and strong relationship means faster claims service and a better chance at obtaining future endorsements for special coverage at reasonable cost, such as for extended cruising or charter usage. A weak agent may not have the resources to handle special coverage, forcing you to go elsewhere later. Remember, once a policy is bound you may be penalized to cancel through a method known as "short rating" which in effect requires a portion of the unused premium (usually 10%) to be retained by the company.(1) If you anticipate any special coverage, find out upfront what is required.

Finally, ask your lender what they think of your insurance selection. Since all lenders require insurance on financed purchases, they can probably give you a good reading on a claims service record. The reason? You'll discover that, prior to closing, the lender will require an endorsement on the policy naming itself as a "loss payee" or "mortgagee as its interest may appear". This so-called "banker's endorsement" gives the lender the right to your claim check up to the amount of its legal interest, or the amount of the outstanding principal balance plus accrued interest, expenses and so forth. For large claims, the bank looks to your reimbursement as the only means of satisfying your debt. Even on small claims, your lender's counter signature will be required on the check in order to cash it. If the lender has poor experience in collecting payment with a particular agent or underwriter, you can be sure they will let you know about it.

The underwriter

Just as you are free to select an agent, so to are you free to pick the underwriter, although the agent is certainly in a better position to do so. Feeling comfortable with the agent should allow you to feel good about his selection of carrier, although there are certain guidelines to consider. First, look at the overall rating of the company. A.M. Best Co. is the largest rating agency for the insurance industry and their "Best's Guide to Insurance Companies" is a compendium of company ratings that takes into account a firm's financial strength, loss experience, diversification and other factors to provide an overall rating, ranging from C (fair) to A+ (top rated). A rating of B+ or above is a good bet; if you seek an "umbrella" policy as well (described later on), generally only an "A" rating will do. You shouldn't accept a poorly rated company just to receive a better quote. A very cheap quote can imply a very cheap policy! Besides, most banks have a minimum acceptable rating for insurance companies protecting their investment.

Next, examine the carrier's recent loss ratio, which is the ratio of premiums collected to claims paid (Best contains this information and your agent can share it with you). A loss ratio of greater than 1.00 means the company is currently taking in less in premiums than it is paying out in claims and expenses. This could (although not necessarily) indicate that a substantial premium increase is on the way at renewal. In 1984 the property-casualty industry as a whole took a drubbing for the first time since 1906, the year of the San Francisco earthquake and fire, due mainly to a six-year price war in commercial insurance. As marine insurance rates have also been forced down due to competitive pressures in recent years, a number of venerable marine underwriters have suffered loss ratios greater than 1.00 in their marine portfolios and it may not be long before their rates begin to climb again.

Finally, you may also request a copy of the policy to examine it prior to purchase. Like most insurance policies, the language may be long and involved, but the time required to review it will be well spent if by doing so you avoid future problems.

The Types and Costs of Coverage

Marine insurance comes in all shapes and sizes. But certain elements are present in a majority of cases. Below, we will detail a number of these standard provisions and describe the costs associated with each. But two things must be kept in mind. First, we are dealing only with a Yacht Policy, and while other kinds of policies will provide certain marine related coverage, only the Yacht Policy (and it is always referred to as such) will provide all the various coverages listed below.

Second, marine insurance carriers do differ in the finer points of each area of coverage. For example, minimum deductibles may vary, or contain a deductible waiver provision upon total loss. Some policies do not include marring, denting and scratching from the "normal wear and tear" exclusion, while others do. Personal property limits may vary by a wide margin, as might medical payment base limits. Because of these differences and because of other factors, pricing will differ by a fair amount. Exhibit 6-1 illustrates some of the fine points to examine in your policy.

Exhibit 6-1

Comparision of Three Yacht Policies

Item	Company A	Company B	Company C
Agreed value coverage	Yes	Yes	Yes
Minimum deductible	$250	1%	1%
Minimum length	20 ft.	26 ft.	28 ft.
Land transport coverage	Yes	Yes	No
Commercial towing	Yes	No	No
Seizure by civil authority	Yes	Yes	Yes
Voided coverage from concealment or fraud	Yes	Yes	Yes
Personal property limit	$1,000	$500	$500
Uninsured boater coverage	Yes	Yes	Yes
Medical payments limit	$5,000	$5,000	$2,000
Capture and seizure endorsement available	Yes	Yes	No
Breach of warranty available	Yes	Yes	Yes

Hull insurance

Hull insurance covers the boat itself, including all spars, sails, machinery, furniture, fittings and electronics that are a part of the boat and which are required to be on the boat for its safe operation and maintenance, whether afloat or ashore. This also includes auxiliary boats or launches that may be included in the policy.

You should always obtain "All-Risk" type hull coverage which covers accidental direct physical loss or damage from any cause, other than what is specifically excluded. Such exclusions normally include war, nuclear disaster, piracy, riots and insurrections, and confiscation. Special coverage is sometimes available for these exclusions. Losses arising from negligence or improper use are also not covered, as is damage from wear and tear and gradual deterioration.

"Named Peril" type policies cover only those risks stated in the policy declarations. While such policies are less expensive, they are also less effective, and thus not often sold. Nevertheless, they may be the only type of policy available for certain special coverages, such as ocean passages or racing, or coverage for certain older vessels.

The maximum amount of reimbursement is stated in the policy declarations.(2) Normally, this is stated as an "Agreed Valuation" and such a policy is therefore an Agreed Valuation Contract (AVC). A deductible is always included and is stated as a percentage of the Agreed Value, one percent being standard. Watch out for an "Actual Cash Value" contract. Upon a total loss, you may be entitled to collect only what the adjuster's boat price guide says is the vessel's market value without regard to the original cash price paid.

Should a loss occur under an AVC, an amount will be paid up to the AVC figure, less both the deductible and a figure representing depreciation on certain equipment, mainly sails, outboards and batteries. Most policies provide for full AVC payment without the deductible should a total loss occur and an insurance company will consider your loss as total if the cost of recovery and repair is greater than the Agreed Value.

Once an Agreed Value is obtained, any additional coverage (such as for new equipment) is added by endorsement. The deductible can similarly be changed by endorsement, but you will find that most lenders, on a financed transaction, will allow a maximum 2% of insured value.

For new boat purchases, the amount of hull coverage obtainable will pretty much be a function of the price you paid for the boat. This figure often includes taxes and commissioning thus covering your total investment. You may be required to document this investment so it's a good idea to keep a complete file of invoices, tax receipts and yard bills. If you feel you received a "special deal" by going factory direct or by receiving special (non-customary) discounts, bring this to the attention of your agent. Additional coverage may be possible.

On a used boat sale, hull coverage is a little more difficult to determine. The price-you-paid rule still applies, but the insurance company will also look at a used boat price guide to see if any large discrepancies exist. The BUC Used Boat Price Guide is still the reference of choice. If a large difference is encountered, you should have a suitable explanation ready. Perhaps the vessel has very low engine hours, or just underwent a major refit. A survey will help determine this and most insurance companies will require one (hauled) on boats five (in some cases ten) years or older. You may also be required to periodically survey the boat if you own it for more than five years.

A note on the topic of surveys is perhaps in order here. Most insurance agents (and lenders for that matter) recognize that marine surveys are somewhat limited as a means of identifying value. There is no federal or state agency regulating surveyors so an enforceable standard does not now exist. For this reason, surveys are generally read with an eye to determining overall condition and equipping of the vessel. Thus, don't be surprised if you are told the boat cannot be insured for its survey market value, especially if that figure is substantially greater than the purchase price. A smart agent knows that the market is the basic determiner of boat prices and values, and there simply is not an abundance of "great deals" out there.

In order to support your contention of a higher-than-paid boat value, prepare information on what similar vessels sold for recently, along with current asking prices. Point out the finer aspects of your yacht and keep in mind that the agent himself has some influence with the underwriter in adjudicating discrepancies, especially if the agent/carrier relationship is strong.

In spite of your best efforts to insure an older boat, you may still encounter some resistance from the agent. In any event, you'll quickly discover a surcharge is assessed for power boats at ten years and sailboats at fifteen years. Since AVCs call for replacement of damage, older boats generally require greater claims payments as a percentage of Agreed Value than newer boats. For example, a 1970 Bertram with a market value of $30,000 costs the same to repair as a 1985 Bertram with a market value of $180,000. Yet, in the absence of a surcharge, the carrier would be providing similar coverage at a fraction of the premium for the older boat.

Also, because many large agents are on a loss ratio related profit sharing plan with their major carriers on the policies placed with them, they may be reluctant to carry coverage on vessels that have a higher incidence of claims experience. Ultimately, you may be required to do a little more shopping to get the right coverage.

The cost of coverage - Insurance companies employ fairly complicated pricing schedules to arrive at premium rates. Hull coverage accounts for about 90% of the quote, so we'll concentrate on its pricing. We'll cover a number of the items affecting this quote, but by no means is the list complete. The figures offered are industry standards but show a fair amount of variance from company to company.

Final premiums are calculated as a base rate less certain credits, both expressed in dollars. The base rates are fairly consistent within a given carrier and are priced as a percentage of the Agreed Valuation. Generally, the size of the yacht does not affect this percentage, although on larger boats, the vessel make could. Sailboat base rates are 15%-20% less due to a more favorable loss history, yet certain types of sailboats, for instance multi-hulls and ultra-lights, are much more difficult to insure. If you do find this type of coverage it will no doubt be substantially higher.

"Go fast" boats, those with rated speeds in excess of forty knots, always command a surcharge which can be quite high depending on the make. Premiums run to around five percent of hull coverage and often carry certain machinery damage exclusions and high deductibles.

Once the base rate is established, certain credits, expressed as a percentage of the base rate, are deducted from the base rate. A short list follows:

Exhibit 6-2

Credit item	Credit amount
Diesel power (vs. gas power)	10%
Power squadron training or a recognized sailing school	2.5 - 5%
VHF on board	5%
Fathometer on board	2.5%
Halon or CO_2 system	5% (gas)
	2.5% (diesel)
Full time skipper	5%
2% deductible (vs. 1%)	10%-15%
Trawler (vs. sport fish or motor yacht)	10%
Inland waters navigating limits	10%

Other credits are also available, but the associated discounts are less standardized. Previous boat ownership, especially if it is loss free, often rates a nice credit. Many insurance companies will shy away from persons who are just getting into boat ownership especially if they are starting out young, with new money, buying large boats with which they may not be entirely familiar.

If your boat is laid up part of the year, for instance in the colder northern regions, additional credits are also granted. The total number of months laid up and the boat's location will determine the actual amount

Anticipated use also determines the cost of hull coverage. If the boat is intended for charter, additional costs will be encountered, with many insurers avoiding this market altogether. If you plan to use your boat extensively for racing, you may be assessed a surcharge and if your boat is heavily race equipped, you may find that certain equipment such as sails, spars and rigging cannot be insured in the basic policy. More will be mentioned on these points later.

Again, these are only very broad guidelines and tend to apply mainly for Agreed Values of up to $200,000. Over that figure, the credits are less and the policy tends to be more custom designed and specially priced, mainly because so many of the large policies are reinsured through other companies. On a large boat purchase, the type of reinsurance policy a carrier has can mean a big difference to you in terms of price so it's a good idea to look to a broker that specializes in the big boat market.

All of the information necessary to receive a quote is usually obtained through the insurance questionnaire. The form will ask you for the year, make, model and length of your vessel along with engine type, model number and horsepower rating. List all electronic, navigation and safety equipment and if your boat doesn't have a VHF and fathometer, buy them. They'll pay for themselves with insurance savings alone.

You should make every effort to be accurate when completing the questionnaire, even if you need to bring out information not requested. Minor points you might easily overlook could save you many dollars in credits. It will also help your agent in placing the policy where it costs the least. Whatever you do, NEVER intentionally misrepresent the facts. Upon claiming a loss, it could void your entire policy. You can rest assured that if an insurer can avoid paying a claim due to a willful misrepresentation, it will.

In order to demonstrate the variation in the cost of hull coverage, the following quotes were obtained from one agency writing through INA Insurance Company during July, 1989. All examples assume completion of Power Squadron safety course, boarded VHF and fathometer, automatic fire fighting system, Atlantic coastal navigation, one percent deductible, and an experienced operator with no losses.

Exhibit 6-3

Vessel	Hull Coverage	Engines	Premium (1 year) Hull	$300K P&I
1985 46' Bertram	$400,000	twin diesel	$4,062	$221
1982 26' Wellcraft (60 mph)	$32,000	twin gas (260hp)	$1,440	$400
1973 33' Morgan	$36,000	single diesel	$416	$64
1978 50' Gulfstar	$200,000	single diesel	$1,443	$158

Protection & Indemnity insurance

Perhaps the most misunderstood component of a yacht policy, Protection & Indemnity (P&I) is most often viewed as simple liability coverage of the type already available through one's homeowners policy. Nothing could be farther from the truth.

P&I insurance is the broadest of all liability insurance for ships, yachts and boats. Originally developed by the underwriters at the Lloyds of London syndicate, P&I represents the type of coverage that most completely provides full protection for marine related liability and accidents. Not only does it "protect" — give legal advice and counsel, defend in court, pay legal fees and determine liability, it will also "indemnify" — pay the court award. Other types of liability insurance are available, and they may sometimes defend an uncovered claim in a civil court. However, in the event a suit is adjudicated under maritime law in admiralty court, such coverage may not indemnify. P&I is then a promise by the insurance company to pay on the owner's behalf for all damages for which the owner is legally liable in any court. This includes both bodily injury and property damage.

Hull coverage **can** be purchased without P&I leaving the insured to think his homeowners policy might pick up the liability. Rarely is this the case. No liability insurance other than P&I will provide complete protection. For example, unlike P&I, your homeowners liability won't cover 1) removal of a wreck from a channel or dock; 2) liability or medical expenses if a business friend or prospect sues as a result of injury sustained while aboard your vessel; or, 3) a friend who does bodily injury or property damage while using your boat.

This last point is perhaps the most important. You may forget many times that your friends and guests are not as familiar with safe boating as you might be. In the event of serious trouble, you, as the vessel owner, can be held responsible for any negligence or recklessness causing the injury or death of a guest. Keep in mind, anyone injured on the water has much greater opportunity for collecting heavily because of the more liberal laws regarding a maritime action.

More specifically, P&I **usually** covers:

1) Loss or damage to any other vessel or other property caused by your boat.

2) Any attempted or actual raising, removal, or destruction of the wreck of your insured boat or its cargo. This includes losses arising from the failure to raise, remove, or destroy the wreck.

3) Loss of life or bodily injury.

4) Payments made on account of life salvage.

5) Losses in (1)-(4) above resulting from your use of another persons boat (as long as you had the other owners permission to use the boat).

6) Loss or damage to another person's boat up to the amount of your hull coverage.

P&I insurance covers all legal costs of litigating a claim as well as the awards arising from the litigation. Thus, it is the insurance company's sole responsible to decide when and how to engage in legal action; regardless of this decision, you're covered.

P&I insurance coverage is most often bound in an amount between $300,000 and $500,000. Few lenders will accept any figure less than $300,000 for financed transactions and, with current trends in court awards, neither should you. Additional coverage for private pleasure use vessels can be picked up under what is known as an "Umbrella Policy" which covers any additional claims over the P&I limits. Umbrellas are often written at $1 million or more and essentially represent a "super" P&I policy with a $300,000 (or $500,000) deductible! For all this extra coverage, the additional premium is quite small — only about $100 extra per year for an individual.

The cost of P&I - It doesn't take a lot of money to obtain this very comprehensive coverage. Pricing is determined in much the same way as hull coverage with the same credits reflected in the quote. Only about 10% of the yearly premium is attributable to the P&I coverage, but unlike hull insurance, the base rate is determined by the vessel LOA (length overall), so the bigger the boat, the greater the cost for the same coverage amount, reflecting the greater damage they cause when a problem occurs or the greater number of people typically aboard.

Federal Longshoremen's and Harbor Workers' Compensation Insurance - Usually included in the P&I insurance, Longshoremen's and Harbor Workers' Compensation covers any compensation payments you might be responsible for under the Long Shoreman's and Harbor Workers' Act (Public Act No. 803, 69th Congress, approved March 4, 1927). Seamen are given much more liberal benefits under this law than are workers under Workman's Compensation on land, and it is surprisingly easy for a guest to be construed as a "seaman" under the law. Such persons are entitled to "maintenance and cure" as well as a liberal right to damages for bodily injury and disability. The cost of this insurance is usually included in the P&I premium.

Medical Payments Insurance - Often, small claims will be entered for medical payments arising from bodily injury sustained aboard the insured vessel. Normally covered under the P&I insurance, they may not be large enough to justify litigation. In this case, at the direction of the policy holder (and with sufficient proof of claim) the insurance company will issue a check for the claim up to the limit of coverage. In effect, this type of coverage represents a "no-fault" policy provision because no liability is admitted by the insured or the company; payment is made simply to keep the matter out of court.

The cost of medical payments coverage is included in the P&I and the coverage amount rarely exceeds $5,000 under normal conditions. If a claim is submitted for a greater amount, it usually justifies a more thorough investigation and possible legal proceedings.

Personal Property Insurance - Personal property insurance covers personal effects, clothing, sports equipment and so forth for you and members of your family while these items are on board your vessel. Some policies will also include these same items belonging to your guests. A nominal limit is set at around $500 to $1,000 although you can purchase more.

You'll encounter a number of personal property exclusions such as money and checks, valuable papers and documents, jewelry, furs, animals, household furniture and goods intended for sale or exhibition. Also excluded is property acquired for use with the vessel although this is covered in the hull insurance.

Your coverage will not include losses due to wear and tear, vermin, temperature and humidity effects, or mechanical or electrical breakdown. Also, if the loss cannot be satisfactorily explained, you may not be able to obtain a claim. If a payment is made, it will be for the replacement cost less an amount for depreciation. In any event, a small deductible usually applies to any personal property loss.

Limitations and exclusions

All marine insurance policies will have initial navigation limits stated in the declarations. They are established by the area you live in and are fairly standard across companies. For instance, if you live on the Eastern seaboard, your limits will probably read "Eastport, Maine to Cedar Keys, Florida". If you reside in Southern California, you'll likely see "Pt. Conception, California to Ensenada, Mexico". This doesn't mean you can't cruise to areas outside these limits; you'll simply have to obtain an endorsement allowing you to do so.

If you do not obtain the endorsement, your coverage will not be effective if an accident occurs in waters outside the stated navigation limits. For this reason, if your purchase was financed, the lender might have required a "438 BFU" endorsement (Breach of Warranty clause) which covers the loan balance if a loss occurs when your vessel is outside the navigation limits. This endorsement does cost a little extra, 10 to 25 cents per $100 of hull value, but it effectively provides worldwide coverage for at least the loan amount.

The cost to obtain special navigation limits coverage is fairly reasonable if you simply wish to travel to other contiguous U.S. coastal areas. Generally, you'll be charged a one time fee of between $50 and $100. On the other hand, if you wish to travel to distant coastal areas, where you have little or no local knowledge, or if you plan to cruise outside U.S. waters (perhaps in the Caribbean or Mexico) the cost will be much greater. It all depends on the size of the vessel, its insured value, and of course, your experience. But even a two week hop from Florida to the British Virgin Islands on a forty foot sloop can run as much as $1,000.

If you wish to make more distant passages, say from California to Hawaii or Florida to Europe, the costs will be commensurately greater. Especially difficult journeys to politically unstable regions or through treacherous waters may not be insurable at all. If they are, the cost could be unrealistically high and the coverage will most likely be on a named peril basis only. If you plan such a trip, your agent can help you obtain coverage through a company that specializes in named peril insurance. But read the policy carefully; be satisfied that you are protected should unanticipated trouble occur, such as vessel confiscation. This type of insurance is available from specialty companies, the London market being preferred.

If you do get this kind of coverage, make sure you have complied with all the requirements stated in the policy, which might include employment of a Coast Guard licensed skipper, an American Bureau of Shipping or similar certificate on the vessel, and special navigation or safety equipment. Not complying could void your policy (at perhaps a very inconvenient time and place!) should trouble arise.

Intended usage represents another major area of restriction. Without special coverage, your policy likely excludes charter use, whether bareboat or crewed. Coverage is obtainable but getting expensive due mainly to the proliferation of poorly run charter management companies that do not properly care for their boats or accurately establish the competency of the users. Self chartering (without the benefit of a charter manager) is also excluded, but of course is much more difficult for an insurance company to track. If you simply let a friend "borrow" your boat, you will be covered but you should always be confident of his or her competency. Remember, negligence or misuse can be grounds to deny a claim.

For sailors, racing may represent another use restriction. Certainly club racing and informal competition with friends is okay. But if you plan to enter this year's SORC or Transpac events, you will need special coverage if for no other reason than to handle the navigation limits.You may also want to look into additional coverage for spars, sails and equipment which are not normally protected on vessels designed for racing.

Paying for your insurance

Upon accepting a quote, the first year's premium is due up front. A couple of options are available here. The first obviously, is payment by cash, but most agents are willing to bind coverage upon receipt of a signed insurance application and approval by the carrier. In fact, the larger and more established agencies have their own binding authority up to a certain dollar amount on insurance packages that conform to overall carrier requirements. Your evidence of coverage is a "binder", a single page document that specifies the terms of coverage. Generally speaking, you will have to put up a deposit with the balance due in thirty days; take any longer and the policy will be automatically cancelled.

A second option involves premium financing. Most agents will have sources available that are willing to lend you the premium money. Actually, it represents a fairly risk free form of lending. Since your premium is earned by the insurance company over the life of the policy, an early cancellation (resulting from say, your failure to make the premium payments) will result in a rebate of the unearned premium, less an amount for short-rating. The lender also makes a fantastic rate of interest, ranging from fifteen to twenty-two percent or more depending on where you live. If this rate seems too high you may find a yacht finance company that will add the premium to your loan contract, thus giving you the benefit of the note rate for your premium financing.

At the expiration of the policy, the agent sends a renewal notice. As long as the insurance company's experience with your policy has been favorable, the renewal should be quite easy. The cost may nevertheless go up; insurance, like anything else, is subject to inflationary pressures and, more importantly, market conditions.

Special Coverages

For the majority of boatmen, the preceding effectively covers most, if not all the issues, that you will encounter when insuring your yacht. However, you may occasionally have need to obtain more specialized coverage, and the options in this case are not nearly so numerous.

Coverage while racing

As mentioned before, racing coverage can be difficult to obtain and often commands a high price. Sailboat racing coverage is generally determined by boat design. For example, a cruising sailboat that is raced will employ a racing coverage endorsement on a basic yacht policy that is standard rated. The carrier may exclude spars and rigging from coverage while racing under the endorsement, but this would be unusual.

An International Offshore Racing (IOR) type race boat is quite a different matter altogether. Because it is used almost exclusively for racing, one must go to a specialty market for coverage. Starkweather & Shipley of Chicago has an USYRU endorsed program that provides coverage, albeit at a much higher premium. The policy also contains restrictive endorsements on the policy such as a mandatory 10% of hull value deductible on the standing rig and sails.

Power boat racing insurance is even more difficult to obtain and coverage is usually for liability only. The sponsoring racing association generally makes the coverage available.

Cargo insurance

Knowledgeable boat buyers are becoming aware that a number of good deals are available by purchasing overseas. Most often, these buys are arranged by a U.S. broker or dealer and the buyer need do little more than arrange for stateside financing and a letter of credit. For the purchaser who wishes to exclude the middleman and take the savings by buying direct, arrangements for insuring the vessel importation must be made.

Coverage for all phases of the yacht delivery is available in an "Ocean Cargo Policy", a type of insurance that protects the boat while it is being shipped aboard a freighter. Because this is a marine coverage, it is handled by the same carriers and brokers that insure pleasure boats.

The cost of the coverage ranges widely from $0.55 to $1.00 per $100 of insured value depending on such factors as the freighter shipped aboard, how the yacht is secured and shipped (deck cargo versus below deck), the overall distance, the ports of entry and exit and so forth. Most shipments are insured at 110% of assessed value and war coverage is available at a slight additional cost.

Charter insurance

If you plan to charter your boat for the tax advantage it may provide, you will want to spend some extra time making sure the insurance coverage fully protects your investment. Charter insurance is becoming more difficult to obtain, for reasons outlined earlier.

During the first six months of 1985, the availability of charter boat insurance diminished significantly. Unfortunately, the reason for this lies in the fact that a number of carriers aggressively bid for the business in 1983 and 1984 without perhaps understanding the pitfalls of the charter boat industry. As a result, losses mounted in charter portfolios that were not covered by premiums; a number of carriers subsequently dropped out of the market.

As a result, the carriers that have remained (and there are few) have raised prices and are more restrictive on what they will accept. For example, there appears to be only two companies in this country that will still write coverage for self charter. However, if that same boat is provided with a captain (a crewed charter), coverage becomes easier to obtain. Pricing is determined by the amount of charter service the boat is expected to undergo.

A much easier way to obtain coverage is through placement of your yacht in a bare boat charter fleet. In this case, coverage is underwritten on the quality of the charter manager. The carrier looks at a number of criteria such as financial viability of the company, years in business, check in/check out procedures, maintenance schedules, and even the wording of the lease-back or management agreement. For more established fleets, the underwriter will even make a close examination of the charter company's loss ratio.

Quite often, the established charter operator will have a master policy with one broker and insurance company. The rate to the operator, and thus the owner, is based on the loss ratio, management ability and type of coverage, and boats and owners are added and deleted from the policy as vessels are sold into or retired from the fleet.

The owner should always be a bit cautious when looking at insurance coverage on a charter boat. The policies are almost always more restrictive than a standard yacht policy although the more reputable and long standing fleets obviously have the best coverage. But extra coverage is available and three particular types are worth looking into:

1) **Capture and Seizure** - This coverage protects the owner if the boat, while out on charter, is captured or seized by a lawful or unlawful party. Whether the boat is never found or is destroyed, you're covered. This coverage is particular useful in certain waters, notably the Caribbean and Gulf of Mexico.

2) **Breach of Warranty** - Covered earlier, a Breach of Warranty endorsement provides protection to the owner if the charterer goes beyond the agreed upon navigating limits.

3) **Loss of Use** - If a charter boat is damaged and becomes unusable due to an insured peril, this coverage will provide the owner or charter company with an amount equal to the lost charter income for charters that had **already** been reserved. There is usually a three days income deductible. The coverage is inexpensive, usually about 15% of the total annual premium, and is very useful in demonstrating to the IRS at tax time that you have every intent to "insure" a profit.

One last word of caution. While you must always be wary of flimsy charter companies, the same is true of insurance companies that insure charter boats. Go for the best here, because a lot of the so called "offshore" companies that provide coverage for offshore fleets might not be around at claims time. Lloyds syndicate carriers are the largest insurer of offshore fleets and about the only safe bet. For U.S. based fleets, the major U.S. marine carriers do a good job.

---

(1) On the other hand, if the policy is cancelled by the carrier, you will only be charged for the number of days the coverage was in effect.

(2) A "declaration" is any policy item contained in the original policy whereas an "endorsement""is any addition or change to the policy effected within the policy period.

CHAPTER 7

BOAT REGISTRATION: The Necessary Paperwork

Before you actually close a boat purchase, the manner in which you provide for legal ownership must be examined. Many factors affect the way boat ownership is registered including the terms of purchase (cash, trade or finance), the state you reside in, where the boat will be docked, and even how long you plan to own it and the options you might desire in selling it. The prudent buyer also needs a background knowledge of boat registration requirements in order to confidently purchase a boat knowing that all the requisite forms and documents are correct, thereby eliminating future problems or even involvement in fraudulent transfers of ownership.

The issue is somewhat complicated by the number of regulations governing boat ownership and the frequency at which law makers enjoy changing them. As the pleasure boat industry continues to grow and tax the resources of present systems, a major overhaul of documentation, registration, and titling regulations will become unavoidable. In fact, a major piece of Federal legislation is ready to be enacted which could change substantial parts of what is about to be said.

Registration and Documentation

There are essentially two ways vessel ownership is evidenced: Through a state registration system, possibly including a "titling" component, and through the Federal registration system. Although both systems were **created** through Federal law, the **administration** of state registration is left to the individual states, and so wide differences are noted among them. Federal registration, or documentation, on the other hand provides a nearly uniform means of vessel registration.

In addition to acknowledging ownership, vessel registration also provides the means in many cases of recording and enforcing lender liens on boats purchased with credit. The casual reader may be tempted to say "So what?" but the fact remains that without some fairly efficient and inexpensive means of establishing and enforcing a secured interest in an expensive asset like a boat, very little money would be made available to buy them. In a very real sense, the strength of the laws surrounding boating, especially the unique Federal laws that apply to the maritime industry, are responsible for putting yacht ownership into the hands of so many who might otherwise never know the pleasure of boating.

As stated before, the primary distinction between registration method lies in state versus federal jurisdiction. At this writing, all states except Alaska have a federally approved registration and numbering statute while twenty-four states and the District of Columbia possess additional vessel titling laws. These laws were written, adopted, and amended over time and as you might guess display wide variations from state to state. In general however they contain several similar features: They (i) evidence ownership, (ii) assure payment of certain fees, assessments and taxes, and (iii) regulate compliance with certain ownership requirements in areas such as safety, usage and residency. Where a provision for a certificate of title also exists, such a document is the actual legal ownership instrument.

Federal registration is very different, providing as it does a nearly uniform and internationally recognized means of evidencing current ownership, chain of ownership, national origin, and lien recordation. Our system of federal documentation dates back to the English maritime system of the 18th century, and provides a fascinating history that puts a number of unique characteristics of the U.S. maritime industry into perspective.

U.S. Coast Guard Vessel Documentation

Shipping has been an integral part of civilization longer than almost any other human endeavor. Evidence of the use of sea going vessels dates back to the dawn of recorded history, and few cultures ever achieved world prominence without a sophisticated shipping industry. The idea of trade amongst nations was a direct result of the ability of men to traverse long, open distances by boat to exchange goods for the betterment of all.

It is no wonder then that the systems of law and commerce regarding trans-oceanic trade and shipping are among the oldest of all industries. More surprising however, is the fact that our American system of registration is a direct descendent of much older methods of controlling and regulating watercraft that have remained basically intact.

Almost since the beginning of the republic, U.S. shipping regulation has been designed to protect and promote the domestic shipping industry. The origins are contained in the mercantilistic philosophy of the European nations of the 1600s and 1700s. As industry and commerce between nations grew, a greater emphasis was continually placed on a country's manufacturing capability and the development of foreign markets for domestic products. England in particular adopted a number of acts that restricted the manner in which goods could be shipped into England and from the early colonies. Central to this policy was the use of only English built vessels for the transport of goods into the British Empire and trade with the colonies. The system was designed to protect and promote the British shipping industry as well as providing a means to regulate it. In this manner the British maritime industry was given a boost that it might otherwise not have enjoyed.

During colonial times, shipbuilding thrived in the American colonies due to a number of very different factors. The colonists were skilled craftsmen who came from countries with a maritime heritage and their location along the eastern seaboard allowed good lines of communication as well as an excellent supply of timber. As a result, America's own shipbuilding industry was very well developed at the time our country won its independence.

Vessel documentation in the United States borrows directly from the British maritime system which itself dates back to the 1500s. That system, and its American offspring, provides a certificate of nationality for any vessel registered under it; a registered ship is a "flag vessel" of its country of origin and represents that country and its law in peacetime commerce or wartime conflict.

The earliest regulations in the U.S. date back to the 3rd Act of Congress although they did not restrict foreign vessels or owners from engaging in foreign or coastwise(1) trade; it was simply more expensive to do so. Tariffs and tonnage duties were least for vessels made in the U.S. and operated by U.S. citizens, and most for foreign vessels (regardless of ownership). In the middle were U.S. built vessels owned and operated by foreigners. Thus, historically, shipbuilding has been favored over ship ownership and operation in America.

Throughout the 19th century, a number of laws were passed that gradually provided for more restrictive regulation of U.S. shipping. In 1817 the first law was passed prohibiting the carriage of merchandise between contiguous U.S. ports in a vessel belonging to a non-U.S. citizen. Gradually, more prohibitions were placed on vessels of foreign origin or that had been registered under a foreign flag or were manned by foreign crews.

Finally, in 1920, Congress passed the Shipping Act, 1920, more commonly known today as the "Jones Act" after its chief sponsor, Senator Jones of Washington. Section 27 of this act provides that no vessel may engage in the coastwise trade (that is, between U.S. ports) unless that vessel (1) is documented under U.S. laws, (2) was built in the U.S., (3) is owned by U.S. citizens (except in the case of a U.S. corporation where 75% of the ownership must be held by U.S. citizens), and (4) has not been previously sold to a foreign citizen or placed under foreign registry.(2)

While there are a number of sub-sections and provisos to this act, it does provide a good back drop to a general discussion on vessel documentation. It is interesting to see how our present system grew out of commercial shipping regulation and it does have a significant impact on certain topics addressed elsewhere in this book, particularly charter.

Federal registration

Regulation and enforcement of the Jones Act comes primarily through the device known as vessel documentation, which provides for registration according to a specific set of eligibility requirements established in federal law. Any boat carrying passengers or merchandise for hire in U.S. waters must have a valid registry and the type of trade being conducted determines whether or not a U.S. registry is needed. Eligibility requirements also determine whether a particular vessel can be U.S. documented. In effect then, vessel documentation both allows and excludes vessel usage in U.S. waters.

Since the passage of the Jones Act, other categories of vessel registration have been established so that foreign built boats may qualify for federal documentation. One of these categories, "pleasure", will be treated in more detail since most private owners will register in this fashion.

Vessel documentation is performed by the United States Coast Guard (USCG) which is a division of the Department of Transportation (DOT). Another DOT division, the Maritime Administration (Marad), regulates the citizenship requirements of documentation although the USCG enforces those regulations as well.

Types of registration

There are five categories of vessel registration under present Federal documentation regulations: Coastwise, fishery, Great Lakes, registry and pleasure. The first four are referred to generically as "commercial documents" (although such a designation does not actually exist) while the fifth affects the vast majority of private pleasure craft eligible for documentation. Each category contains different qualifying elements, rights and responsibilities. In all cases, the boat must be owned by U.S. citizens, as that term is defined in the regulations (addressed further on). A vessel is not limited in the number of registrations it may carry, so long as all relevant requirements are met.

Coastwise - A vessel that carries merchandise or passengers for hire between any two U.S. ports in the coastal waters of the U.S. must be documented Coastwise. A crewed charter aboard a pleasure yacht for example, would require a Coastwise registration for use in U.S. waters. Only U.S. built vessels qualify.

Fishery - Entitles the vessel to engage in commercial fishing operations in the coastal waters of the U.S. and to land that catch, whatever caught, in the United States. This license is subject to applicable federal and state law regulating the fisheries and only vessels built in the U.S. qualify.

Great Lakes - Permits a vessel to engage in the coastwise trade and the fisheries on the Great Lakes (and their tributary and connecting waters) and in any other employment for which a registry, coastwise or fishery license is not needed. Only U.S. built vessels qualify.

Registry - Entitles the vessel to engage in trade between a U.S. port and a foreign port. No restrictions on vessel origin are placed on registry documents.

Pleasure - Entitles a vessel to pleasure use only (not to be used in commercial operations). No restrictions on vessel origin are placed on pleasure documents.(3)

Documentation Today

As mentioned earlier, vessel documentation is a way of showing a vessel's nationality. A U.S. documented yacht certifies its citizenship to the world at large; it becomes a piece of the United States, not unlike a foreign embassy.

Documentation also provides the means to establish a central registry for boats in the same manner that, say, a state Department of Motor Vehicles provides registry for automobiles. Also, specific provisions exist in federal law regarding the mortgaging of documented vessels. The existence of a central registry makes it possible to effect those provisions more efficiently; clearly this is a crucial factor in bringing more lenders into the field of yacht financing.

The vessel homeport

The central registry referred to above actually takes place at one of fifteen regional Coast Guard documentation locations. Prior to 1983, the total number of ports handling documentation was almost a hundred. Under the budget reduction plans of the Reagan administration, the Coast Guard was forced to reduce the number of offices and personnel devoted to the task of vessel documentation. These designated "homeports" (and their predecessor locations) aren't necessarily ports at all in the strict sense of the word. They are locations where the USCG has found it convenient to process the considerable paperwork required by law to properly register a vessel. Any documented vessel will have its basic record, known as an abstract, kept at one of these fifteen locations. Each of the Coast Guard homeports covers a territory roughly equivalent to one, or a portion of one, of the ten national Coast Guard Districts. Appendix F shows these homeports, their addresses and the territory covered.

Admeasurement

Not all vessels are eligible for documentation. In order to qualify for **any** form of documentation the boat must have a "tonnage" measurement of at least five net "tons". Keep in mind, the term ton and tonnage does not reference the weight of the vessel. Rather, being derivative of the old English term "tun" (meaning a cask or similar storage receptacle), the term tonnage refers to the internal displacement of the vessel with one register ton equal to 100 cubic feet.

Tonnage is determined by the Coast Guard through the process of admeasurement in accordance with fairly complicated formulas that compute internal capacity on a gross and net basis. The formulas were designed to provide very accurate measurement of large commercial vessels, but seemed to be rather tedious for smaller pleasure craft. For many years, the actual measuring of a boat's dimensions had to be carried out by a documentation officer, regardless of how many times the same boat had been measured before. For that reason, under new rules adopted in 1982 for pleasure boats, this process has been greatly simplified and usually no longer requires on-site inspection of a vessel by a USCG agent for admeasurement purposes.

The Coast Guard can now compute the tonnage of a pleasure boat on which it has specifications in its files by taking the product of the vessel length, breadth and depth, multiplied by a factor.

More specifically, the formula is:

For gross tonnage:

    power boats: [(LxBxD)/100] x .666

    sailboats: [(LxBxD)/100] x .5

For net tonnage:

    power boats: Net tonnage equals gross tonnage x .8

    sailboats: Net tonnage equals gross tonnage x .9

where:

"L" is the vessel length, defined as the horizontal distance between the foremost part of the stem and the aftermost part of the stern, excluding bowsprits, bumpkins, rudders, outboard motor brackets and similar fittings or attachments.

"B" is the vessel breadth, defined as the horizontal distance, excluding rub rails, from the outside of the skin (outside planking or plating) on one side to the outside of the skin on the other, taken at the widest part of the hull.

"D" is the vessel depth, defined as the vertical distance taken at or near midships from a line drawn horizontally through the uppermost edges of the skin at the sides of the hull (excluding the cap rail and trunks, cabins, or deckhouses) to the outboard face of the bottom skin of the hull. This excludes the keel **unless the keel is covered by the skin.** (author's emphasis).

If the resultant figure for net tonnage is five or greater, the vessel is documentable. Otherwise, it is not. No exceptions. As you can see, the simplified admeasurement process has little to do with the actual internal capacity of a pleasure boat. While generalities are difficult to draw, most power boats over about 27' LOA (length overall) will be documentable while fixed keel (fin type) sailboats of 25' LOA will qualify. Shoal draft and centerboard type sailboats will obviously have to be of greater length.

Citizenship requirements

Only U.S. citizens are entitled to the rights of U.S. vessel documentation. For individual owners, the test is very straight forward. Either citizens by birth or naturalized citizens are eligible.

Corporations may also own U.S. documented vessels although the definition of what constitutes a citizen in the case of a corporate owner does vary. For a pleasure document, the stock of the corporation may be held by foreigners as long as U.S. citizens act as President (or Chief Executive Officer) and Chairman of the board of directors, and non-citizens cannot constitute a quorum of the board of directors. In other words, the USCG wants to see that management control of the corporation is vested in U.S. citizens. In the case of a coastwise registration a corporation must have at least 75% of its stock held by U.S. citizens.

The Official Number

Once the vessel is found to meet the size and ownership requirements, it can be registered. When it is, the USCG awards it with an Official Number, a six digit number that will subsequently follow the vessel for the remainder of its "life". Regardless of where the vessel goes or how many times it changes ownership, the Official Number, once awarded, never changes for a particular vessel. This also includes any decertification of the boat. Should it ever have the U.S. registry closed and later reopened, the original Official Number will again be used.

Official Numbers are awarded according to an international system that involves British and Canadian vessels as well. U.S. vessels all carry six-digit numbers that begin with 2, 5, 6, or 9 while British and Canadian vessels are reserved numbers beginning with 3, 4, 7, and 8.

So important is the Official Number to the documentation process that the Coast Guard requirement for placement on the vessel states that it "must be marked by a permanent method which cannot be obliterated or obscured ... on some clearly visible interior structural part of the hull."[4] At one time the Coast Guard wanted this number actually cut into the hull itself or cut into a plaque that was then made integral to the hull. Now, they will accept decals that are epoxied over in a location that is readily accessible.

Marking the vessel

Coast Guard regulations require that a documented vessel be clearly marked. Just as the Official Number must be marked, so too does the name and a designated "hailing port". The hailing port must correspond to either (1) the domicile of the registered owner (city and state) or (2) the Coast Guard homeport that serves the domicile of the owner. For example, an owner living in Griffith, IN could use that location or Cleveland, OH (as the corresponding homeport) for the hailing port.[5]

The rule for marking pleasure vessels is very simple: "...the name and hailing port of the vessel must be marked together in clearly legible letters not less than four (4) inches in height on some clearly visible exterior part of the hull."[6] Out of tradition, most persons choose the transom of their boat. On any vessel documented other than pleasure, the name must be marked on both sides of the bow.

The Certificate of Documentation

Referred to informally as the ship's license or document, the Certificate of Documentation has been a part of U.S. registration since its inception. At one time it came in five different forms: Over/under 20 tons for pleasure; over/under 20 tons for coastwise; and registry. Later, a uniform certificate was used which was endorsed for the particular type of registration. In 1987 the certificate was revised a final time so that it now looks like the following.

Exhibit 7-1

UNITED STATES OF AMERICA
DEPARTMENT OF TRANSPORTATION
UNITED STATES COAST GUARD
Certificate of Documentation

VESSEL NAME				OFFICIAL NUMBER		HOMEPORT	
GROSS	NET	LENGTH	BREADTH	DEPTH	HULL MATERIAL		SELF PROPELLED

PLACE BUILT   YEAR BUILT

OWNER   THIS VESSEL IS PRESENTLY DOCUMENTED FOR

COMPLETE RECORDS ON FILE AT HOMEPORT

MANAGING OWNER

RESTRICTIONS

ENTITLEMENTS

REMARKS

ISSUED AT   SIGNATURE AND SEAL

ISSUE DATE

THIS CERTIFICATE EXPIRES ON THE LAST DAY OF
UNLESS RENEWED BY DECAL ON REVERSE.   DOCUMENTATION OFFICER

DEPT. OF TRANSP., USCG, CG-1270 (Rev. 10-87)
PREVIOUS EDITIONS ARE OBSOLETE   SN 7530-01-GF2-9870

The Certificate of Documentation indicates a number of things. First, it evidences the owner of the vessel, whether it be an individual, partnership or corporation. Second, it identifies the vessel by name, official number, and homeport along with the vessel's dimensions, tonnage (displacement) and hull material. Next, it specifies the type of registration and thus the activities the vessel can engage in, and any restrictions in registration. Finally, the certificate on the reverse shows all recorded ship mortgages against the vessel including amendments, assignments and satisfactions of those mortgages.

A ship mortgage is deemed "preferred" when it is endorsed on the certificate of documentation in accordance with certain rules. Mortages accorded preferred status accrue additional rights and benefits to the lender, which is one reason why boat lending terms are so liberal. Changes resulting from an extensive recodification of the relevant documentation and mortgage statutes will further modify the form and the required endorsements to it.

The Certificate of Documentation is not a title instrument; it only evidences title. Actual title to a documented vessel is a recordable bill of sale. Any such bill that meets Coast Guard requirements is usually referred to as a Coast Guard bill of sale. The type most often used looks as follows:

Exhibit 7-2

DEPARTMENT OF TRANSPORTATION U.S. Coast Guard CG-1340 (Rev. 12-83)	BILL OF SALE	OMB APPROVED 2115-0110
1. VESSEL NAME		2. OFFICIAL NUMBER¹

3. NAMES(S) OF SELLER(S) AND INTEREST OWNED BY EACH

3a. TOTAL INTEREST OWNED _____

4. NAME(S) OF BUYER(S) AND INTEREST TRANSFERRED TO EACH

4a. TOTAL INTEREST TRANSFERRED _____

5. CONSIDERATION RECEIVED

6. I (we) do hereby sell to the buyer(s) named above, my (our) right, title, and interest in the vessel together with the following necessaries and appurtenances:

This sale is made to the buyers in the proportion specified, subject to the following warranties and conditions:

7. SIGNATURE(S) OF SELLER(S) OR PERSON(S) SIGNING ON BEHALF OF SELLER	8. DATE SIGNED

9. NAME(S) OF PERSON(S) SIGNING ABOVE AND LEGAL CAPACITY IN WHICH SIGNED

10. ACKNOWLEDGMENT (Insert such acknowledgement language as is required by state law.)

The acknowledgement may not be taken by an officer or employee of the Coast Guard.

¹If vessel has never been awarded an official number, complete those items of vessel data on reverse of form as are known.

Previous Editions May Be Used   SN 7530-00-F01-1020

Possession and renewal of the certificate - Once your boat has been documented and you are in possession of the license, you are required to know all the regulations pertaining to that license. For a pleasure license, this requires an understanding of the proper marking of the boat, including name, port and official number. But it goes beyond that. For instance, a documented vessel must always be under the command of a U.S. citizen. While this does not prohibit foreign citizens from enjoying the pleasures of boating aboard such a documented vessel, it does preclude a non-U.S. citizen from being the sole operator of the vessel.

Unless surrendered to the Coast Guard, the certificate must be on board the vessel at all times; after all, it is **the** license for the boat. The only exception to this rule is if the vessel is out of the water or in storage or if the document has been submitted to a documentation officer for the purpose of surrender, replacement or the endorsement of a preferred mortgage. Enforcement of this rule seems to vary from port to port. Nevertheless, it's a good idea to keep the document along with other valuable ship's papers. Since the penalty for any major violation of these regulations is vessel forfeiture (the Coast Guard doesn't mess around with fines), technically the boat is subject to seizure if the document is not aboard.

There are a number of events that could occur rendering a license invalid and possibly requiring its surrender to the Coast Guard. They include:

1) A change in the ownership of the vessel in whole or in part.

2) The homeport of the vessel changes.

3) The gross or net tonnage of the vessel, or her dimensions, changes.

4) The name of the vessel changes.

5) The legal name of any owner of the vessel changes.

6) A self-propelled vessel becomes non-self-propelled or vice versa.

7) A tenet by the entirety owning any part of the vessel dies.

8) The trade endorsements (type of registration) for the vessel change by addition, deletion or substitution.

9) A substantive or clerical error made by the issuing documentation officer is discovered.

10) The vessel is placed under the command of a person who is not a United States citizen.

Under provisions 1-7 above, the certificate remains valid but is still subject to surrender if a preferred mortgage is recorded against it. In such cases, the mortgagee must consent to the surrender and subsequent change.

A Certificate of Documentation is valid for one year. At the end of a year a renewal is required and noted on the certificate by the attachment of a small sticker provided by the Coast Guard. The expiration date is the last day of the anniversary month regardless of the original date of issue and the renewal is free.

Rights and responsibilities of documentation

With what has gone before, some persons may be inclined to ask, Why document? There are a number of very good reasons. The first is that you may have to. Any boat over five net tons used commercially in U.S. waters, either coastwise or in the fisheries, **must** carry a U.S. document.

For pleasure documented vessels there are several advantages. First, in the absence of any guarantees of title, or title insurance that would protect an owner's interest in the event of a title dispute, the Coast Guard documentation process is still the best way to evidence title and thereby protect an owner's interest. Since documenting a boat involves obtaining a clear and acceptable chain of title, any prior claims or clouds on a boat's ownership are more likely to be revealed. A good documentation service is very useful in preparing an application for documentation precisely because of their experience in searching out the chain of title. And, to the extent they possess a good Error and Omissions insurance policy, you can come as close as possible to having a guarantee of title when you buy a pre-owned vessel. Nevertheless, there are certain "invisible" liens that can follow a boat literally forever, and no method of registration can reveal or clear them with absolute assurance. More will be mentioned on this point in Chapter 9.

Second, U.S. documented vessels are recognized as U.S. property when in foreign waters. In the event of arrest or seizure of the vessel you have the right to expect the U.S. State Department to intervene on your behalf (whether they actually do is another matter). In some cases, medical services are available abroad for crew members of U.S. registered vessels. For anyone contemplating cruising in any foreign waters, whether it be the Caribbean, Mexico, Canada or the Mediterranean, documentation is a good idea.

Finally, the best reason to utilize documentation is the fact that it will open your purchase up to a much larger number of lenders. Most national yacht financiers, whether banks, service companies or finance companies require a preferred mortgage as a condition of the loan. Typically, these mortgage-based lenders offer flexibility in rates and terms that is entirely owing to the superior lien position they have in their collateral by virtue of the existence of a special federal law governing the mortgaging of documented vessels.

State Registration

State registration is a fairly recent phenomenon which roughly traces the growth of the pleasure boat industry. State vessel registration grew from a requirement contained in the Federal Boating Act of 1958, recodified as the Federal Boat Safety Act of 1971. In terms of registration, the act attempts to bridge the gap between state and federal systems.

Vessel numbering and registration

Every state must have a vessel numbering system approved by the Secretary of Transportation. Under the Safe Boating Act, if the state's system was approved by the federal government, it was turned over to the state for administration, where additional regulations could be added. If not approved, the U.S. Coast Guard was responsible for state numbering, and only the basic registration provisions of the act were enforced. Today, all states except Alaska have some form of registration law.

As states set up their numbering systems, the laws that followed were adopted initially as a means of regulating boat usage, especially with regard to safety awareness and facilities development. Most reiterated the USCG safety devices and operating equipment schedules. But enforcement cost money and boat registration fees seemed the fairest way to pass these costs on to the actual users and so fees began to rise. Because the variability between states does not allow treatment of each system in detail here, Appendix G has been provided to highlight the most important aspects of each set of laws.

Numbering generally applies to vessels that are not federally documented. Some states appear to require that even federally documented boats be registered, in apparent conflict with federal statutes which suggest that federal and state registration are mutually exclusive. The reason some states require this is obvious since state registration provides a means to track payment of various taxes (especially sales tax) and user fees. Some states, such as Florida, have adopted a compromise system whereby a vessel receives a documented vessel decal, but does not receive a state number or title. Again, the effect is to insure payment of applicable fees and taxes.

Also exempt from state registration (or subject to different laws) are foreign vessels, commercialy used vessels and boats owned by a government entity (or a political subdivision of one). Generally exempt from registration are lifeboats, ship's tenders, surf boards, racing shells and rowing sculls.

Under federal law, reciprocity exists between states. A vessel properly numbered in the state of principal use is considered in compliance with the numbering requirements of any state in which it is temporarily used. If the vessel is permanently moved to a new state there is at least a sixty day period to obtain a new number. Some states offer ninety days, but in all cases, the state of primary use is where registration must occur. In certain coastal states the authorities actively check the registration status and time in port of out-of-state boats to insure compliance with this regulation. This is why out-of-state registration for sales tax avoidance is not very effective these days.

Safety regulation - Most states, in their establishment of boat registration laws, outline various safety and usage rquirements. Generally, they require certain operating equipment such as lights, bells, horns, flotation devices and the like, while spelling out for the novice boater proper operating procedures, "Rules of the Road" and so forth. Although too numerous to mention here, Appendix G also provides the names and addresses of the state authority where such regulations may be obtained. By either writing or calling, a brochure or hand book listing all regulatory requirements is usually available free of charge.

Fees and assessments - Most states charge fees, taxes or assessments for the privilege of using boats on their waterways. This revenue generally is put back into waterway maintenance and improvement, boating safety and education. The fees vary widely from state to state and are usually paid upon registration with annual renewal charges. Often times, registration (and titling, below) is the means to insure compliance with state, county and local sales, use and property tax payments. While these amounts vary (and some states do not use vessel registration as a means to enforce tax payments) the requirement when present is the most strictly enforced. While little if any of these payments find their way back to boating, state taxing authorities have gained the cooperation of state boating offices (and even the USCG lately) in policing payment. So generally a boat can't be registered until the money is paid.

Youth education - Although no state yet requires a license for adults to operate a boat, several do have mandatory youth education and certification requirements for youthful operators. At present, ten states (Connecticut, Illinois, Maryland, Minnesota, North Dakota, Wisconsin, New York, Indiana, Alabama) and the District of Columbia have a youth education provision in the registration law. Given the current concern over several recent well publicized boating accidents, more legislation in this and other areas is certain to be added to current laws.

State titling

Where a title provision exists, it does so as an adjunct to the registration law but supersedes it in terms of establishing proof of ownership, and at this time twenty-four states issue titles. The title provision of the law merely provides a means to more clearly (that is, with more legal "force") identify the owner. In addition, the existence of a title requires a lender to file notice of a security interest or lien in a vessel in a different manner than that used in the absence of a title. In the latter case, the filing of a lien is through the provisions of the Uniform Commercial Code, as adopted by that state. Once issued, the title is delivered to the lienholder; if no lien exists, it is held by the owner. Appendix G lists the states with titling laws and details on fees, documents and transfer.

In order to obtain a title, the owner must first apply on the appropriate form. Some states automatically issue a title upon registration - the same form is used in these cases. An original Certificate of Origin (also known as a Manufacturer's Statement of Origin) is often required for new boats. If a used boat, the previous registration or title must be presented along with a bill of sale, unless the title itself can be endorsed to the new owner. Once a new title is issued, it becomes the means by which all future transfers of ownership are recorded. In addition, all information on vessel liens, including assignments and releases are recorded. The filing for title may also be the basis for the payment of taxes or special fees.

As a certificate of ownership, your title becomes a valuable means of indicating liens against a boat; since a title conveys legal ownership, any sale of a boat with a lien recorded against the title would be subject to that lien. This appears to be the chief reason that boat titles were introduced into state law. Should a titled vessel be entered for documentation, the title will have to be surrendered to the Coast Guard.

National titling - At present, there is an effort underway to establish a national titling law, in order to cover all states in as uniform a manner as vessel documentation provides. Interestingly enough, the proposal calls for the same "preferred status" of liens recorded under the system as presently exists in vessel documentation. Not only would this save the USCG time and taxpayer money, but it would probably add even more lenders to the field of boat finance, and liberalize lending terms still further! Only time will tell.

---

(1) "Costwise" is a term that implies carriage of passengers or merchandise for hire between contiguous ports of a particular country.

(2) There is an exception however to the "U.S. built" rule in existence today. Under certain conditions and with special Congressional approval, foreign built yachts may be admitted to U.S. registry for commercial use. This is referred to as "Documentation Pursuant to Extraordinary Legislative Grant". Although such cases are rare, sixteen different vessels will likely make it into U.S. registration in 1989 during a proposed recodification of the Ship Mortgage Act.

(3) In this section of the Federal Regulations an interesting note appears: "A vessel operating under a pleasure license endorsement only may be bareboat chartered for pleasure use only. Guidance on the elements of a valid bareboat charter should be obtained through private legal counsel."

(4) Code of Federal Regulations, Title 46, Sub part 67.15-1.

(5) Sound confusing? Apparently enough people thought so that in 1984 Marad proposed a regulation change that would eliminate the homeport/hailing port marking requirement in favor of the ship's name along with its official number marked on the vessel. Some wags in the marine industry think this has less to do with Marad's concern for the confusion of boaters than it does for their distaste of the current marking of government owned vessels. You see, when the USCG homeports were collapsed down to fifteen, the port of Washington, D.C. was absorbed into the Norfolk, VA homeport. Thus, all ships owned by the Federal Government must now carry that location marked on their hull, something Marad is apparently not too keen on.

(6) Code of Federal Regulations, Title 46, Sub part 67.15-3.

CHAPTER 8
CHARTERING: A Business Opportunity

Most people don't think of pleasure boating as a business. On the contrary, it's usually a way to escape the pressures and the cares of everyday work and business activities. Sometimes, though, boat owners find less time than they like to indulge their boating interests. Consequently, they may find their expensive dream boat sitting at the marina most of the year gathering dirt, barnacles and more expenses.

One main reason people choose to buy a boat even if they don't plan to use it frequently is the satisfaction and prestige of ownership. Boats often are clearly visible signs of financial success and as such they bring to the owner considerable prestige. Unfortunately, any vessel deteriorates very quickly if it is not used. Maintenance costs will run high if the boat is always kept in a seaworthy condition. Whenever the owner uses the boat for vacation, he may spend much of the time cleaning teak, scrubbing fiberglass or making some other needed repairs. Most of us would rather be cruising, fishing or whatever and not substituting one type of work for another.

Many boating enthusiasts turn to chartering a sail or power boat rather than pay the big expenses of a boat they hardly use. However, it may be possible to enjoy all the pleasures of boat ownership and still gain from income and tax advantages while functioning within the guidelines of the Federal tax system.

What Kinds Are Suitable For Charter?

Not all boats are suitable, however, for the charter trade. If your particular boating objectives call for a boat different than is typically chartered, then there may be no market for it. The boat's design and construction determine largely if it will prove to be durable enough for constant charter use. What type of boat should you consider if chartering is in your future? Most charter companies rent sailboats from about 25 feet up to 70 feet. Many of these same companies also charter powerboats ranging from 30 to 50 feet.

The length of the vessel is not the only consideration, though. Many other factors such as hull type and construction, sail rig, engine type and cabin layout must be evaluated for charter service. The features that a person frequently looks for when chartering a boat are a tight, safe craft; an easy to handle rig; a dependable engine that starts at the push of a button; four or more bunks; standing headroom; an enclosed head; a workable galley and adequate refrigeration; a swim ladder; a good dinghy; and a stereo and/or television. If your specific objectives don't include these features, then your boat may not be a candidate for chartering. It is wise to discuss your objectives with a charter management company before buying. They can give you many hints as to what type of boat they would be willing to accept into their fleet.

Since most charter operators sell boats as part of their business, they may have new or previously owned yachts available for sale that are equipped for chartering. Comparing boats available from dealers or brokers and those from the charter/dealers will point out a big difference in price. The charter boats are often completely outfitted with almost $20,000 worth of options (see Appendix H). Much of this equipment you probably wouldn't buy for your own use at the outset. Instead, you may wait a year or two. A charter boat, on the other hand, is expected to be completely furnished and equipped as soon as it arrives in the fleet. A list of equipment is normally specified by the company and the individual items are standard on all boats in their fleet. If you choose to buy a new boat from a dealer and equip it at your convenience, you will be expected to complete the outfitting by the beginning of the second year of chartering. As property required to run your charter business, these required items may be depreciated on your Federal tax return.

Powerboats of the displacement or semi-displacement hull type, fiberglass construction with a minimum of external woodwork, and diesel power are the ones most frequently chartered. A cabin layout that allows for the privacy of two or three couples in double berths is the most favorable arrangement. Those hull designs that have a keel running the length of the hull which protects the rudder and propeller are ideal for shallow waters such as the Chesapeake Bay. Motor yachts with semi-displacement hulls operate up to 18 knot speeds with a twin engine installation. Diesel engines are favored for their long life, reliability and low maintenance. The nonexplosive nature of diesel fuel is an added safety benefit. Such boats are relatively easy on fuel with consumption rates varying from two to ten gallons per hour.

Sailboats typically have a sloop rig but some over 30 feet may have a ketch or yawl rig. There is either a fixed fin or shoal draft keel, a small diesel auxiliary engine and accommodations for two to eight. Some larger sailboats often have a crew with a liveaboard captain and mate/cook. There are fewer restrictions on sailboat types for chartering as compared to power boats. Thus, there is less likelihood that your boating objectives will be compromised with a sailboat should you choose to place it into charter service.

In spite of personal preferences, it is important to remember that charter demand, resale value, durability and lower maintenance costs are the primary considerations. Whether you plan to keep your vessel, give it to your children, or replace it with a newer model in the next few years, selecting the right boat initially will help keep your options open.

The Business of Chartering

You can gain in two ways from chartering your boat, namely the added income your boat can produce and the tax benefits you accrue from running a business. These long term tax benefits are the key to chartering. The income helps offset the ongoing expenses such as maintenance, dockage and insurance. Fuel costs are paid by the ones who charter your boat except for the time that you use her. A word of caution is important at this point: It may seem as if you can get something as big and expensive as a power or sail boat for little or no money while Uncle Sam pays the bulk of the cost. But there are prices you have to pay which may convince you that chartering is not for you.

First, you have to prove that you are conducting a charter boat operation as a trade or business. The Internal Revenue Service has many rules which you must follow to ensure you can take the tax deductions. As you may expect, there have been many abuses of "vacation home"[1] and "hobby loss"[2] rules in which owners have evaded taxes on the presumption of operating a business. In order to minimize tax losses, the IRS requires that a profit motive be established. This can be demonstrated if the charter operation is profitable three out of five years. This is a sufficient but not necessary condition.

Factors that are important in proving profitability include the experience a taxpayer has in other business operations and the expertise of his advisors; the time and effort devoted to the activity including participation in maintenance and promotion, bill paying and record keeping; the expectation that the boat will appreciate in value (you can assume this based on the track record of like vessels); and the history of the charter income or losses (a trend toward profitability is particularly useful). The amount of personal use is another factor that the IRS can consider in allowing your deductions.

Charter income forecasts are somewhat elusive as there are no guarantees as to the number of weeks that you will be able to charter your boat regardless of management's experience in previous seasons. Many factors influence the number of weeks of chartering, including weather in your chosen charter location, proximity to transportation for your clients, amount of down time for repairs and the number of repeat customers a boat can establish. Conservatively you should count on only 50% of the average predictions in the first year, 75% in the the second and finally, 90% in the third year. In the fourth and fifth years use whatever seems reasonable for your initial income forecasts. Once you establish a five year income projection list all the major anticipated expenses for each year. Add up the expenses and subtract the total from the income to find your net income by year. Table 8-1 lists examples of charter income in various locations as well as by size of boat.

Table 8-1

Average Weekly Charter Rates

Location	20-30'	30-40'	40-50'	50-60'	over 60'
Caribbean	$800	$1800	$2400	$4320	$6000
Florida	n/r	$1150	$1720	n/r	n/r
Mid-Atlantic	$630	$860	$1600	n/r	n/r
California	$630	$1200	$1400	$2300	n/r
Mediterranean	$800	$1150	$2000	$3430	$5700

Note: n/r — not reported. These rates are the results of a worldwide charter management company survey. See Appendix I.

Exhibit 8-1 shows how to record and compute your projected income and estimated expenses. It is assumed that a charter company manages your boat and splits the income with you while charging you for all the expenses (Exhibit 8-2). A cash flow projection for both sale-leaseback plans and crewed yacht alternatives is covered later in this chapter (Exhibits 8-4 and 8-5).

Exhibit 8-1

Bareboat Charter Cash Flow Assumptions
Type of boat: 35 - 40 foot, power or sail

1.	Cost of boat as delivered (assume January purchase)	$125,000
2.	Downpayment (20%)	$ 25,000
3.	Loan balance	$100,000
4a.	Term	15 years
4b.	Rate	12.5%
5.	Prepaid interest (3 points)	$3,000
6.	Documentation fee	$400
7.	Total loan (includes points and fees)	$103,400
8.	Monthly payment	$1,274
9.	Charter revenue per week (4%/yr. increase)	$1,570
10.	Management fees per year	$500
11.	Income split: Owner / charter management	70% / 30%
12.	Dockage/storage per year	$2,200
13.	Insurance per year	$1,500
14.	Useful life (assumed for illustration only)	5 years
15.	State sales tax	0%
16.	Marginal tax rate	28%
17.	Cost of equipment	$7,500

Exhibit 8-2

Assumed Charter Cash Flow Without Taxes

	Year 1	Year 2	Year 3	Year 4	Year 5	Total
Assumed Income						
1. Charter weeks	6	9	12	12	12	51
2. Gross revenue	$9,420	$14,695	$19,594	$19,594	$19,594	$82,897
3. Management company share	2,826	4,409	5,878	5,878	5,878	24,869
4. Net revenue	$6,594	$10,286	$13,716	$13,716	$13,716	$58,028
Assumed Expenses						
5. Slip fee (+3%/yr.)	$2,200	$2,266	$2,334	$2,404	$2,476	$11,680
6. Maintenance (+8%/yr.)	5,600	6,048	6,532	7,054	7,619	32,853
7. Insurance (+5%/yr.)	1,500	1,575	1,654	1,736	1,823	8,288
8. Management fee	500	500	500	525	525	2,550
9. Loan interest payment	12,785	12,452	12,076	11,650 *	11,168	60,131
10. Cost of equipment	7,500	7,500	1,750	950	500	18,200
11. Points	3,000	0	0	0	0	3,000
12. Documentation	400	0	0	0	0	400
13. **Expense Total**	$33,485	$30,341	$24,846	$24,319	$24,111	$137,102
14. **Cash profit (loss) from operations**	($26,891)	($20,055)	($11,130)	($10,603)	($10,395)	($79,074)

* Refinancing assumed in fourth year to take advantage of a lower interest rate.

Operating cost: **$1,318/month** (over 60 months)

In the first two years, the costs of outfitting your charter boat may cause you to have excessive expenses. It's possible to avoid this by equipping your boat for charter before you buy it. In this way, all the equipment costs are contained within your mortgage and spread over the period of the loan. Finance companies will usually work with you on this method of meeting the equipment needs of a charter boat. An alternate approach is to equip as you go. This results in a lower monthly mortgage charge but requires that you stay on top of your equipment list so as to get the items installed within the first year. This is a normal period in which most charter management companies want everything in place. Ideally, they would like it all on board before you turn your boat over to them. In this way, they can standardize on the options and best meet (in their opinion) the needs of the charter customers.

Tax Considerations

In the past 10-15 years, tax laws were enacted in order to make capital purchases easier for business so as to stimulate the economy. Many boat owners have taken advantage of these new laws to charter their yachts as a business. At the same time, chartering boats became a major recreational activity for thousands who just wanted to get away but did not have the time or money for a boat of their own. As a consequence, charter management businesses grew quickly as an industry.

As you would expect, there have been abuses of the sections of the Tax Code dealing with charter boat ownership by often well meaning but naive owners who thought that Uncle Sam was going to buy their boat for them without any strings attached. As we all know, that just doesn't happen. Consequently, Federal tax changes in 1986 made the tax advantages of charter management less attractive. Investment credits are eliminated, depreciation schedules are lengthened and there is now a need to establish owner "activity" in the chartering business. The effect of the current tax laws will be to make charter management programs less attractive than they were. Owners who personally act as crew are, of course, active participants in the business. It would be wise to evaluate the impact of the current tax law on one's own charter yacht ownership program. You and your tax advisor must jointly assess whether charter yacht ownership can be a viable business opportunity for you and whether it makes economic sense or not.

Yacht expenses

Expenses for the charter yacht can be categorized as recurring (maintenance, dockage, insurance costs and management fees) and one time (outfitting costs). In addition, trips to your boat to inspect her are normally recurring. All these are deductible in some way from your Federal income tax return. Recurring costs are costs associated with running your charter boat and are deducted as normal expenses attributable to the business. They are recorded as reductions on IRS Schedule C, Profit or (Loss) From Business or Profession, along with the rental income received.

The current tax laws allow owner use up to 14 days or 10% of the total days the boat is chartered during the tax year, whichever is higher. If you use your yacht for greater than these periods then the deductions are limited to the gross income.

Depreciation

One time equipment costs are depreciable as "Recovery Property" (Section 168, U.S. Tax Code: Property that is acquired by purchase for use in a trade or business). This generally applies to charter boats. You have three choices: (1) expense the property under Section

179 (currently you may expense up to $10,000 of qualified property but limited to the charter profits); (2) depreciate it under the rules of the Modified Accelerated Cost Recovery System (MACRS) or (3) if your yacht does not qualify for MACRS, consider depreciating it on a seven year schedule.

IRS Form 4562, Depreciation and Amortization, is the recording media for depreciation. Before completing it you should see the appropriate instructions in the Federal tax returns or IRS briefs covering the most recent tax law changes that affect the way you report depreciation. This knowledge will help you plan for the completion of the form with your tax preparer.

Depreciation recapture - Unless you plan to keep your boat for at least five years it may not make financial sense to charter it and take the tax benefits. The Internal Revenue Service has the right to "recapture" or require you to pay back a portion of the depreciation.

Depreciation is recaptured if you fail to meet the requirement that 50% of your yacht's usage is for "qualified" business purposes. Depreciation is then recalculated on a twelve year straight line schedule, according to the Tax Reform Act of 1984. This act applies to all yachts placed into management service after June 18, 1984. Thus, all depreciation taken on a five year accelerated basis which is in excess of the twelve year schedule is then taxed as ordinary income. If you convert your charter boat to personal use after the five years you stop claiming depreciation but carry the liability until the boat is sold. It is, in essence, a self-perpetuating deferral which will discontinue when you contract for outright sale.

Relative appreciation - If your yacht appreciates relative to your original purchase price over a five year period, you can expect to sell your boat at a gain and the amount of the gain is taxed as ordinary income. If the boat is traded for another boat used in charter service, the gain will not be recognized unless cash is received as part of the trade. However, the new depreciable basis will be the new cost of the vessel minus the depreciable basis of the previous vessel. For example, if the market for your old boat is $50,000 and you purchase a new boat for $150,000, the depreciable basis is $100,000 (net amount after trade-in). This assumes that the older boat is fully depreciated.

Assuming that your boat will appreciate (this should have been one of your original selection criteria), you then can buy a larger vessel and pay only the difference between the old and the new.

Passive and active income

The major negative factor in the current tax law is the passive loss limitations included in Section 469 of the law. Income is now classified into one of three categories, namely, investment income and income from active or passive activities. Charter boat rental income is classified as passive. While there is a limited exception for losses from rental activity in which the taxpayer is active, the loophole applies only to real estate rentals.

Expenses from passive activities cannot exceed the income from these same activities until passive income profits are earned or the activity is abandoned. This passive loss rule is being phased in over four years, 1987 through 1990. Such partial allowances were only permitted for investments prior to October 23, 1986. For all practical purposes, losses after the 1988 tax year are effectively worth little on the current year's taxes.

In order to avoid automatic passive classification you must provide significant services as part of the activity. It may be possible for you to escape classification as a passive income activity in a charter rental, but if you do not "materially participate" (quote from the tax law), the charter activity may be called passive. Material participation is defined as involvement in operations on a regular, continuous and substantial basis and is based on the same material participation standards of Section 1402(A).

If your charter business were your principal business activity in time and effort, it would presumably be active. As a second or third business, it will come under close scrutiny. The primary concern of the law is whether the taxpayer is at the place of the activity. For example, are you working on your boat and crewing or maintaining it? Involvement in management decisions is not considered adequate participation in the activity to confer active status. The exception is when the work is done on a regular basis and the success of the operation depends in a large part on the business judgement of the taxpayer.

If you merely approve the work of an agent in caring for your charter boat or in deciding upon the suitablity of charterers, this does not establish a substantial role. "Even an intermittent role in management, while relevant, does not establish material participation in the absence of regular, continuous and substantial involvement in operations."(3) The law does not rely upon management participation to determine whether an income activity is "active" because it is difficult to verify.

The second home alternative

For years, owners who have rented their vacation home had to count the days of personal use of that home. If personal days exceeded fourteen, a complex allocation had to be done in order to split the expenses between personal and rental use. Since personal use days did not include days on which the owner's use involved normal rental functions such as cleaning and painting, a log was a necessity to show activity.

The IRS has generally concentrated on issues such as personal/rental use, and value of land versus depreciable value of buildings because real estate usually appreciates in value. With the adoption of the passive loss rules in Section 469, most vacation rental investments have lost their current tax appeal but many are still viable for the long term. Some owners, consequently, no longer rent their properties and have instead converted them to personal use since the homes now qualify as second residences with interest and taxes still deductible.

Fortunately, larger boats were placed into the same category. You have several options:

(1) You use your boat strictly for personal pleasure. You may deduct your interest paid on the loan and nothing more. When you sell your boat for less than you paid, no loss is deductible. If you make a profit by selling for more than you paid, the profit must be reported. The major disadvantage is that you must carry all the costs yourself.

(2) You may limit your personal use to less than fourteen days, and charter the boat. In this case, you will generate tax losses which the IRS will label passive, and loss deductions will be deferred until the boat is sold. Your major advantage is that the charter income helps pay for the boat. The key disadvantage is that you do not receive tax benefits.

(3) You may operate a charter boat and ignore the fourteen day rule. This permits you to use the charter income to help pay for the boat and allows limited tax advantages in the tax years when the boat is held. Excess expenses, however, do not qualify for write off, and is the major disadvantage.

The advantage of the second home deduction is that tax and interest are deductible, and there are some income possibilities that can help you defer some of the ownership expenses.

Perhaps more important, though, is the satisfaction of having relatively greater personal use of the boat than if it were solely purchased for a charter business.

Sales taxes

One important aspect is state sales taxes. These range up to 7.5% with the average equal to 4%. (4) On a $100,000 boat this is a $4,000 bill that can be included within your loan. If you choose to charter your boat, many states allow you to defer this tax in exchange for sales tax from the charters, but you must register your boat with the state as a boat rental business. You are then authorized to collect sales tax which you must report at least quarterly. If you are chartering the boat yourself, then you both collect and report the tax. If you contract with a charter management company, they can collect and submit the tax for you.

If you convert your boat to personal use sometime in the future, you may be subject to paying the state sales tax. Each state has their own rules regarding such personal use conversion, and you should investigate your state's policy before making any decision to buy. A $4,000 tax bill is a hefty price to pay for the personal use conversion.

Summary

In order to maximize a charter boat's effect on taxes, considerable planning before purchasing a boat is necessary. First, be definite about your motives and your abilities to prove them. Second, spend some time determining the probable charter cash flow picture over a five year period (Exhibit 8-3). Use this to discuss with your tax advisor the financial pros and cons of chartering in light of your current and projected tax situation. Lastly, discuss your intentions with your financing company. They need to protect your boat as their financial "asset." Consequently, they will want to have a say in how you plan to charter your boat.

Exhibit 8-3

Assumed Charter Cash Flow with Taxes

	Year 1	Year 2	Year 3	Year 4	Year 5	Total
Assumed Income:						
1. Charter weeks	6	9	12	12	12	51
2. Gross revenue	$9,420	$14,695	$19,594	$19,594	$19,594	$82,897
3. Management company share	2,826	4,409	5,878	5,878	5,878	24,869
4. Net revenue	$6,594	$10,287	$13,716	$13,716	$13,716	$58,028
Assumed Expenses						
5. Slip fee (+3%/yr.)	$2,200	$2,266	$2,334	$2,404	$2,476	$11,680
6. Maintenance (+8%/yr.)	5,600	6,048	6,532	7,054	7,619	32,853
7. Insurance (+5%/yr.)	1,500	1,575	1,654	1,736	1,823	8,288
8. Management fee	500	500	500	525	525	2,550
9. Loan interest payment	12,785	12,452	12,076	11,650*	11,168	60,131
10. Cost of equipment	7,500	7,500	1,750	950	500	18,200
11. Points	3,000	0	0	0	0	3,000
12. Documentation	400	0	0	0	0	400
13. **Expense Total**	$33,485	$30,341	$24,846	$24,319	$24,111	$137,102
14. **Cash profit (loss) from operations:**	($26,891)	($20,055)	($11,130)	($10,603)	($10,395)	($79,074)

* Refinancing assumed in fourth year to take advantage of a lower interest rate.

Tax Affect: (Assumes "active" income/expenses)

	Year 1	Year 2	Year 3	Year 4	Year 5	Total
15. Taxable income @ marginal tax rate (MTR)	($19,362)	($14,439)	($8,014)	($7,635)	($7,485)	($56,935)
16. Depreciation rate (%)	40	25	15	10	10	0
17. Depreciation	53,000	36,125	22,450	15,193	14,700	0
18. Depreciation at MTR	14,840	10,115	6,286	4,254	4,116	39,611
19. Debt reduction	(2,509)	(2,841)	(3,217)	(3,643)	(4,125)	(16,335)
20. Downpayment	(25,000)	0	0	0	0	(25,000)
21. **After tax cash flow:**	($32,031)	($7,165)	($4,945)	($7,024)	($7,494)	($58,659)

Operating cost: $978/month (over 60 months)

Continued on next page

Exhibit 8-3 (continued)

The following are the tax effect computations:

(1) Taxable income at marginal tax rate (Line 15) = cash loss (line 14) x (1 — MTR) with MTR assumed to be 28%

(2) Depreciation (line 17) is derived as follows (the annual depreciation percentages are shown for illustration only):

Depreciation Item	Year 1		Year 2		Year 3		Year 4		Year 5	
	Amount	%	Amount	%	Amount	%	Amount	%	Amount	%
Boat	$125,000	40	$125,000	25	$125,000	15	$125,000	10	$125,000	10
Equipment	7,500	40	7,500	25	7,500	15	7,500	10	7,500	10
Equipment			7,500	40	7,500	25	7,500	15	7,500	10
Equipment					1,750	40	1,750	25	1,750	15
Equipment							950	40	950	25
Equipment									500	40
Line 17	$53,000		$36,125		$22,450		$15,193		$14,700	

(3) Depreciation at MTR (line 18) = line 17 x MTR

(4) Debt reduction (line 19): From amortization tables

(5) After tax cash flow (line 21) = sum of lines 15 and 18 through 20

The difference between being able to support your intent to make a profit or not can often be found in your plan and the records you keep to substantiate the profit motive. Be certain that you are committed to the concept of offering your yacht for charter service in order to satisfy the IRS requirements regarding personal use. While an IRS audit may occur, it may be faced easily by following the rules and guidelines and keeping a good set of records. You wouldn't do any less for your other personal or corporate business.

Location, Location, & Location

The choice of chartering location depends on many factors. It doesn't matter whether you are contracting with a management company to handle your charters, living aboard as captain, or renting your boat out of your backyard, the proper location will determine largely how successful you will be. There are four major elements that have the greatest influence on your charter boat's location — the weather and climate, the amount of sheltering to the waters, tourist accessibility, and the availability of service and supply facilities.

Get a chart of the world which you can lay flat. Draw heavy lines at 25-30 degrees north and south latitude if you like warm weather. More temperate climates range to 40-45 degrees latitude. You can find numerous places around the continental U.S. including the Atlantic, Pacific and Gulf of Mexico coasts that are excellent for chartering. Inland waters such as the Great Lakes, and estuaries like the Chesapeake Bay are other fine U.S. locations for chartering. The greatest difference between north and south is the length of the season. In southern Florida, you can reasonably expect 20-22 weeks of charter per season. Ten to fourteen weeks is tops in the more temperate areas. Depending upon where you live, you may choose to locate your boat closer to your home rather than over the horizon. Although IRS rules limit personal use of your charter boat to a percentage of its charter time, occasionally you may want to inspect her or perform some needed chore. Closeness to home allows you to make these trips with some frequency.

Sheltered waters attract more customers than open ocean passages. Most people come away with the idea of sailing, swimming, sunning and relaxing. Seasickness resulting from an open ocean crossing doesn't fit in with these ideas. Prevailing winds are important as changes in them can make it impossible to sail to the most popular areas at certain times of the year. Similarly, water conditions may turn bad in thunderstorms caused by late summer heat and humidity. Can the charter sailors seek refuge in leeward, deep water anchorages? Tidal ranges also may be a problem if they are excessive. It may be difficult for a charter party to land in water too shallow for the boat.

Accessibility to a charter area by customers from far away is a major consideration. You may love your new found charter paradise, but if no one can get there, your business will be bad. This is not likely to be a problem for charter operations in the continental U.S. but it may be one for the operator in the South Pacific islands groups. People will take a jet, small plane hop, and taxi ride to the boat but not much more.

Supplies, repairs, laundry, water, communications, fuel and other services may be plentiful in your chosen area. If they are, restocking, maintaining and filling up will be easier than having to sail around for your supplies. Most charter management companies have all the facilities your charter boat will need. On the other hand, owner/operators must be well aware of the necessity of having services available to make their customers happy and their charter business profitable.

Chartering Arrangements

There are three arrangements by which charter boats can be operated and it is important to understand their fundamentals before you get involved. The choices are charter management, owner-managed and crewed. Any one of the ways to enter the charter game can justify a book unto itself. The objective of the following is to provide for you the essentials of the different types of chartering operations so you can choose the best one for your needs.

Choosing a management company

An owner who charters his boat must be reconciled to the fact that the vessel, which may occupy a place close to his heart, is now a workboat, earning her keep and experiencing wear and tear as a result. It may have taken twenty years to afford her, and now he may have to give her up to the uncertainties of renters. Chartering a pleasure boat is similar in most respects to renting a vacation home and boat owners are just as protective of their property. Separating yourself from your prospective charter clients is done by hiring a charter management company. They can take a more business like approach to renting your boat. For example, they are less emotional in screening clients and more thorough than you can be. Beyond selecting the right people for your boat, charter management companies provide a variety of other useful services to the charter boat owner.

It is generally recognized that placing your yacht with a company that will keep her in tip-top condition not only attracts more charters but also protects your investment. Finding that company is not a simple task as there are many charter firms in business today. Unfortunately, there is no rating service for them. It is up to you to select the best one. The most obvious starting point is the reputation of the firm. Your financing company may have the names of several charter management companies they believe have the best reputations for protecting the boats in their fleet. Other than that, you are pretty much on your own. A good source of company names can be found in boating magazines. Frequently, advertisements placed in the magazine call your attention to various management programs.

Before contacting any of the companies, it is a good idea to make up a list of questions. Among these should be the questions shown in Table 8-2. Comparing the answers from several companies in your area of interest should give you some benchmark for choosing one. The answers can most likely give you some clues as to whether the particular firm meets your business objectives. Finally, a face-to-face discussion with one of the principles is essential.

Table 8-2

Charter Management Company Questionnaire

1. Name of principals and their experience
2. Locations of principal operations
3. Type of vessels
    a. Sail or power
    b. New or previously owned
    c. Bareboat or crewed
4. Years in business
5. Number of boats and sizes in fleet
6. List of charter rates by size
7. Management program
    a. Annual management fee
    b. Split on income in %
8. Sale-leaseback program — lease % per year
9. Emphasis on maintenance
    a. Parts/labor discounts
    b. Labor rates
        skilled in $/hour
        unskilled in $/hour
10. Average cost of maintenance per year
11. Pay charter sales tax to state
12. Income and expense reporting monthly
13. Fleet insurance available and deductible amount
14. What type of advertising and marketing is done
15. Are charter brokers used
16. Amount of security deposit required
17. Pre-charter inspection and orientation trips
18. Provisioning for charter

Note: See Appendix I for the results of a charter management company survey.

What you want to find in a charter company is how close it comes to defining mutual goals that you want for your yacht. It should be maintained and presented in a manner that attracts the charter market and will ultimately bring the most value when you are ready to make a trade or sell your yacht. As an owner, you are in a position to delegate as much or as little control as you see fit. Most reputable management companies are qualified and agreeable to handle anything from the smallest part replacement to the details of an extended charter. How well they do these things and how they are financially able to meet the seasonality of chartering and normal business cycles are important questions they must answer.

Split income charter management - The charter company usually provides maintenance, advertising, and charter bookings in return for a split on the income. The range of the split is from 50-70% for the owner. The remainder goes to the company for advertising and commissions. In addition, the company may require an annual management fee to cover their administrative expenses. Charter management companies usually provide a complete accounting of all income and expenses. Such monthly statements are extremely valuable to back up your tax claims (Exhibits 8-1, 8-2 and 8-3 assumed a split income management company).

Sale-leaseback charter management - An alternate to splitting income with the owner and having the owner assume reponsibility for all expenses is the "sale-leaseback program." The charter company (usually the one selling the yacht) sells someone a yacht, and then leases it from the owner for a fixed sum and term. This amount is normally 8% of the original purchase price per year. Thus, 40% of the purchase price or $40,000 would be returned over a five year period assuming a $100,000 purchase. Under this program the company receives all charter income but is also responsible for all costs such as maintenance and repairs, dockage, insurance, etc., incurred by the vessel. A potentially negative aspect of sale-leaseback programs is a lack of motivation to adequately maintain the charter vesssel. All maintenance expenses are borne by the charter company, and, consequently, directly affect their profitability.

In comparison to the charter management method there is less paperwork with sale-leaseback programs. The payments from the company to you offset a large percentage of the annual mortgage costs, but there are no major tax advantages such as you have by deducting expenses. While a sale-leaseback program would probably generate less flack from the IRS, it may still generate a Section 183 problem unless the residual and cash flow pictures promise a profit high enough to pay off the loan and yield some cash. Nevertheless, sale-leaseback should be evaluated as an alternative way to charter your boat. With the advice of a tax advisor, you can make a decision as to which program is best for you (see Exhibit 8-4).

Exhibit 8-4

Sale-Leaseback Cash Flow

Assumptions:

Fully equipped yacht $100,000
Monthly payments $1,047
Sale-leaseback percent 8%

	Year 1	Year 2	Year 3	Year 4	Year 5	Total
Annual payments	$12,564	$12,564	$12,564	$12,564	$12,564	$62,820
Sale-leaseback	$8,000	$8,000	$8,000	$8,000	$8,000	$40,000
Net cost per year	$4,564	$4,564	$4,564	$4,564	$4,564	$22,820

Net monthly cost: $380

Protection of your boat (which is now a business asset) should be high on both your priority list and that of the charter company. Since you are paying them to effectively manage your charter vessel, you should expect nothing less than the best protection. This comes in three forms: Insurance, maintenance and customer checkout.

Insurance

Most charter companies have a fleet insurance policy with a specific insurance agent which is in turn underwritten by a large insurance carrier. Typically, they endorse a standard yacht policy for charter service. The rates are significantly higher than for an individual policy, as much as two to three times. The policy's risk is determined by the charter area. Premiums for chartering on inland lakes are among the lowest for charter operators. Among tidal waters the Chesapeake Bay is the lowest. On the other hand, chartering along the southeast coast of Florida carries the highest premiums in the U. S. Contrary to what one might think, vessel collisions are not the major causes of claims, rather, theft and onboard accidents are. Unfortunately, damage awards for such accidents are high, particularly if awarded by a court. Insurance coverage for charter use is covered further in Chapter 6.

Maintenance

The management company is responsible for the upkeep of your charter boat. The company has an incentive to keep your boat well maintained as parts and labor are an additional source of revenue. Your biggest problem may be in the over zealous pursuit of these contributions to their bottom line. Consequently, you may have to keep a watchful eye on your monthly statements so that unnecessary work isn't being performed or that the time spent on relatively simple jobs doesn't appear excessive.

One of the advantages of charter company maintenance over ordinary yard work is the discount you should get on the work done. If there are a number of boats in the charter fleet, then it's possible for the company to pass volume discounts on to the owners. A reasonable discount should be 10-15% on both parts and labor. These discounts are applied to both basic and skilled labor rates. Discounted rates will vary by location and should be approximately $20.00 and $30.00 per hour, respectively. Along with planned and other repairs, maintenance includes the clean up charges necessary after each charter. These are flat rate charges that run from $2.00 to $3.00 per foot of length. This charge is deducted from your net income per charter.

A good working relationship with your charter company is beneficial, particularly insofar as maintenance is concerned. Joint planning will help even out the cycles of repairs and this will smooth your cash flow making budgeting easier. Occasionally, some repairs will have to be done immediately for safety or operational reasons. These unexpected expenses can be better handled if your budget has some slack built in. This is possible if you are able to keep control on the planned and periodic maintenance requirements of your charter vessel. Annual or semi-annual meetings with your maintenance supervisor will pave the way for better relations and fewer surprises.

Customer screening

Careful screening of those people who want to charter your boat will help eliminate the ones with no experience or ability to operate her. The management company must be selective about who operates its fleet. Damage caused by improper operation has to be repaired, otherwise the boat is not available for charter and no money can be made — an equally bad situation for you and the charter company. The cost of the repairs may be borne by the ones who caused the damage, but they aren't liable for your lost revenue.

There are more opportunities for a charterer to damage a boat than for a renter to mess up a vacation home. Consequently, management companies are highly motivated to screen potential customers who have not chartered with them before and may not have a chartering record. Proof of sailing ability and overall seamanship by at least one member of a charter group according to some standard should be required before they go sailing off in your boat.

Some methods to determine competance used by companies, brokers and individuals handling bareboat charters include proof of previous sailing or powerboat experience or ownership of similar size vessels; a certificate from a recognized sailing school; or a practical demonstration of ability. At the beginning of each charter, the company representative should take clients for a three to four hour orientation run to familiarize them with the boat. This outing should include handling her in a variety of situations, particularly docking. Improper docking procedures can do as much damage to a vessel as a collision at sea. You may want to review the familiarization training with your company so that you feel comfortable about the operational points they are covering.

A good idea is to have the charter company provide a handy notebook which contains the operating instructions for the vessel's systems, radiotelephone calling procedures, a chart showing rules of the road, blank cruising and maintenance log sheets, an equipment inventory list, documentation paperwork and miscellaneous descriptions and procedures. This notebook can be used as a reference when on a cruise.

The completion of the charter should include a survey by your company representative and the charterer. All damage and equipment losses should be noted and the costs deducted from the security deposit of the client. The charterer is often required to place $500 to $1000 security deposit (including the insurance deductible) for any damage or loss that he causes. The deposit is often kept for several weeks after the charter in the event that latent damage is discovered. The company's cleaning persons should be on the lookout for damage as well as missing equipment.

Damage to the boat above the water is usually easy for a practiced eye to spot. Below water damage, however, is a different matter and there have been cases where a bareboat has hit a rock, reef or underwater obstruction during her charter. The subsequent damage to her hull or underwater equipment may go undetected by the inspector and unstated by the charterers. A quick way to deal with this is to send a diver below the waterline to inspect for any damage incurred during the charter.

There are many equipment items that can make a charter trip very pleasant and they should remain onboard. After all, as a charter boat owner you have spent many thousands of dollars outfitting your boat for charter service. Unless an inventory is kept rigorously by the charter company, it is likely that many items will disappear either through outright theft, mistakes or loss overboard. Standard operating procedure should be for the company representative or broker along with the client to locate all the equipment onboard so it is returned to its proper location.

Bareboat charter management companies may offer other services, too. They may provision a boat for charterers, pick them up at the airport, give them a book on where to cruise and anchor, and provide towing service should the vessel break down.

CHARTERING: A Business Opportunity

Owner managed

All of the factors that have been previously discussed apply equally to the individual who wants to keep his boat at his backyard dock and bareboat charter her. This person advertises in a variety of publications or by way of his own brochure, or may use a broker for bookings. Maintenance, clean up and perhaps provisioning are some of his chores. Such chartering is similar to the owner who captains his own boat except that the bareboat owner allows someone else to operate her. Some say that the most difficult aspect for this person is proving to the IRS that it is really a business and not just a hobby. If you are new to chartering, you may not be able to defend your case since you don't have the experience to operate such a business. It would pay you to learn the charter business with a charter management company before setting off on your own. All the same IRS rules will apply to you when you finally establish your own operation as they do to others in the charter business.

Selecting a captain and crew

Bareboat charters usually apply only to boats less than fifty feet. There are two reasons for this: They don't draw enough income to pay for a crew and boats up to fifty feet or so can be handled by relatively experienced charterers. A third reason may be the lack of space in a smaller boat for a captain and his cook/mate who may be a husband and wife crew.

In his book, *The Charter Game*, Ross Norgrove describes beautifully the ability to have a job as captain of your own boat in the charter trade, doing what you may have always wanted to do and getting paid for it. It may be the ultimate getaway for a husband and wife. You do have to work to make your boat a financial success, but think about all the fun you'll have doing it.

Of course, operating your own boat is just one way you can have a crew for your boat. The other is to arrange for one through a charter management company. You have to make the final crew selection but the company will aid you in doing this. In this case, the captain and mate are paid a salary with a performance bonus by the charter company and they alone are charged with the duties of proper yacht care. Success of the charters is their responsibility. Additionally, they have to perform preventive and curative maintenance, provision before each charter and keep the yacht looking its best. The charter company will handle the charter accounting and reporting for the crew. The captain will be working through a controlled checking account supplemented with a yacht credit card. All his expenditures are readily audited and must fall within reasonable limits.

Advertising, client contacts and booking is done through an international charter brokerage system that has been in effect for 100 years. This well established method sells charters and books the yachts through a central booking agent in St.Thomas, U.S. Virgin Islands. It is strongly recommended that a crewed charter operation not deviate from this recognized practice of booking as few individual chartering companies have ever been successful in capturing the crewed charter market. Many independent owner-operators derive their sole source of income directly from their charter business, thus, it's in their best interest to ensure that the existing system continues to function without dilution by crewed yacht fleets.

Your charter related finances should be handled the same with a crewed yacht as with a bareboat. Crew's salaries are an additional line item. This should be reported to you along with the other operational expenses. The exception, of course, is if you plan to crew your own boat. In this case, your principal business activity is your boat and your taxes would be reported accordingly. Serving as a crew member may be the only safe way to write off a charter boat so as to keep the income active.

Exhibit 8-5

Sample Income/Expense For A Crewed Charter Boat

Income:

Weeks of charter	20	
Rate per week	$3,000	
Total income		$60,000

Expenses:

Food, drinks and ice ($550/week)	$11,000	
Fuel ($50/week)	1,000	
Dockage	550	
Haul out	1,200	
Maintenance	3,000	
Insurance	3,000	
Motor transport	350	
Commission (15% booked income)	9,000	
Clearing agent	300	
Total expenses		$29,400
Net income (before taxes)		$30,600

Assumptions for Exhibit 8-5:

▸ 45-50 foot vessel in Caribbean charter location

▸ Owner/wife are crew

▸ Four charter guests per weekly cruise

▸ Expenses are based on reasonable estimates from various sources and from the author's experience.

If you are considering crewing and operating your own boat, you should seek special advice to determine how to best go about this. Basic questions you need to answer are whether you have the skills necessary and can totally sever yourself from your existing lifestyle. If you feel confident about both answers, then press on. Who knows, it may well be the best move of your life.

(1) Section 280A, U.S. Tax Code

(2) Section 183, U.S. Tax Code

(3) Tax comments drawn from the report of the Staff of the Joint Committee on Taxation, 1987

(4) *BOATING COST GUIDE*, Annual Edition, R.S. Means Company, Inc., Kingston, MA., 1984

Bibliography

1. Norgrove, Ross, *The Charter Game*, 1978, International Marine Publishing Company, Camden, ME

2. Chartering and the IRS, Elaine Kersels, *CHARTERING* Magazine,Inc., October 1984

3. Yacht Management, anonymous, *CHARTERING* Magazine, Inc., October, 1984

4. Yacht Chartering and the IRS. *CHARTERING* Magazine, Inc., August, 1984

5. *Boating Cost Guide*, Robert Sturgis Godfrey, Ed., R.S. Means Company, Inc., 1984, Kingston, MA

6. "Yacht Management: Its Time Has Passed", *Practical Sailor*, Volume 11, Nr. 5, March 1, 1985

7. Tax Report, Staff of the Joint Committee on Taxation, 1987

Acknowledgements

1. David Lidle, CPA
    Segal & Segal
    Philadelphia, PA

2. Mike Landers
    President
    C&C Charters, Ltd.
    Point Pleasant, NJ

3. Len Smith, Partner
    Withum, Smith, & Brown, CPA's
    Princeton, NJ

CHAPTER 9

SELLING YOUR BOAT: Preparing to Move Up

It's a favorite saying of yachtsmen, that one of the two happiest days in their lives is the day the boat is sold — the other of course being the day the boat was bought! Conventional wisdom notwithstanding, if you've planned carefully and thoughtfully, and not encountered adverse personal or economic conditons, you most likely thoroughly enjoyed your boat ownership experience.

But for one reason or another, the time arrives to sell your dream possession. Hopefully, because of careful planning and the help this book offers, you find yourself selling in order to trade up to an even bigger boat. Maybe your charter boat is fully depreciated and it's time to roll over into a new boat. Perhaps you just wish to switch from sail to power, or vice versa (it does happen!). Or maybe you just want to give boating a rest for a few years as you pursue other interests.

Whatever the case, it is always easier and more pleasant to sell a boat when ownership was planned carefully; forced selling never commands as good a price or terms as does selling at leisure. And because some day nearly everyone who owns a boat will sell it, a proper wrap up to a book on boat ownership is detailed information on how to properly dispose of a boat. While there are a lot of ways to accomplish this objective, the same careful planning should prevail.

As you read through this material, you will no doubt notice that some of the buying issues mentioned in Chapter 1 are again discussed. This should come as no surprise obviously; for every boat sold, one is bought. Buying and selling are two sides of the same coin, so many of the boat selling issues brought out in this chapter will also be discussed in terms of their impact on the boat buyer.

The Prevailing Price

Most surprising to the first time boat seller is the price his vessel will likely fetch. A myth has sprung up in the marine industry over the last ten years that boats are appreciating assets. In reality, the vast majority tend to depreciate like other consumer durable goods, although at a somewhat slower pace. The increase in resale prices during the late 70s and early 80s contributed to the myth. Yet evidence suggests price appreciation had more to do with the severe inflation of that period and a subsequent shortage of product during the ensuing recession, than with any factors intrinsic to boats themselves.

There are a few exceptions to boat value depreciation, but precious few. With luck, you may discover that your boat is actually worth more than you paid. Temporary supply/demand conditions could cause this, as might changing consumer preferences. In general, it's a good idea to check local prices periodically during your ownership period to see what direction your boat's price is moving; it may influence your decision as to how long you wish to own it. But the sad fact remains that, over time, these shifts tend to equal out, producing a declining value for most boats.

Be prepared then for a somewhat lower (maybe much lower) sale price than you paid for your yacht and **don't be discouraged.** Remember, you received a great deal of use in the vessel and likely enjoyed it very much. That enjoyment has a value which should not be overlooked.

Probably most disconcerting for an owner anxious to sell is how little all that fabulous equipment and decorating increases the price of the boat relative to similar, less equipped boats on the market. Don't be shocked when you discover this. To a certain extent, the way a yacht is equipped is a matter of personal preference. A potential buyer may not need that fifty mile radar you installed, but may instead wonder why your yacht doesn't have a cruising generator. A rule of thumb: The more you equip your boat, the less you'll get back for each new piece of equipment you add. This is especially true if you **over** equip your boat, that is, add equipment that is truly superfluous to the boat's operation or intended use.

Interior decor generally represents another nonrecoverable cost. Most buyers have their own tastes and preferences. When looking at your boat, they probably have already added in the cost to redecorate.

If a single factor stands out from the rest in obtaining the best price for a boat, it is probably condition. Most yacht brokers advise sellers that the initial impression is everything when buying a boat. The better maintained your boat and the more presentable it appears while marketing, the better the price you will receive. A wise investment at time of sale is a good boat detailing job; the money will be well spent.

Regardless of how you plan to sell your boat, it's a good idea to get an idea of prices before you go to market. Several methods of price determination should be employed to develop a full view of your yacht's value. The first and most simple consists of calling various area yacht brokers and asking for prices of similar listed boats. If you own a popular make of boat and live in or near a large marine center, there will probably be a number of like boats already up for sale. The best indication of your boat's price is, of course, what these boats are actually selling for.

You can also check one or more of the multiple listing services that work direct with the public. These lists aren't always as "fresh" as information provided by a broker, but at least they provide an indication. At least two national on-line computer listing services also now make available listing prices and, in certain cases, actual sale price data. At this time however, they are available only through yacht brokerages.

Some waterfront tabloids devote entire sections to current listings and most marine periodicals have brokerage advertising with extensive lists that often include asking prices. These listing prices must be discounted by 15-30% to reflect a likely selling price but it does tend to establish a range.

Finally, information from the industry price guide, the BUC book, can be used (see the footnote in Chapter 3). As mentioned earlier, such information is not quite as reliable as that obtained from local sources, but it can help establish a general range.

Once you have determined what your boat is worth on the current resale market in your local area, **accept that figure.** Even if you're not thrilled with the number, consider what it will cost you additionally to hold the boat waiting for a better price e.g. loan payments, slip fees, maintenance and insurance. You'll find timing can become very problematic if your new boat is on order with a set delivery date and owning two vessels is financially impossible. Thus, be realistic about price up front.

If the investment can be justified, you may consider moving your boat to another area (or at least marketing it in another area) where prices are better for that particular model. Such price discrepancies are sometimes seen on the resale market for geographic areas that are relatively proximal. The price of trawlers, for instance, may be better in Seattle than San Francisco, with the cost to move a vessel between the two markets less than the value differential.

Dealer, Broker or Direct?

There are several methods of selling your boat and different guidelines for each. If you are trading up from your used boat to a new one, you are probably working through a dealer for both boats. If you simply wish to sell on the open market, a broker must be employed. And if you take on the entire responsibility of selling yourself, you are direct marketing. We'll look at each of these avenues in turn.

Selling through a dealer

A dealer is any boat seller that handles new product, usually from stock kept at their place of business. Dealers are affiliated with a particular manufacturer but will often carry several complimentary lines, usually at different points in the price spectrum or displaying different use characteristics, though not very often do dealers carry both power and sail (the differences between the product and the buyers purchasing them are usually too pronounced to coexist successfully in the same dealership).

Manufacturers generally establish dealerships in accordance with their overall marketing objectives for rational product distribution and pricing. For this reason, dealers of a particular product are strategically placed to provide the greatest coverage while still allowing sufficient market area to obtain reasonable boat sales and profit figures. Thus, if you are seeking a specific brand of new boat, you may have to buy from a certain dealer. Manufacturers encourage their dealers to respect territorial lines; from the standpoint of after market service and warranty, it's most efficient that way.

A dealer earns his living by selling his product for more than he pays the manufacturer, creating a profit margin. Obviously, dealer margins are not published for the public but there are means to determine them. Gross profit margins in boats range from around 15% on larger, higher quality boats to as high as 40% on smaller boats and boats built overseas. Knowing the margin can be helpful to you when trading up through the dealer as noted below. The discount structure of some builders can easily allow a volume dealer to sell a 20% margin boat for as much as 30%. There is also a substantial profit made on optional equipment the dealer may be asked to obtain for the buyer. Profit margins on these items run as high as 50%.

"Selling" to the dealer - This is the easiest way to dispose of a boat; the dealer simply takes it in trade. If a loan is on the boat, the dealer pays it off using a previously established line of credit with a bank or finance company. The difference between that loan and the agreed trade price goes against the new boat purchase price. If there is no loan on your trade boat, you get value against your new boat at whatever figure you and your dealer agree upon. The following example illustrates this:

Exhibit 9-1

New boat price		$72,000
add: Freight		2,500
Commissioning	+	500
Sub total		75,000
add: Sales tax @ 5%	+	3,750
Total		78,750
Trade boat	−	40,000
Net price		38,750
add: Trade boat loan payoff	+	29,500
Net cost of new boat		68,250
New boat loan (80% of boat + tax, freight, commissioning)	−	63,000
Net cash down		$5,250

In the example, the used boat is sold and the new boat bought with only $5,250 out-of-pocket. Of course, the loan payments are likely now considerably higher.[1]

You may feel that by employing a trade you will receive a better price on a new boat, especially if you inform the dealer of your current boat after negotiating the new boat price. But most boat dealers who have been around for awhile understand very well new boat/trade boat pricing and they have considerable experience in protecting their profit through the use of price trade offs. Because all of their profit is usually tied up in the trade boat, they will be very careful to price that boat to lock in that profit. Often times this conflicts with a seller's opinion as to the worth of a trade boat. You may bargain for a higher trade value, but it will usually be offset by a closer-to-retail price for the new boat.

Most dealers therefore tend to underestimate the price a boat will bring on the trade market (they are not interested in holding on to it either!). You may feel in the end the trade value given is not fair, and decide to market the boat yourself. But you will then certainly have additional expenses to pay as we'll see later.

Completing the trade - Once the dealer accepts your trade at an agreed value, you must sign over title in the boat to the dealer. But beware, because some dealers will resist taking that title. If title remains in your name and the dealer simply promises to make the payments until the boat is sold, you could be on the hook for both boats indefinitely. If a trade is part of the deal, make sure it is complete. Transfer title and worry about only one boat.

Boat dealers, unless they are very large and financially solvent, will not take large boats in trade. The amount of bank credit required to pay off your loan along with the time it takes to sell the boat (not to mention the amount of profit tied up) usually don't justify their effort. Small boats, however, are more readily sold with smaller variances from expected value and thus represent less risk to the dealer.

Selling through a broker

A broker differs from a dealer in that a broker handles the sale of boats, either new or pre-owned, on a commission basis only. A new boat dealer often brokers boats not accepted on trade, or on listings obtained from previous customers, referrals and so forth. Almost all dealers at some time or another handle brokerage boats and some are as good at it as the well established "pure" brokerage houses.

Just as in real estate transactions, a broker is the agent that brings the parties together. Never will the broker take a title (ownership) position in the boat, but they will do literally everything else short of that. Arranging advertising, showing the boat to prospective customers, supervising surveys, repairs and sea trials; all these duties can be professionally handled by a good yacht broker.

A broker's primary concern is selling your boat; no income is earned until he does so. Yacht brokers are rarely salaried employees of a brokerage firm. In fact, most are self described "independent agents" who are using the facilities and reputation of a particular brokerage house in return for a portion of the sales commission. They prospect for customers through advertising, referrals and their general familiarity with the yachting community. Most are fairly aggressive; one must be to stay in the business long!

Brokers also tend to favor larger boats because, of course, the fees are higher. In fact, if you have small boat (say under 25') you may discover that you must sell direct. Few brokers will handle this type of boat because the commission earned upon sale simply doesn't justify the cost of selling. Unless the broker has few listings and little else to do, you'll find it hard to shift the selling responsibility for a small boat. But don't panic. The market for smaller boats is much wider so buyers are more readily available. Smaller boats also sell well using some of the inexpensive techniques outlined in the next section. And dealers are more likely to take them in trade since they will normally represent only a small portion of the new boat sale.

Quite often, the broker takes the place of an attorney or escrow company in passing funds and title documents. Although only California and Florida regulate the licensing of yacht brokers, which thus provides a modicum of protection to the consumer, most sellers and buyers accept the integrity of the well known brokerage houses and thus allow them to handle these large sums and important title transfer documents.

Brokers will also perform valuable services in the areas of finance and insurance for persons buying or selling boats. Some are very skilled at arranging creative sales that may involve seller financing or property exchanges (dealt with in a later section). Of course, it's always a good idea to have an attorney involved, but sometimes the contracts and basic structure of a deal can only be worked out by a broker. In this case, find one with experience in the area you need; check out credentials by speaking with previous customers.

When it comes to finance, the broker is uniquely qualified to put the borrower with the right lender. Since they work with many lenders over a period of time, they often develop a good "instinct" as to which lender to point a particular type of credit profile. For that reason, a number of brokers now attempt to pre-qualify their clients by inquiring into income, past finances, credit problems and so forth so they can better direct the financing. Don't be upset by this inquiry; it's actually a good sign and demonstrates your broker's more thorough knowledge of what it takes to put a transaction together.

Once a boat sells, the broker receives his paycheck. Unlike a dealer, whose profit ultimately depends on both the sale price of the boat and his business expense control, a broker makes money on every transaction. The standard commission in the industry is ten percent, a figure which is not discounted very often. Occasionally, on very large transactions, some concession can be gained in the commission percentage, or a seller can ask for a net price allowing the broker to obtain whatever extra, (up to 10%) he feels necessary to compensate his effort.

In a later section we'll examine the commission split between the buyer's broker and the seller's broker (if they are not the same) and the respective brokerage houses. Suffice it to say, if you plan to sell through a broker you will receive ten percent less than the purchase price. To compensate, you may want to increase the listing price of the boat or raise the lowest price you will accept.

Listing your boat

Once you have selected the dealer/broker, a listing agreement with that firm must be signed. Different brokers use different listing agreements of varying complexity, but the majority contain similar terms and provisions. Listings are generally of three types; exclusive, central and open.

Exclusive listing - An exclusive listing grants the listing broker the sole right to sell the boat. Anyone bringing a buyer to you must deal through that broker who is then entitled to a ten percent commission if he successfully concludes a sale. If a different broker finds a buyer for your vessel, the listing broker still receives by custom thirty percent of the sales commission, which generally covers initial advertising and other marketing costs. The outside broker originating the sale (also known as a "co-op broker") receives the remaining seventy percent. Subject to any time limitations in the listing, when the boat is sold the broker receives a commission regardless of the customer origin. In other words, once an exclusive is signed, you are obligated to pay a commission even if you, by chance, find a buyer for your own boat.

Central listing - A central listing is similar to an exclusive with one exception; you retain the right to sell the boat, without payment of commission, to any buyer you obtain. A central still gives the broker the sole right to bring in offers. Any other broker with a buyer must deal through the listing broker. The same commission split applies in this case as well.

Open listing - An open listing grants a nonexclusive right to sell the boat in exchange for a commission, again usually ten percent. As many open listings can be signed as there are brokers to sign them. The terms are less restrictive because the open listing is generally one-sided; it merely protects the broker's commission if they find a buyer. Thus, your strategy might consist of granting a series of open listings thereby allowing a large number of brokers to see the potential of a full ten percent commission.

Which should you sign, exclusive, central, or open? It depends on a number of factors and may be influenced by your confidence in or prior experience with a particular broker. By way of example, let's look at the commission split again. As we stated, the typical commission arrangement between selling broker (buyer's broker) and listing broker (seller's broker) is a seventy/thirty split. But the split of the commission between the salesman completing the sale and the brokerage firm he represents is handled on a somewhat different basis. A broker who develops a central or exclusive is usually guaranteed one percent, regardless of who sells the boat. The house gets the other two percent. If the broker **sells** his own central, another 4% goes his way with the remaining 3% to the house. On a co-op sale however, the selling broker will usually get only half of the selling commission, or 3.5% while the house takes the other half. So, an exclusive is really a bonanza for the broker if he sells his own listing, as it generates about 43% more commission for himself!

And that is really where the difference in type of listing lies: The amount of effort a broker will exert to sell the boat. A central listing will usually get you better notice in the brokerage firm's weekly or monthly newspaper and magazine advertising. Salesmen will promote the boat more aggressively and consistently. It seems reasonable to expect this since a sale of a central listing earns significantly more commission! Thus, if you plan on spending 10% of the sale price in commission, spend it wisely — sign a central listing.

Signing a central may also gain you extra consideration from the brokerage house in keeping and maintaining the boat. Quite often a broker who has available slip space will give priority first to boats centrally listed with his company. The slip may still cost you but in areas where such accommodations are at a premium, it could be worth it. Depending on your bargaining skills and the listing price, you may actually get the slip and routine maintenance for little or nothing. If the brokerage house believes the boat will move fast at the price you want, such concessions are possible.

In fact, you may be able to get a good location at a desirable marina by offering a central listing at a price that will insure it stays **unsold** for awhile. Why would a broker accept such an arrangement? Because it allows him to use the boat as a means to attract buyers to his office where other more realistically priced boats may be shown and sold.

Provisions of a listing - The provisions of a typical listing agreement are fairly simple and straight forward. If a central, the agreement allows the central agent to accept offers from any broker it chooses (who are referred to as "sub-listed brokers"). These offers are then passed through the central agent to the owner. Should the vessel be sold through a sub-listed broker, the central agent has the responsibility of paying the commission due. Always, unless there is a provision in the listing to the contrary, if the vessel is sold by anyone except the owner (unless the listing is exclusive) to anyone during the term of the agreement, the commission is paid. Thus, if you have a person in mind who might buy your boat but you want to list it anyway on an exclusive basis, it would be wise to obtain an exclusion for that one person.

An open listing allows the sale of the boat by another broker or by the owner but protects the broker's commission on any sale to a buyer who was made aware of the boat through that broker's advertising or other marketing efforts. An open allows you to sell the boat through any other broker or through your own means without paying commission to more than one party.

Any listing will also have two provisions relating to the term of the agreement. The first will reference the listing expiration and is expressed either as a termination date or as a required notification period prior to termination. For example, you may grant a six month listing thinking that is sufficient time for a broker to find a buyer for your boat. Or you may make the contract open ended with a thirty to ninety day cancellation period. Both a termination date or required notification period are negotiable elements of the listing and you may want to keep them relatively short especially if you feel the boat is being offered at a reasonable sale price.

The second provision relating to term will specify a period after termination of the contract during which a commission must be paid if the boat is sold to any person that the central agent or a sublisted agent brought to the seller. This period varies anywhere from ninety days to a year with 120-180 days being fairly common.

A listing will always release the broker from any obligation to care for, maintain or control the listed yacht. If you want such responsibilities to be handled by the broker or the marina the brokerage operates from, you must generally sign a separate agreement.

The listing will state an initial price at which the seller must accept an offer. You should always establish a figure that is higher than you feel the boat can sell for in order to create some room to negotiate. A figure of 20-25% is realistic and does not create the impression among buyers that the seller is expecting an unrealistic price that will impede negotiations. While no one really expects any boat to sell at its original listed price, that number is important as it establishes a range that prospective buyers will look at when deciding which boats warrant examination.

The listing will allow the boat, at the seller's discretion, to be sold at whatever lower price he may choose to accept. Upon presentation of any offer to the broker, the seller has the right to accept, or reject and counter with a new figure. It's a good idea to have a "lowest" acceptable figure in mind at the outset of negotiations. But keep this number private. Otherwise you may guarantee it as the **highest** price you obtain.

Selecting a broker - The brokerage community is a fluid one with individuals working for many different houses in the course of a career. Because of this, the best reference on a house or particular individual is from a fellow boatman who has worked with them before. Referrals are absolutely invaluable because just as in every field of endeavor, there are those who exhibit honesty and integrity and those who don't. It is well worth your time to investigate whom you should be buying or selling through.

The yacht brokerage field is largely unregulated so caution is recommended in selecting a broker. But there are some signs to observe. First, how long has the firm been in existence? The more reputable houses have a track record and a history that derives from providing good service and value to buyers and sellers.

Second, does the house put on a professional appearance? While appearance isn't everything, a company that professes to deal with a largely upscale and professional market should attempt to be perceived in the same way. Watch out for disorganized, untidy offices with brokers that lounge around and seem unconcerned with your boat buying needs. Read the listing agreements. Do they cover all the bases and are they fair? Examine their actual listings. Are they central or open (more centrals mean more owner confidence in the house). Are they representing quality boats and late models, or older, less desirable product?

Discuss price with the broker and notice how his figure compares with what you have already determined through independent investigation. A broker who is not fond of working hard is very likely to tell a seller that he wants too much for his boat no matter what the asking price. After all, the lower the price, the easier it will be to sell and the difference in overall commission is not that great.

If you believe, or even suspect, that the price you are hearing is not correct, ask for evidence. Don't accept a statement like "Well, this boat is just not that popular right now" or "It's interest rates you know, the market is just too soft". A knowledgable broker will obtain real prices of similar boats recently sold in your area. Ask for more than one. There is always that one flukey price — high or low — that may seem to justify his estimate, so get a representative sample of boat prices.

Selling direct

After examining trade and brokerage options you may decide to give direct selling a try. In effect, you eliminate the middle man and try to obtain the best price possible utilizing whatever means available. Boat owners are often tempted to go this route for two reasons. First, they feel ten percent is too large a commission to pay for selling a boat. After all, the standard for residential real estate is only six percent. Why should a yacht be higher? Second, a seller might feel he or she can do just as good a job as a broker, perhaps because they had luck in selling their own automobiles or real estate.

To decide if direct selling is best for you, look carefully at the costs, time and effort involved before you make a choice. A simple analysis should precede this decision.

Direct selling analysis - On the one side of the equation is the commission you save, ten percent of the price of your boat, an easily quantifiable figure. Of course this assumes you can obtain a price equal to or better than that obtainable by a broker, and the odds are you can't. Why? Simply because a broker can expose your boat to a wider market. This is especially true in the case of a larger yacht where potential buyers are likely to start their shopping with a favorite broker. For arguments sake then, let's assume your direct price will be an average 5% less than a good broker can obtain.

Direct selling requires advertising your boat in various ways. You can do this without great cost (only time) through your local yacht club, an area yacht chandlery, at various marinas and at boat shows. Prepare an inexpensive brochure with pictures that describes the vessel, her equipment and so forth along with your asking price. Don't worry about printing in color on high gloss stock (unless perhaps you wish to sell a 100 foot Italian motoryacht!). You simply wish to present the boat's vital statistics in a clear and comprehensable manner. Emphasize condition, mention equipment and include at least two photographs of both the interior and exterior. Shoot in black and white, well lit, so the print shop that makes your brochures can reproduce them on paper.

The number of people that are likely to see the brochure is of course small, unless you have the time and inclination to post it in all the marine centers close to your location. Boat shows are an excellent place to distribute them; lots of people who are there to buy! But how to get them out to the audience? Two suggestions. First, you can ask to drop a few off at a "neutral" exhibitor's booth for placement on a table or stand so passers-by can pick them up with all the other literature collected at the show. Insurance companies, lenders, surveyors and hardware companies are all good bets, especially if you have purchased services from them in the past. Let them know you will also recommend them to interested buyers and they will probably not object to a few additional leaflets in their exhibit.

Second, you can put them at the main entrance to the show, next to the stacks of show programs that are always left on a nearby table. You may even get creative and headline the flyer with something catchy like:

BOAT SHOW SPECIAL !!

Imagine yourself

Sailing away today . . .

Sabre 42

Like new condition, roller furling, stow-away main
Loaded with all new electronics three private cabins and two heads,
teak interiors, contemporary galley

$159,900

Call (212) FOR-SALE

Clever marketing has sold many a boat that would otherwise still be in the hands of the owner. Dare to be different is selling **your** boat!

Advertising can also be placed in a variety of media both in and out of the marine industry. National magazine classifieds, local waterfront tabloids, newspapers and listing services are among the best choices. If you live in a large urban center such as New York or Los Angeles, you can probably utilize a special boating classified section in a Sunday paper. Local editions of the Wall Street Journal also have special boating sections from time to time.

Display ads with bold headings or pictures are better attention grabbers but cost more than classified type advertising. The larger the boat, the more you can spend on advertising and the following table gives some sample rates as of November, 1988.

Exhibit 9-2

Media	Display (one column x two inches)	Classified (five lines)
Wall Street Journal - per day	$332.08	$59.30
L.A. Times - Sunday	$350.18	$80.00
L.A. Times - one week	$1,732.00	$125.00
N.Y. Times - Sunday	$172.48	$61.60
N.Y. Times - one week	$795.06	$283.95
Yachting Magazine (national - 1/16 pg)*	$730.00	$315.00 (2 in.)
Soundings (3 months/ 20 words)	$105.00	$60.00
Sea Magazine (California)*	$130.00	$29.75
Southern Boating (Florida 1/8 pg)*	$395.00	$ 40.00 (1 in.)

* Single issue

As you can see, the cost of advertising varies with the periodical selected and of course depends on how long the ads run. For this reason you want to go in with an attractive price so as to generate a number of inquiries in the shortest period possible. Once you commit yourself to this expense you must follow it through. Even a small advertising program, copy only without professionally prepared graphics, will run around $2,000 for the space alone. This will allow for sufficient exposure to sell a larger boat, say in the forty to sixty foot range. Smaller boats will require less advertising but you can still count on spending $500 – $1,000 for any significant exposure.

The next thing you must do to sell your boat is answer a lot of questions, over and over, and show it to interested persons. This is of course the most time consuming and expensive part of the direct sale process. Unlike selling your own home, where you can show prospective buyers the property after working hours when you are home anyway, a boat will demand time you can probably ill afford to spend, such as weekends and during work hours. If your time has a high value, this alone may make the cost of direct selling prohibitive.

Finally, every serious buyer is going to want a sea trial. You can minimize unnecessary outings by requiring a signed contract and deposit before taking anyone out on your boat. It's fair to ask and may eliminate "joy riders". As a general rule you too should try to qualify anyone who gets to the contract stage. With the permission of your buyer, you may get a credit search firm to run a credit report, to see if there are any past problems that might prevent a loan approval.

Once you have looked at all that is involved with selling your own boat, you can do a simple analysis to determine cost effectiveness:

Exhibit 9-3

Sale of 36' Sailboat

Assume: Selling through broker for $50,000 (gross selling price)
Selling direct for $47,500 (net selling price)

Initial Savings:

Commission @ ten percent	$5,000.00

Costs:

Price differential (5%)	$2,500.00

Expenses (direct and estimated)

Brochure printing	+	200.00
Advertising costs	+	1,000.00
Showing the boat		
4 hours telephone time	+	60.00
6 buyer inspections	+	300.00
3 sea trials	+	300.00
Total estimated cost	+	4,360.00
Plus: Personal time	+	$? ? ? ?
Net savings		$ 640.00

From the above it appears as if, for the contemplated sale, it may be more practical to sell the boat through a broker. For a smaller boat you may not have a choice. For larger boats it really doesn't make a lot of sense unless you have something selling for say, $200,000 or more. Of course, if you are making enough to afford a $200,000 yacht, your time alone might not justify it. In short, it appears as if only a real "do-it-yourself" seller with a lot of free time will find direct selling viable.

Documents and Paperwork

When selling your boat, or buying one for that matter, you should pay very close attention to your documents and paperwork. A boat closing is not so complicated that you need a lawyer to work up the contracts at considerable expense. The exceptions include a special purchase or loan structure necessary to obtain special tax advantages, or if the sale involves seller financing, asset/property trades or involves a lender repossessed boat. In order to control costs, you may wish to shop for a broker/lender combination that has experience in these areas. Some of these "trick deals" are actually quite common in the boat business and certain brokers and lenders may possess the proper techniques and know-how; even if they are not directly qualified, they most likely know legal and accounting experts with experience in the field to assist you at reasonable cost.

In planning your closing there are four documents you should be very familiar with as they constitute the center of the sale and transfer of the yacht. To ignore them could end up costing you a lot. This is especially important in direct sales where no broker, dealer or lender is involved.

Purchase agreement

The most simple item to overlook, the purchase agreement, should be the first step in actually closing your sale. A purchase agreement is a legal contract; it alone establishes the terms of sale and can be quite useful should any disagreement arise over who was responsible for what long after the boat is sold and the elation of both parties has subsided. Every purchase agreement should address:

(i) *Price of the boat*: Should state the total cost of the boat and who has responsibility to pay any applicable taxes, fees, etc.

(ii) *What is included in the boat*: For example, electronics, miscellaneous equipment, dinghy, sails, furnishings, etc.

(iii) *Deposit and the terms of its refund:* Since you will incur expenses in closing the sale, should the buyer be unable to perform, you will want some money to cover those expenses.

(iv) *The time in which the purchase must be consummated and provisions for any extensions*: Always set a deadline to give the buyer a sense of urgency and to avoid losing other prospects if your buyer can't perform. Once the contract is signed, you cannot summarily ignore it if a better price comes along. If you want to extend the period to consummate, you can always do so later with a simple modification agreement.

(v) *Any warranties provided by seller*: Usually there will be none. Used boats are almost always sold on a so called "as is, where is" basis meaning effectively, Buyer Beware. As we'll see later, this is why a marine survey is so important in a closing.

(vi) *Contingencies for cancellation of the contract*: There are usually three.

   ▸ Financing - allows the buyer to withdraw if financing is not obtained. Since financing often comes last, avoid the term "acceptable financing" as it provides an easy out if your buyer has a change of heart. For example, "sale is contingent upon buyer obtaining financing of at least $100,000 for fifteen years at a fixed rate of not more than 14%."

▶ Survey - here you probably have to live with the term "acceptable survey". But if the boat is found to have no **material** defects then you should be able to enforce the sale.

▶ Sea trial - your contract should also specify a sea trial and again the term "acceptable" is unavoidable. But after the sea trial you should have your buyer sign off immediately on the acceptability.

(vii) *Warranty of clear title, or limit of liability if title is defeated or encumbrances remain*: This last point is especially crucial. In a moment, we'll look at so called "invisible liens", and how they affect your boat. If your purchase contract stipulates no liens or encumbrances, you may be liable in the future for those you did not know about. A seller who is doubtful of the vessel's full history may wish to limit liability to registered liens and see to it that all appropriate lien searches are conducted.

Generally, it is up to the buyer to satisfy him or herself that all liens and encumbrances are removed at the time title passes. If the purchase is financed, the lender will investigate this carefully as they will have a secured interest in the collateral. But while the seller may guarantee the clear title in the purchase agreement, that representation is only as good as a buyers ability to collect on it; there is no fully effective title insurance available for boats. This is one of the reasons U.S. Coast Guard documentation is so useful when buying or selling a yacht, providing a clear indication of legal title to and a secured interest in a vessel.

The purchase agreement must be signed by both parties. Don't accept the other party's broker signature, and if a Power of Attorney is used, ask to see the original, notarized form.

Bill of sale

The means by which title actually transfers is by a bill of sale. In most states with a title law (see Chapter 7) the bill of sale is on the title itself. You simply sign it as current owner to the new owner, unless of course a lien is noted on it. If you plan to document the vessel under the Federal system, a bill of sale in a form recordable by the Coast Guard is required. It is common these days for the purchase price to read "ten dollars and other valuable considerations"; although in some states, if a new state title is to be obtained, the actual purchase price must be noted on the bill of sale.

Current ship's registration

In order for the buyer to register the vessel and to help ascertain current ownership and liens, you should always volunteer the vessel's current registration papers. This will consist of either a valid (current) Coast Guard license (ship's document) or a current state registration and/or title. Nothing else indicates valid registration. And Federal law states that every boat not held for resale must be registered under **either** state or Federal law. Obviously then, it is very important for the buyer of a boat to inspect these papers, in order to ascertain legitimate ownership.

The registration may also indicate any lien holder against the vessel although as we said before, only a current lien search will establish all parties that might have an interest in the boat at the time of sale.

As part of the sale process, in addition to bills of sale, the registration must also be delivered to the buyer. For a documented vessel, the license (which has been held aboard the vessel by the owner) is delivered to the buyer who must then surrender it to the Coast Guard in order to effect a transfer of ownership, change of name, etc. If a lender is involved, they will usually handle the details of this so as to record a mortgage against the license when the change over is complete.

For a titled vessel, the certificate of title is held by a lender usually and can be delivered as soon as the outstanding lien is paid. If no lien is on the boat, the current owner will be in possession of the certificate. In either case, if the title is to be maintained, a new state registration must be filed in the name of the new owner. If the title is to be replaced by a ship's license under federal registration, then it must be surrendered to the Coast Guard.

Lien satisfaction

Probably the most important condition to satisfy your buyer on is the absolute assurance that the boat is sold free and clear of liens or encumbrances, so far as you are aware. While most state law protects you from buying a boat from a dealer and finding out later he did not pay off an inventory loan against it, no such laws exist to protect buyers in the event a private seller sells a boat without paying off its mortgage. In this case the lien very likely could follow the vessel to its new owner who may find himself without the money and the boat. As seller, it is your legal and ethical obligation to disclose any and all claims against your vessel.

A seller then should be aware of any liens placed against his vessel prior to sale, such as yard bills or crew's wages. Remember, if you represent in a purchase agreement that a boat was sold free and clear, you could be held liable for committing a fraudulent sale.

Forms of lien satisfaction - To be fully satisfied that no other liens are registered against the boat, it is the buyer's responsbility to do thorough and accurate lien searches against the boat. If the transaction is financed, the lender will probably do this in the ordinary course of a closing. On the other hand, if you are selling for cash, it will be the buyer's sole responsibility to do the checking. There are essentially three ways to check for outstanding liens against a vessel:

(i) **United States Coast Guard** - In Chapter 7 the subject of Coast Guard documentation was discussed with reference to securing a marine loan with a preferred ship mortagage. Any such mortgage against a vessel, or any subsequent Notice of Claim must be registered against the vessel at its designated homeport if it is a documented vessel. Checking for these liens and/or claims is simple. Simply contact the proper homeport with the name and official number of the vessel and ask for a lien search. Most will give you the information right over the phone. If you have to write, a small fee will usually be charged. Appendix F lists the U.S. Coast Guard documentation homeports.

(ii) **State title** - If a title is on the boat (and there likely will be if you live in a title state and registration numbers appear on the bow of the boat) you will have to do a search through the state agency responsible for boat registration and titling (see Appendix G). Each state differs in how this is carried out; you simply contact the agency, pay any required fee and let them walk you through it.

(iii) UCC - If a boat is neither titled nor federally documented, a lien could only exist if it were established under the laws of the Uniform Commercial Code (UCC), as adopted by a particular state (except Louisiana which never adopted it). It is not likely this has occured, although certain situations could lead to it. The law is a bit too involved to go into here; suffice to say a search is done at the level of Secretary of State of the state where the boat is domiciled. There are a number of commercial firms that will perform these searches for a fee.

Invisible liens

Boats are unique also, in that certain "invisible liens", liens that do not have to be recorded **anywhere** and still be perfectly enforcable, may attach to the boat and be near impossible to detect. These encumbrances, referred to as "maritime liens", are generally in the area of crew's wages (not too much to worry about), vessel repairs, salvage and torts (claims for physical injury).

These liens take priority according to the point in time the services were rendered that create the claim, **in reverse order**. The legal expression of this doctrine is "last in time, first in right". It is unique to boats and is derivative of the same body of law that was examined in Chapter 7. By giving the last vessel supplier the first right to collect when the vessel reached the destination, discharged any cargo and collected its charges, the doctrine helped disabled or troubled vessels reach that final destination.

Thus, if repairs have been made to a disabled vessel and subsequently a tort lien is placed on the boat because of injury to a passenger, both claims will attain superiority over any previous lien, and because they are maritime liens will take priority over any mortgage on the boat. Neither needs to be recorded in order to be enforceable.

Closing The Deal

When closing a boat sale, buyers customarily request a marine survey and a sea trial. Indeed, both are often a contingency found in the purchase agreement, meaning that the buyer must sign off on each before being required to take delivery of your boat.

When a survey is called for (and it almost always is on a used boat sale) it is at the request of the buyer, at his expense. Most marine surveys may not contain the detail that you may be accustomed to seeing in a real estate appraisal. And like real estate appraisers, there is no governmental licensing authority for marine surveyors — it is a rather weakly self policing business.

You may wish to discuss with the buyer the selection of a surveyor. Ultimately though, since the buyer is footing the bill, he will have the final say. Also, since most boats are sold on the "as is, where is" basis with little or no recourse for defects discovered after the fact, the buyer has a right to the most thorough survey he wishes. Also, you don't want to provide the buyer with your own survey, even if it shows the vessel to have a higher market value or no defects. Such a survey, provided and paid for by you, could constitute an implied warranty for which you could be liable to make restitution if the vessel has defects or cannot be sold later for its "market" value.

If any defects are found, the buyer can either (i) reject the vessel and receive the refund of any deposit or (ii) negotiate with the seller for a reduction in price or the correction of any flaws.

The sea trial is usually conducted by the listing broker or the owner. You have every right to require a signed offer to purchase and a full deposit (10%) before taking any buyer for a "free ride". You may even wish to establish his or her financial credentials, although a deposit covers you fairly well.

Once the survey and sea trial are found acceptable, and any required title transfer documents are drawn up, you are ready to close. Generally, title documents are exchanged for certified funds; if a lender is involved they will perform the "escrow" function. At other times the broker will do the same. It is at this point that the broker's reputation is most important. Since the majority of states do not regulate yacht brokers, you and the buyer must place a great deal of trust in the brokerage house to hold a large sum on deposit until title documents are exchanged for the net selling price. One solution is to hire an actual escrow agent, although there does not appear to be a true escrow service within the marine industry like that in real estate. But any licensed and bonded escrow agent can perform the service if very specific instructions are written.

But watch out for . . .

Nine out of ten closings occur without incident. But it only takes one bad scene to lose a lot of money. When selling your boat, here are a couple of things to watch out for.

Watch out for a buyer, on a direct sale, who wants to pay you on a weekend. Some recent scams involving bogus cashiers checks suggests you should never let go of your boat until you have determined the validity of a check at the issuing bank.

Watch out for the dealer who offers to make your payments on a boat taken "in trade". As was said before, unless title is transferred, you still own it and are responsible for the debt. By the same token, watch out for "consignment" sellers who offer to put your boat on their lot while promising you your asking price. If you plan to broker the boat, sign a bona fide brokerage agreement.

Watch out for buyers offering generous lease-purchase arrangements to take a boat off your hands. You may never see more than a few payments. The same is true for "seller financed" deals brought in by brokers unfamiliar to you. Check out thoroughly any buyer who asks you to carry his credit. And always secure the loan with the boat itself or some other valuable asset.

And finally, always watch out for your new boat deal while you are selling your old boat. You can get real close to the market during your negotiations and save a lot of time if you sell and buy at the same time. Use this as an opportunity to spot a sharp deal.

Wrapping it up

So you got into and out of boating in one piece! If you planned your ownership carefully, chances are your boating experience was extremely satisfying, and likely you will repeat it. Be aware that you are a part of one of the fastest growing segments of the leisure industry. Close to 75 million Americans are involved with boating in one form or another, and that number is likely to grow.

The emphasis of this book has been on planning. All too often, people in the marine industry declare that buying a boat is an "emotional decision" or that boat owners are "impulse buyers". Nothing should be farther from the truth. Without proper planning, you run the risk of under insuring, improperly registering, having little or no equity at trade up time, being unable to make loan payments, etc., etc. With proper planning, you're in for the time of your life with family and friends!

---

(1) Paradoxically, this is not always the case. With the declining rates and lengthening terms seen in marine finance the last several years, we could imagine a situation as follows in our Exhibit 9-1:

Original loan balance of $36,000 for 10 years at 14% interest has a payment of $559/month and produces the $29,500 payoff in the example after 38 months, an average holding period.

The new loan, at $63,000 balance for twenty years at 11% produces a payment of less than $100 more, or $650!

APPENDIX A
Shopping For A Boat

The purpose of this appendix is to clarify some key points of design and relate them to how you will use your boat. You should be able to better interpret (according to your objectives) varying hull designs, engine offerings, sail and rigging, and cabin layouts. An in-water test, however, will prove if the boat's design truly meets your needs.

Four elements need to work together in the design of any vessel, namely design and construction, sails and rigging, power, and accommodations. Whether a small, flat bottom sailboat, an ocean racer, outboard powered runabout or a 20 ton cruiser, these same elements must be considered together. The combinations of these elements are almost endless. Several of them, over the years, have become somewhat standard with minor variations to gain some advantages in the way you use your boat. For example, trade-offs have to be made among seaworthiness, comfort, speed and cost depending upon a boat's use as shown in Exhibit 1-1 in the first chapter.

Hull Types

Hull types are divided into three general categories: Displacement, semi-displacement (or semi-planing), and planing. Displacement hulls are typical of the "trawler" design powerboats and sailboats. These hulls obtain no lift from their speed. Additional power beyond a specified amount only serves to push a larger wall of water ahead of the boat. The "hull-speed" of the boat determines its speed through the water. The longer the displacement hull boat, the faster it will go as its hull-speed is determined by its speed-length ratio. This can be calculated by dividing the boat's speed in knots by the square root of the length of its waterline. The speed limiting ratio for all displacement hulls is 1.34:1. All boats operate as displacement hulls at slow speeds no matter what their design.

Semi-displacement hulls are characterized by rounded bottoms (U cross section), and a transom wide enough to give it some lift from the water flow beneath the hull. The attainable speed-length ratio is 2.5:1 which means this hull design is capable of greater speeds than the displacement types. Power cruisers of many designs have this type of hull.

Planing hulls obtain a great deal of lift from the water flow due to a typically wide transom and their attainable speed-length ratios vary from 3.0:1 to 8:1. Most V-bottom cruisers, outboard runabouts and specialized ocean racing powerboats are of this kind. Planing hulls are inefficient at slow speeds and kick up a large wake as they push a big wave under the hull. It is not until they "step up" onto the wave that they achieve higher efficiencies of operation resulting from reduced water drag on the hull. At planing speeds, the primary component of drag is friction with the water.

The cost of keeping a large boat on plane is measured in gallons per hour of fuel consumed. For example, a fast planing cruiser 35 feet long may well use 30 gallons per hour at 22 knots where a 35 foot displacement cruiser may only use 3 gallons per hour at 7.5 knots. The fast cruiser takes almost three and a half times as much fuel to go the same distance. When you are trying to beat the others out to the fishing grounds, a fast boat is what you need. On the other hand, if you want to cruise for extended periods, it is hard to beat a displacement or even semi-displacement hull for fuel economy. Exhibit A-1 gives hull speeds for differing speed-length ratios and hull lengths.

Exhibit A-1

Speed-length Ratios

	Hull speed		
	Displacement	Semi-Displacement	Planing
Ratio	1.34	2.5	3.0 to 8
length (ft.)	hull speed (kn.)	hull speed (kn.)	hull speed (kn.)
20	6.0	11.2	13.4 to 35.8
25	6.7	12.5	15.0 to 40.0
30	7.3	13.7	16.4 to 43.8
35	7.9	14.8	17.7 to 47.3
40	8.5	15.8	19.0 to 50.6
50	9.5	17.7	21.2 to 56.6

Midship sections

Three distinct categories of midship sections are flat, V, and round bottom hulls. Flat bottom boats are further divided into the scow (garbage hauling), punt (cargo and work boats), skiffs (work boats, sailboats), and dory (sailboats) (Exhibit A-2a). These boats are generally for coastal use in protected waters. The skiffs and dories are excellent as small sailing craft. The dory type is noteworthy for its excellent seaworthiness due to a flared topsides which provides an added measure of stability. Dories also make seaworthy low speed power boats and can be economically driven with small engines. The narrow bottom of all dories causes them to be somewhat unstable initially. Because of this they have short deck houses and weight must be kept low in the hull.

Exhibit A-2a

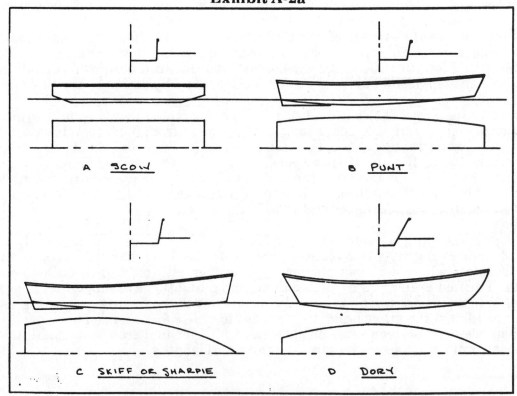

The points to look for in flat bottom designs are fairly low freeboard (height from the waterline to the top of the side rails) and short upper works to reduce weight aloft and windage. Sailboats should not have excess curve to the keel (rocker) as this is detrimental to speed. A fine entrance (an angle off the vertical) is desirable for both sail and power and a fairly deep forefoot (length of bow that continues below the waterline before turning horizontal) will help reduce pounding particularly in power boats.

Modifications of a flat bottom hull results in a V-bottom hull, also known as "deadrise" hulls (Exhibit A-2b). The amount of the V is measured in degrees from the horizontal. Typical V-bottom boats are the high speed powerboats but many other types including high performance sport fisherman have made excellent use of this design. The chine (where the sides meet the bottom) is fairly high forward and dips below the waterline well aft. The stern is wide to enable the vessel to plane. A chine that is too low in an attempt to obtain more interior space causes excessive pounding and is very inefficient at slow speeds.

Exhibit A-2b

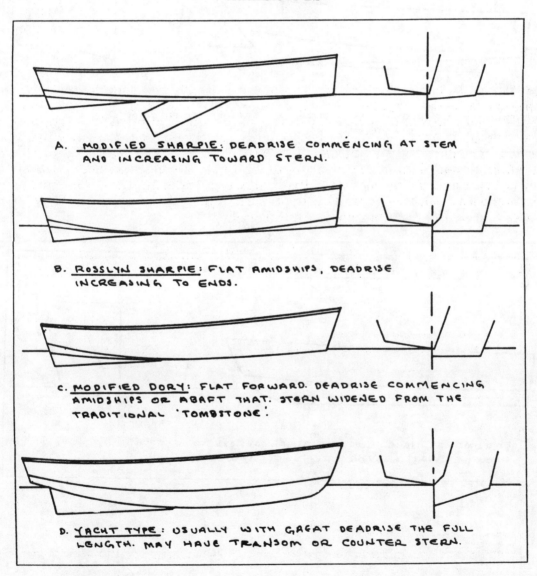

A. MODIFIED SHARPIE: DEADRISE COMMENCING AT STEM AND INCREASING TOWARD STERN.

B. ROSSLYN SHARPIE: FLAT AMIDSHIPS, DEADRISE INCREASING TO ENDS.

C. MODIFIED DORY: FLAT FORWARD. DEADRISE COMMENCING AMIDSHIPS OR ABAFT THAT. STERN WIDENED FROM THE TRADITIONAL 'TOMBSTONE'.

D. YACHT TYPE: USUALLY WITH GREAT DEADRISE THE FULL LENGTH. MAY HAVE TRANSOM OR COUNTER STERN.

Two additional points to consider are a 25 degree V in the forward hull section to reduce pounding in heavy seas and a spray rail to deflect water off to the sides. A dry boat should show some flaring to the topsides in the forward area. This lets the boat deflect spray and solid water as it drops from a wave particularly in a following sea (traveling with the waves). Deep V hulls carry the V shape all the way aft as in (Exhibit A-3). These hulls are noted for soft riding in choppy conditions and have proven themselves in power boat racing in open water.

Exhibit A-3

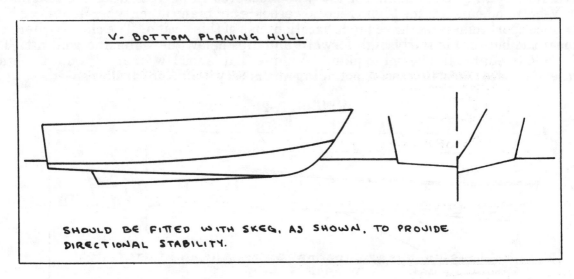

V- BOTTOM PLANING HULL

SHOULD BE FITTED WITH SKEG, AS SHOWN, TO PROVIDE DIRECTIONAL STABILITY.

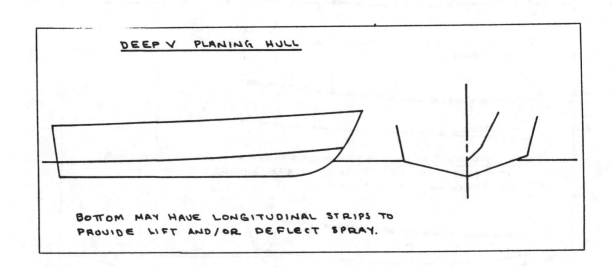

DEEP V PLANING HULL

BOTTOM MAY HAVE LONGITUDINAL STRIPS TO PROVIDE LIFT AND/OR DEFLECT SPRAY.

Deep V hulls don't have skegs attached while other planing hulls require one. This is to help prevent the wide, flat hulls from yawing at lower speeds and to improve steering in heavy weather. Skegs also contribute to protecting the propellor in the event of a grounding.

Exhibit A-4

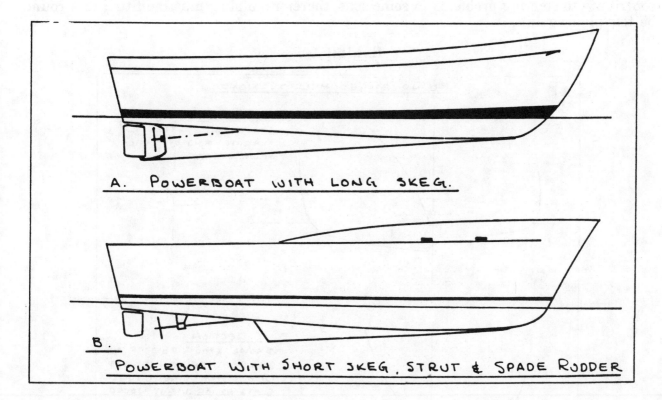

A. POWERBOAT WITH LONG SKEG.

B. POWERBOAT WITH SHORT SKEG, STRUT & SPADE RUDDER

Round bottom hulls fall into two categories: U section (daysailers, small cruisers and semi-displacement and planing powerboats) and Y section (tugs, fishing vessels, sailing auxiliaries and motor sailers). In general, the round bottom hull is superior to flat or V bottom types for offshore and rough water use. For sailing, the shape reduces wetted surface (friction drag) and eliminates turbulence along the chines. Planing powerboats gain from better rough water ability but lose speed and economy. Wide transoms contribute to steering problems in some seas, therefore, a skeg must be fitted to a round bottom planing hull.

Exhibit A-5

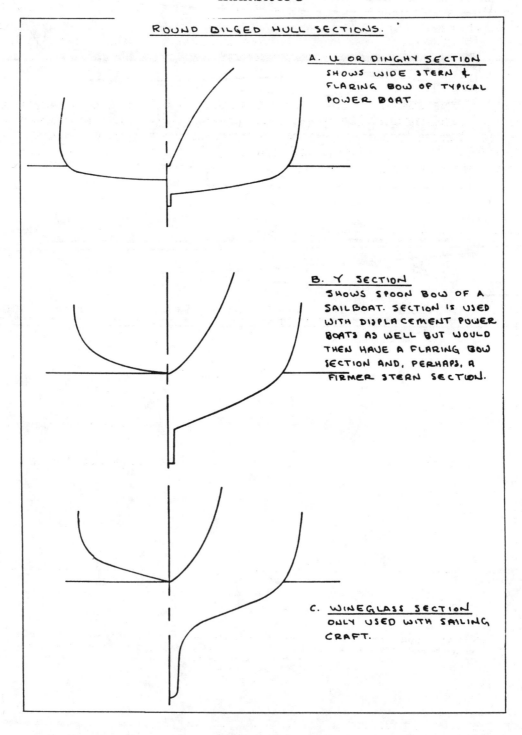

ROUND BILGED HULL SECTIONS.

A. U OR DINGHY SECTION
SHOWS WIDE STERN &
FLARING BOW OF TYPICAL
POWER BOAT

B. Y SECTION
SHOWS SPOON BOW OF A
SAILBOAT. SECTION IS USED
WITH DISPLACEMENT POWER
BOATS AS WELL BUT WOULD
THEN HAVE A FLARING BOW
SECTION AND, PERHAPS, A
FIRMER STERN SECTION.

C. WINEGLASS SECTION
ONLY USED WITH SAILING
CRAFT.

Ocean racing sailboats benefit from the Y section in both stability and seaworthiness. These yachts have ballast equal to 40-50% of total displacement in their keel for tremendous sail carrying power. The wineglass section is a modification of the Y and is better for deep keel sailing yachts as performance is enhanced by the reduction in wetted surface and the elimination of turbulence where the hull meets the keel.

Other design considerations

Another design consideration includes the beam, which is the widest part of the boat. Wider boats have more interior space but width in a power displacement hull is a negative factor as the added beam increases resistance. Sailboats gain from the added stability of a wider boat in two ways: The driving force on the sails is increased because the boat heels less and the keel's efficiency is increased. At the same time, the wetted surface is increased which affects performance. Balancing these factors is largely why yacht design is more art than science.

Previously it was stated that a flaring topsides on a V bottom power boat was advantageous. In sailing craft the opposite is true, especially if they are driven at large heeling angles. Excess turbulence can be created and the bow may dip under a wave leading to broaching (rolling sideways and capsizing). The opposing shape to flare is flam, and is preferred for craft seeing this kind of use.

Exhibit A-6

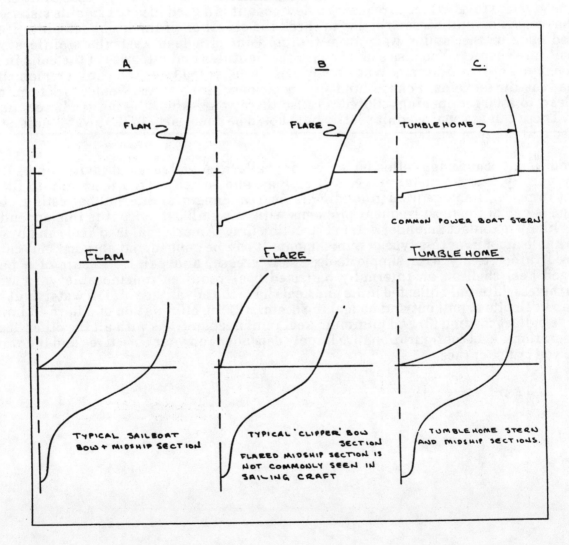

Freeboard is an important factor in both sail and power boats as good freeboard provides reserve stability. Normally, a yacht will continue to pick up stability until her deck edge submerges. Freeboard provides for extra room below decks and is especially advantageous for cruising yachts. In sailing craft, look for freeboard that will keep the deck edge from getting buried at low angles of heel. In power boats, good freeboard will be sufficient to assure a dryer boat. Aft freeboard will help prevent taking a wave over the transom when running before a sea.

Keels

Sailboat keels have evolved over the years as science and new technologies have been applied to increase speed, improve handling and provide greater flexibility in boat usage. The fin keel with balanced rudder and built-in skeg is most frequently seen on production craft. This combination allows for a better and more balanced handling and steering vessel.

Whenever you look for a sailboat with a ballasted keel, there are several key points to consider. The ballast should be lead as it is dense and relatively resistant to different waters. It can be attached to the hull either with bronze or stainless steel bolts or put inside a hollow keel that is part of the hull molding. The simplest solution is often to bolt the ballast keel directly to the hull molding — assuming the boat is of fiberglass construction. When examining a fin keel boat, look to be sure a bilge has been installed. Attaching the keel directly to the boat usually eliminates the bilge and special attention must be given to this. When purchasing a new boat, it is a good idea to examine sisterships that have seen several seasons of use to check the condition of the hull/keel joint. If it is cracked open or rust stains weep from the top joint of a lead keel, the stainless steel keelbolts are suspect. You also should check the tightness and integrity of the bolts in any used boat you are considering. When a new boat is delivered have the yard foreman check the lead casting for voids. Poke around any suspicious chinks or small holes to determine if they lead to a larger opening. Bubbles cause these voids when the hot lead cools in the mold. These can be repaired quite easily but should be done early so that water doesn't get trapped and freeze in winter.

Traditional boat designs often have internal ballast. A molded keel cavity can be filled with a variety of scrap metal and concrete plugs, and sealed with a resin mix to fix the ballast in place. Damage from grounding is the real danger to internal ballasting. Keel damage is one of the most frequent problems with any sailboat since it is this appendage that is likely to contact an underwater obstruction first. An external lead keel can absorb a remarkable amount of this type of punishment. It can be gouged and abraded, but can be repaired rather easily with simple tools, elbow grease, and paint. Repair of a badly damaged keel shell on an internally ballasted boat requires considerable yard work. Nevertheless, internal ballasted hulls and keels have the advantage of (1) a watertight hull with no keelbolts to pull out and no leaking seams; (2) the elimination of a hard-to-handle massive ballast casting; (3) and minimum keel reinforcement. As with all the other design considerations, keel configurations are largely dependent on your objectives and the waters where you cruise or race.

Exhibit A-7

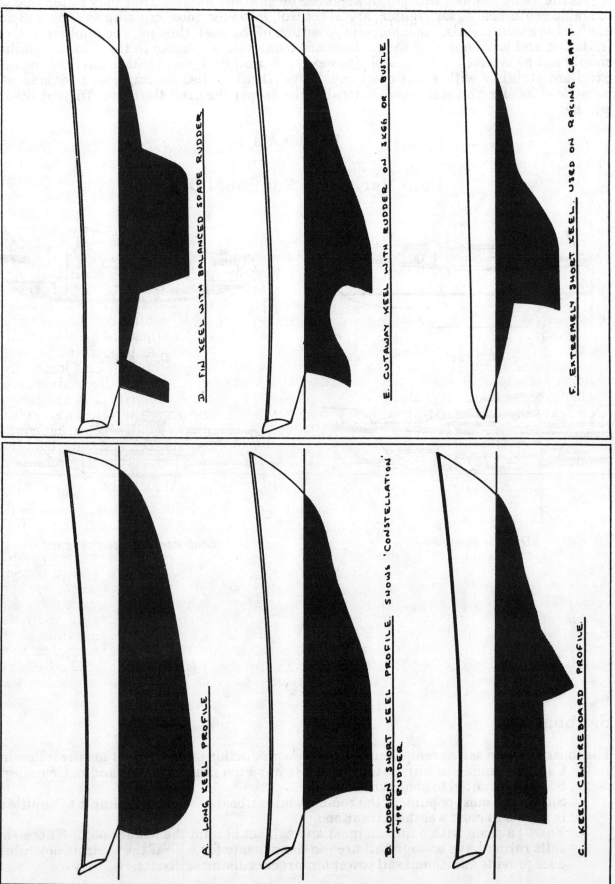

As the name implies, shoal draft keels are for shallow waters. They may be teamed with movable centerboards for greater lateral control, however, most cruising sailboats usually don't have centerboards. As a hole in the bottom of the boat, they may be another source of irritation and problems, and the centerboard trunk takes up room in the cabin. A sailboat should not be rejected on this basis, however. A well designed centerboard/keel combine excellent stability with shoal draft capability. Draft is also an important consideration because of its effect on stability. Generally, the deeper the draft the more efficient the keel will be.

Exhibit A-8

Four Variations For Shoal Draft

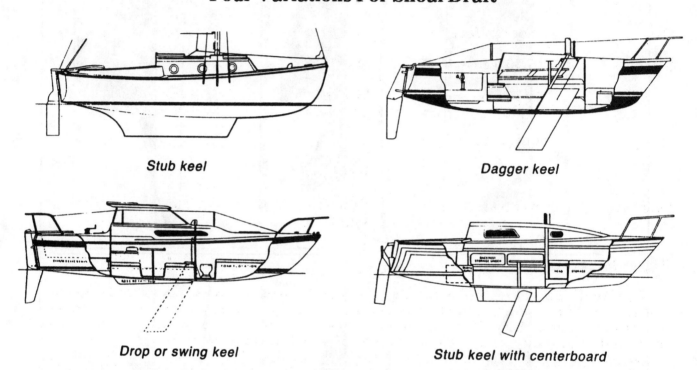

Stub keel

Dagger keel

Drop or swing keel

Stub keel with centerboard

Sailboat Rigs

The most common sail arrangements on today's production sailboats include the following:
- ▶ Cat rig - simple to sail, but larger boats have too much sail to handle. Cruising cat boats are limited to about 25 feet.
- ▶ Sloop - the most popular of the commercial sailboats. This rig is simple to handle and is usable in most weather situations.
- ▶ Yawl - a sloop with a mizzen mast and sail set behind the rudder post. These small sails rarely have enough sail area to compensate for a jib if the main is down but it does provide additional sail power for larger cruising sailboats.

▶ Ketch - the mizzen on a ketch is stepped farther forward than on a yawl. Balanced sails in heavier going is the main advantage.
▶ Schooner - these come in a variety of sail arrangements, but the most common are the foresail or staysail schooner.

Exhibit A-9 summarizes the pros and cons of these five rigs.

Exhibit A-9

Sailboat Rig Types

Rig type	Length range	Wind conditions	Racing/cruising
Cat	under 25 feet	Downwind	Cruising
Sloop	15-40 feet	Most all	Cruising/racing
Yawl	35-75 feet	Most all	Cruising (under 50 feet) Racing (under 75 feet)
Ketch	30-100 feet	Downwind Reaching	Cruising
Schooner	over 50 feet	Reaching Light	Cruising

Rig-to-hull relationship

The "lead" of a sailing hull is the distance that the driving force of all the sails is ahead of the center of the longitudinal fore and aft hull line. The amount of lead varies with hull design as well as sail rig. Too little lead creates a condition called "weather helm" where the vessel continually tries to round up into the wind. Compensating for this condition is tiresome. The opposite condition, called "lee helm", occurs when the vessel won't round up into the wind to relieve pressure on the sails if the helm is left unattended. Mild weather helms are desirable from safety and performance standpoints. A small amount of weather helm gives the helmsman a better feel of his boat when working to windward. Meter type boats have leads of about 6%, cruising boats of 10% and beamy or centerboarders have up to 15%. Exhibit A-10 shows how lead varies with vessel characteristics.

Exhibit A-10

Lead of a Sailboat

Short	Long
Narrow (fine) hull	Beamy hull
Short keel	Long keel
Deep draft	Shoal draft
Fine forward waterlines	Full forward waterline
Stable vessels	Sensitive (tender) vessels
Low aspect ratio rigs	High aspect ratio rigs

Courtesy of International Marine Publishing Company, Camden, ME

Standing and running rigging

The simplicity of the masthead single spreader sloop makes it the overwhelming choice on production boats under forty feet. Under this size, a divided rig (yawl and ketch) adds excess windage and cost. The theoretical gains in handling ease from a divided rig are relatively insignificant until the boat exceeds forty feet. In general, the more performance oriented the rig, the more suitable the boat as a cruiser.

Mast steps and chainplates

These components are the most important in determining if the mast will stay up. The majority of U.S. production boats under 35 feet are equipped with deck stepped masts. This requires a support system that transfers the majority of the rig's compression load to the hull. A compression column under the mast, strongly tied to the hull and deck, usually serves this purpose. Under severe conditions the loading on the compression column may equal the boat's displacement. Thus, a well engineered and constructed system is essential to avoid unnecessary stresses on the deck and hull components. The mast step of a through-stepped mast also must be properly suppported and strongly tied to the hull. The area of the mast step must be strongly reinforced in order to properly distribute the load.

Exhibit A-11 (i)

Chainplates may be attached to either the inside or outside of a properly reinforced hull. Modern wide beam boats need to have their chainplates moved somewhat inboard to avoid compromising performance, however. Fastening these to the deck requires that the deck be reinforced in the area of attachment, or that a bulkhead be located under the chainplates. U-bolts through the deck connected to a tie rod inside the boat are another solution. Some

U-bolts are fastened through the deck-to-hull flange and strongly reinforced. The main problem all these systems face is withstanding the tremendous loading on the shrouds when a boat is heeled hard on the wind. This force can approach the displacement of the boat. Backstay and forestay loading is not quite so great, thus, throughbolts and heavy backing washers at the transom and stem, respectively, are usually adequate.

Exhibit A-11 (ii)

Spars

The modern extruded aluminum spar is strong, inexpensive, light and relatively maintenance free. Untapered masts are the least expensive. Tapered spars, however, reduce weight and windage aloft. For example, five pounds saved at the top of the mast times a mast length of fifty feet is equivalent to fifty pounds of compensating ballast in the keel five feet below the center of gravity. Weight saved aloft means that more sail can be carried which translates into improved performance.

Exhibit A-12

Exhibit A-13

Internal halyards are just about essential on a racing boat, but are a mixed blessing on a cruising yacht. The convenience they provide and the savings in windage may be offset by the difficulty in reeving new halyards should the internal ones break. On the other hand, internal running rigging on a boom is essential to both racing and cruising boats. The outside of a boom should be as uncluttered as possible so there is less chance of injury should the boom swing wildly during a tack or jibe.

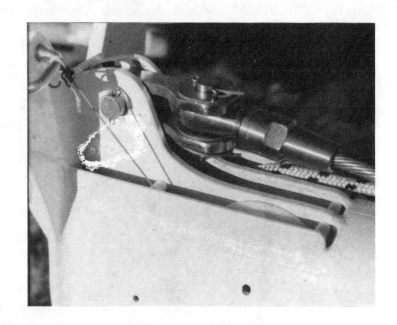

Other rigging components such as wire rope, tangs, toggles, turnbuckles and matching clevis pins should be on the conservative side. This provides an extra margin of safety and is inexpensive insurance. Pay particular attention to the swaged terminal ends on wire rope and other elements. Poor workmanship on these parts can cause the rigging to fail, oversize or not. Fortunately, defective rig components can be replaced rather easily. As long as the chainplates and mast step are adequate, you can change just about everything else. On an older boat this may be necessary and advisable.

Exhibit A-14

Construction

The predominant material for small boats and yachts is fiberglass. The manufacturing cost breakdown for a typical fiberglass boat looks like the following:

Materials	40%
Labor	20%
Tooling	5%
Marketing	5%
Overhead	15%
Profit	15%

Fiberglass is almost indestructable, requires little maintenance, can be polished to a high gloss, colored in many hues and with many kinds of paints, and is relatively easy to repair. Fiberglass hulls do not require the large number of stringers that wooden boats have and interior space is, consequently, much more usable.

The usual stock craft is a hand lay-up of solid fiberglass and resin, and may vary from 3/16" to 1/2" thick. Many variations are possible. These include double hull with balsa, polyvinyl chloride (PVC), or wood cores.

The advantage of the core is that it produces a hull with less of the "drum head" characteristic of solid fiberglass panels. Cores add stiffness and allow for a thinner skin to be used which is a possible weight saver. Labor costs, however, considerably drive up the expense of cored hulls. Wood core hulls differ from balsa or PVC cores in that they depend on the core for strength. The core is usually a strip planked hull with no framing using fairly thin planking and covered with fiberglass both inside and out. This protects the core and provides additional strength while helping to create a one piece unit. Edge grain balsa cores are extensively used in decks and cabin roofs of solid fiberglass hulls providing stiffening in large flat surfaces such as the cabin roof and decks. PVC does the same as balsa but does not soak up water, won't rot and is lighter in weight.

More common in the U.S. boatbuilding industry has been the use of a relatively thin fiberglass shell with stiffness provided by a molded hull pan liner or the bonding to the hull of internal components such as bulkheads and berth tops. Major furniture components — cabin sole, settee fronts and tops, galley cabinets — can be molded outside the boat. This greatly reduces labor costs but creates other problems. For one, the liner doesn't fit exactly into the hull. It must, therefore, be bonded into place where the liner touches the skin. The quality of this secondary bonding is often suspect no matter how carefully the work is performed because it develops less strength than a primary bond. Such bonds may develop weaknesses after several years of flexing. This type of failure does not mean that the hull is necessarily too weak but it does imply an understandable degree of hull flexibility. Coring, liners and secondary bonding are all acceptable methods of improving stiffness.

The hull to deck joint is the most difficult to seal and has caused problems in the past. If you are buying a new boat, find out how the builder handles the hull to deck joint. The recognized best way in terms of simplicity and strength is the inward turning hull flange at the deck level. The deck is laid over it and the two are thoroughly glued and bolted at close intervals. A wooden toe rail can cover the joint and provide extra strength. The main consideration for a well built fiberglass yacht is the skill of the builder and a major focus on quality control during manufacturing.

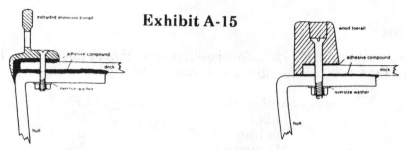

Exhibit A-15

   Other materials used in boat building include wood, aluminum and steel. Few wooden boats are being made these days and are usually either custom boats, small runabouts or replicas of early speedboats. Used wooden boats are very inexpensive as there is a weak market for them. The newest of the old "woodys" was built in the early 1970's. Although they have a nostalgic charm about them, they are difficult to maintain and insure.

   Aluminum is one of the finest materials for boats but its cost is 20% higher than a comparable wooden craft. Advantages include lightness, corrosion resistance and strength, and on balance, aluminum is worth the added cost. Steel, on the other hand, is subject to high corrosion in sea water. Epoxy finishes have been used advantageously to prevent this. The primary advantage of steel is low cost, up to 40% less than aluminum. Both metals react to copper based alloys such as bronze. Stainless steel fittings, seacocks, shafts and propellers must be used to prevent electrolysis. Whenever a bronze fitting is essential, it must be insulated from the hull.

Powerplants

Power boats

   The array of engine options on modern powerboats is large indeed. Whether you are considering an outboard, inboard or I/O drive, you have a bewildering number of choices. Even within one manufacturer's product line there exists several options of engine sizes as well as choices between gas or diesel. Opinions abound as to the best kind of engine for a particular boating application. Selecting the correct engine for your needs means deciding on which criteria are the most important and the kind of hull into which the engine will be installed.

   Size has much to do with the selection of a drive system. Smaller boats, under 25 feet, often perform well with an outboard because of the favorable weight-to-horsepower ratio. Conversely, larger boats are typically ordered with diesels because fuel efficiency becomes of prime importance as hull weight increases.

   Five engine/drive combinations are possible for powerboats:

   1)   Outboard

   2)   I/O Gas

   3)   I/O Diesel

   4)   Inboard Gas

   5)   Inboard Diesel

   Each system possesses strengths and weaknesses about which you must be informed to make the right decision. Several years ago a well-known boating magazine conducted an informal survey of nine categories in which each of these five combinations of engine/drive were ranked by twelve boating industry experts. Exhibit A-16 shows the survey's results.

Exhibit A-16
Engine/Drive Survey Rankings

	I/O gas	I/O diesel	Outboard	Inboard gas	Inboard diesel
Speed	2	4	1	3	5
Reliability	4	3	5	2	4
Purchase Price	2	4	1	3	5
Maintenance	5	3	1	4	2
Fuel Economy	3	1	5	4	2
Resale	4	2	5	3	1
Longevity	4	2	5	3	1
Seaworthiness	1	1	3	2	2
Control	1	3	2	4	5

Note: 1 is highest ranking and 5 is lowest.
Reprinted from *Boating*, copyright 1984, CBS Magazines.

Speed is determined by a system which establishes a greatest speed per rated horsepower in a given hull. Speed is dependent on weight and drag, all other things being equal. Outboards have one of the best power-to-weight ratios compared with other power options and there is a minimum of underwater hardware. In general, inboard/outboard drives minimize submerged hardware while inboards are slowed because of the struts, shafts, rudders and rudder posts.

Reliability is a characteristic of the system that tends to make it is less likely to break down over its lifetime with proper maintenance. Generally, diesel inboards are considered to be the ultimate in marine engine reliability. The survey participants felt that outboards would be less likely to survive based in part on previous bad experiences. Outboards also operate at high RPMs which may contribute to their perceived early demise. Modern outboards have good reliability if they are properly maintained, however, there is probably more potential for abusing an outboard and for improper maintenance.

Purchase price includes all necessary rigging and accessories and takes into account the likelihood of a discount from a dealer. Two facts are obvious: Outboards provide maximum horsepower per dollar and diesels are expensive.

Maintenance means which engine/drive combination is the least costly to maintain as specified by the manufacturer. This includes normally expected but unscheduled maintenance. It does not include repairs. Generally, outdrives require the most maintenance, in part because they can't be tilted fully out of the water. Further, they may have as many moving parts as the engine itself.

Fuel economy specifies the combination least costly to fuel given identical hulls and loads (excluding the weight of the engine) traveling at identical speeds. The critical factors are underwater drag and weight. The diesel I/O combines the most efficient powerplant with the minimum amount of underwater surface and an optimum thrust angle. The outboard is considered inherently less fuel efficient and includes the cost of adding oil to the fuel.

Resale value identifies the engine/drive combination in identical hulls will most likely return the highest percentage of its original value when traded or sold. Resale value is closely tied to longevity. The I/O suffers from its inherently complex nature while diesel power is widely accepted as the most long lived. The outboard is considered to have the shortest life span but it's also the cheapest to replace.

Longevity assumes that the owner maintains the engine/drive combination to manufacturers recommendations. The longevity of the diesel derives from its industrial applications. Typically a marine diesel operates at high horsepower levels which ultimately decrease its life span below that for industrial needs. Still, diesels are noted for longer life than their gas powered counterparts.

Seaworthiness means which of the engine combinations is most favorable in heavy seas and bad weather. I/O was preferred in smaller boats because of its more precise and instantaneous reaction to steering changes. Outboards, conversely, were felt to be prone to swamping in heavy seas. Twin installations were considered to be the best for such conditions and the combinations were similarly ranked.

Control looks at the engine/drive combination that gives the best throttle response and controllable features. The gas I/O receives high marks because of its excellent throttle response, ability to trim, power and manueverability under slow speed docking conditions and trolling.

Would be powerboat owners are often torn between the choice of single or twin engine craft. There are advantages of both that should not be overlooked as the following demonstrates:

Single Screw

- economy of first cost and operation
- simplicity and lower cost of maintenance
- placed deeper in the hull and occupies less space
- propeller and rudder are better protected by being behind the skeg
- reduced drag of a single strut, shaft and rudder

Twin Screw

- back-up ability in case one engine fails
- better maneuverability at low speeds
- engines and propellers are higher in hull permitting shallow draft
- higher maintenance costs

Courtesy of International Marine Publishing Company, Camden, ME

Sailboat power

Sailboat auxiliary engines are usually outboards on boats up to twenty-five feet in length. Beyond that, diesel engines are the predominent choice. Even though more expensive initially, diesels are considered safer and more reliable than gas engines. Since speed is not important to the displacement hulled sailboat, a slow turning diesel is more than adequate. Sufficient horsepower is about 4-6 per ton of displacement. A continuous rating is important so that the engine can run for an extended period without undue effort or strain.

Exhibit A-17

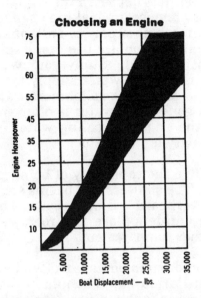

Graph to determine approximate engine horsepower for a sailboat hull displacement (pounds). Shaded area represents a spread in sizes of engine with 2:1 reduction gear. For instance, for a boat with 14,000 lbs. displacement, engine horsepower would range from 14 to 25, with the larger engine probably providing more than ample power and the smaller engine minimal power. In some boats an engine choice outside of the suggested range may also prove satisfactory. *This information is copyrighted by Robert Snow Means Co., Inc. It is reproduced from* Boating Cost Guide *with permission.*

As a general rule, most engines — whether for power or sail operation -- are most efficient at peak torque (twisting power) produced by the engine. Gasoline engines typically achieve this in the range of 2500 to 3500 RPM and diesels at 1800 to 2500 RPM. In virtually all engines torque falls off at the redline speed but horsepower continues increasing because the lesser torque is applied at a faster rate. The point is to keep torque notions in mind when assessing an engine's performance and capabilities. A well designed power package (engine, shaft, propeller, etc.) should combine the right torque, RPM and transmission gear ratios that puts the engine at an optimum point on the torque curve. The package should also include a propeller that complements the other components.

Accommodations

Unless you are solely concerned with racing, you will most likely spend a good deal of time considering the cabin layout, number of berths, galley equipment and location, size and type of head shower facilities and so on. It is extremely important to do so for a variety of reasons.

Cabins and below decks

First, a boat "shrinks" when it is placed in the water; that is, there is never enough room to store things, to move around, to sleep and to entertain. When you've been out on the water for a while and members of your party can't get away from each other even for a few moments, there's likely to be some grumbling. Storage space is another thing of which no boat owner ever has enough. Separate bins or lockers should be provided for each of the following: Navigating instruments, spare lines and blocks, food and galley gear, towels and linens, fenders and mooring lines, sails, spare parts, rain coats and other equipment.

Second, the galley layout may deter all but the most stalwart cooks from making more than a peanut butter sandwich. Cabinets not set in the right location or of improper height, ranges that are neither safe or easy to operate, leaking or inadequately insulated iceboxes and refrigerators and an inadequate water supply can all make "KP" duty unpleasant. The latter is tough to live with especially if you are used to, like most Americans, a virtually unlimited water supply, both hot and cold. Study your water needs carefully to avoid running out at a critical time. A minimum water supply for a cruising boat should be 50 gallons. Drinking, cooking and showering take a lot more water than you might think and it doesn't take long before it's all gone. Hot water is often provided by a heat exchanger type of heater that operates off the engine's cooling water or by one that uses dockside power. An eight to ten gallon capacity is satisfactory.

Third, marine heads should have the capability of being pumped overboard as well as into a holding tank via a Y valve. The showers and basins should drain overboard or into a sump for subsequent pumping overboard. Elbow room is often the one essential that floating toilet rooms lack. Some builders place this room across the forward part of the vessel in place of a vee-berth or other compartment.

Finally, ventilation on many production boats can often be improved. Every port should open and have screens and a ventilation hatch should be installed in the main cabin of sailboats. Small battery powered cabin fans can circulate both warm and cool air (provided by an air conditioner). These little fans move a fair amount of air for their size. Some owners mount a larger fan in the forward hatch to pull air through the cabin. Remember though, a boat is not a condo. Many compromises must be made in the design of a boat. If the interior is allowed too much influence, performance and seaworthiness usually suffer.

Cockpits

Interior space, while quite important to most skippers, is usually secondary to outdoor living either on the deck, flybridge or in the cockpit. Sailboat cockpits, for example, serve compromising purposes: Entertaining at dockside or at anchor versus boat handling and operating efficiencies while underway. Deciding upon the best arrangement for your needs means knowing your objectives and what trade-offs you are willing to make.

Long distance cruising, racing and entertaining are mutually exclusive for most sailboat accomodations, especially the cockpit. Some of the specific cockpit features that must be considered for each of these uses include drains, companionway protection, lockers, seating, steering, sheet leads and sail handling, engine controls and sailing instruments. Combining them the right way to meet your needs will largely determine your sailing enjoyment.

Exhibit A-18

Avid fishermen need a cockpit on a power boat as their workshop. In most cases cabin space is sacrificed in order to provide for maximum fishing equipment in the cockpit. Large sportfisher boats with their fighting chairs are functional works of art. From transom doors to spare rods and tackle, live fish wells to iceboxes, they are decked out for all day excursions to the underwater canyons in search of big game fish. Even very large yachts (75' to 90') often have some cockpit space for the fishing whims of the owner or his friends.

Power boat cockpits are often the center of outdoor entertainment. Many marina or rafting parties are centered on open cockpits. Setting up a table for dinner and drinks or friendly conversation helps make for an enjoyable lifestyle. Those power boats that do not have cockpits are usually the aft cabin types. Above the cabin is a sundeck for lounging or entertaining. This deck along with a flybridge are extensively used by sun-worshipers. The aft cabin arrangement adds to the spaciousness of the interior cabin and sleeping accommodations.

Use these design descriptions to help you complete your own selection charts for the boats that most closely meet your objectives. The charts in Chapter 1 should be filled out with your criteria and priorities. The information in this appendix will help you to establish that criteria.

APPENDIX B

Checklist for Selecting a Boat

Review your objectives
- ☐ Decide if you are really doing the right thing
- ☐ Be sure that this is the best way to spend your recreation dollars
- ☐ Talk it over with your family
- ☐ Make a commitment to adequately prepare yourself

Select the most knowledgeable sources of information on:
- ☐ Boat selection
- ☐ Ownership costs
- ☐ Financing alternatives
- ☐ Ownership responsibilities
- ☐ Insurance and registration
- ☐ Chartering and taxes

Select your boat
- ☐ Be sure it truly meets your objectives
- ☐ Do not overcommit
- ☐ Consider if you will be happy with it five years from now

Choose your dealer or broker
- ☐ Focus on their reputations
- ☐ Be sure the deal is right
- ☐ Understand the contract terms and conditions
- ☐ Know your warranty and service options

Wrap up your financial plan
- ☐ Net worth statement
- ☐ Cash flow analysis
- ☐   Current
- ☐   Boat owner's overhead
- ☐   Maintenance costs
- ☐   Operating expenses
- ☐ Tax return data
- ☐ Desired loan terms

Pre-qualify your credit

- ☐ Three Cs of credit
- ☐ Your debt to income ratio
- ☐ Sources of down payment
- ☐ Presenting your plan in a cover letter

Choose a lender

- ☐ Look carefully at **your** needs
- ☐ List your lender and plan options
- ☐ Compare program numbers

Assess your insurance options

- ☐ Pick the right angent/underwriter team
- ☐ Coverage amounts
- ☐ Important policy features

Evaluate the registration options

- ☐ Alternative I: Documentation
- ☐ Alternative II: State registration
- ☐ Fees, taxes and paperwork

Decide on chartering or other business potential

- ☐ Consider carefully the forms of chartering
- ☐   Mangement companies
- ☐   Crewed operations
- ☐   Self-chartering
- ☐ Gather all the financial data needed to make an informed decision
- ☐ Understand the tax laws and their advantages and limitations to your charter business

Close the deal

- ☐ Bring the parties together
- ☐ Complete the paperwork
- ☐ Pay your money
- ☐ Cheerfully accept a new debt
- ☐ Drive off in your dreamboat

APPENDIX C

Consumer Lending Laws

Equal Credit Opportunity Act (ECOA)

Purpose: The ECOA provides that it is unlawful for any creditor to discriminate against any applicant on the basis of Race, Color, Religion, National Origin, Sex, Marital Status or Age.

Major provisions affecting boat loans:

▸ A written application is not required unless the boat is a liveaboard.

▸ The application must contain a notice regarding the option to disclose alimony, child support, or separate maintenance income.

▸ Information concerning the spouse of an applicant cannot be requested unless:

(1) Spouse will be contractually liable on the loan.

(2) Applicant is relying on spouse's income for loan repayment.

(3) Applicant resides in a community property state.

(4) Applicant is relying on alimony, child support or spearate maintenance payments for repayment.

▸ Creditor may request information about number and ages of an applicant's dependents.

Truth In Lending Act (TILA)

Purpose: Primary purpose is to require a meaningful disclosure of credit terms to the consumer. Provides detailed disclosure requirements with which a creditor must comply.

Major provisions affecting boat loans:

▸ Covers any boat loan up to $25,000 made to an individual for nonbusiness purposes.

▸ Requires full discloseure of APR and finance charges, points and loan fees, insurance premiums, investigation and credit report fees, application fees and late payment charges.

▸ If the APR is free to increase (i.e. variable rate loan) the following must also be disclosed:

(1) The circumstances under which the rate may increase.

(2) The limitation on any possible increases.

(3) The effect of an increase in the rate.

(4) An example of payment terms resulting from an increase in the rate.

▶ A discloure of any prepayment penalties or procedures.

▶ A disclosure of any Sscurity interests taken in the boat.

Fair Credit Reporting Act (FCRA)

Purpose: To insure that consumer reporting agencies adopt reasonable procedures for meeting the needs of commerce for consumer credit information in a manner which is fair and equitable to the consumer with regard to confidentiality, accuracy, relevancy and proper utilization. FCRA imposes obligations both on consumer reporting agencies and on the users of consumer reports.

Major provisions affecting boat loans:

▶ A consumer reporting agency can furnish a consumer report only in the following circumstances:

(1) In response to a court order.

(2) In accordance with the written instructions of the consumer.

(3) To a person which it has reason to believe:

  i)   Intends to use the information in connection with a credit transaction with the consumer.

  ii) Intends to use the information for employment purposes.

  iii) Intends to use the information in connection with the underwriting of insurance.

  iv) Intends to use the information in connection with a determination of the consumer's eligibility for a license or other benefit granted by a governmental instrumentality required by law to consider an applicant's financial responsibility.

  v)   Has a legitimate business need for the information in connection with a business transaction involving the consumer.

▶ A consumer reporting agency must not include any obsolete information in a consumer report. Examples:

(1) Bankruptcies more than ten years prior to the report date.

(2) Suits and judgements which predate the report by seven years or by the applicable statute of limitations period, whichever is longer.

(3) Any other adverse information more than 7 years old.

APPENDIX D

Loan Payments and Payoff Table

Payoff of $1,000 loan held for the number of years indicated. The loan payment is provided next to the original loan term. For loan amounts greater than $1,000 multiply the figures by the loan amount in thousands of dollars.

Example

Two year payoff on $53,500 loan, 12.5% for 20 years:

$$\$974.39 \times 53.5 = \$52,129.87.$$

To determine the amount of interest paid, subtract the difference between the payoff amount and $1,000 from the total of payments made.

Example

Interest paid in three years on 14% loan, 15 year original term:

$$[(36 \times \$13.32) - (\$1,000 - \$926.67)] = \$406.19.$$

9.0% Loan Rate

Loan Term	Payment	1 year	2 years	3 years	4 years	5 years	6 years
				Prepaid In			
7	16.09	892.57	775.07	646.54	505.95	352.18	183.98
10	12.67	935.37	864.67	787.34	702.76	610.24	509.04
12	11.38	951.47	898.38	840.31	776.80	707.33	631.34
15	10.14	966.95	930.79	891.25	847.99	800.68	748.93
20	9.00	981.27	960.79	938.38	913.88	887.07	857.75
30	8.05	993.17	985.70	977.52	968.58	958.80	948.10

9.5% Loan Rate

Loan Term	Payment	1 year	2 years	3 years	4 years	5 years	6 years
				Prepaid In			
7	16.34	894.35	778.22	650.55	510.22	355.97	186.40
10	12.94	937.03	867.81	791.71	708.07	616.12	515.05
12	11.66	953.02	901.39	844.63	782.23	713.64	638.25
15	10.44	968.34	933.53	895.27	853.22	806.99	756.17
20	9.32	982.39	963.03	941.76	918.37	892.65	864.39
30	8.41	993.83	987.06	979.60	971.41	962.41	952.51

10.0% Loan Rate

Loan Term	Payment	Prepaid In					
		1 year	2 years	3 years	4 years	5 years	6 years
7	16.60	896.11	781.34	654.55	514.99	359.76	188.83
10	13.22	938.66	870.89	796.03	713.33	621.97	521.05
12	11.95	954.54	904.33	848.86	787.57	719.88	645.09
15	10.75	969.68	936.19	899.19	858.32	813.17	763.29
20	9.65	983.45	965.17	944.98	922.67	898.02	870.80
30	8.78	994.44	988.30	981.52	974.02	965.74	956.60

10.5% Loan Rate

Loan Term	Payment	Prepaid In					
		1 year	2 years	3 years	4 years	5 years	6 years
7	16.86	897.85	784.44	658.54	518.75	363.56	191.28
10	13.49	940.26	873.93	800.29	718.54	627.78	527.02
12	12.24	956.03	907.21	853.01	792.84	726.03	651.87
15	11.05	970.98	938.77	903.00	863.29	819.21	770.27
20	9.98	984.46	967.21	948.06	926.79	903.19	876.98
30	9.15	994.99	989.44	983.27	976.42.	968.82	960.38

11.0% Loan Rate

Loan Term	Payment	Prepaid In					
		1 year	2 years	3 years	4 years	5 years	6 years
7	17.12	899.57	787.51	662.49	523.00	367.37	193.73
10	13.78	941.82	876.92	804.50	723.70	633.55	532.97
12	12.54	957.47	910.02	857.08	798.01	732.11	658.58
15	11.37	972.24	941.26	906.70	868.14	825.12	777.11
20	10.32	985.42	969.15	950.99	930.74	908.14	882.93
30	9.52	995.50	990.48	984.87	978.62	971.65	963.86

11.5% Loan Rate

Loan Term	Payment	Prepaid In					
		1 year	2 years	3 years	4 years	5 years	6 years
7	17.39	901.27	790.56	666.43	527.25	371.19	196.20
10	14.06	943.36	879.86	808.65	728.81	639.29	538.91
12	12.83	958.88	912.77	861.07	803.11	738.11	665.24
15	11.68	973.45	943.67	783.83	872.86	830.89	783.83
20	10.66	986.32	970.99	953.79	934.51	912.89	888.65
30	9.90	995.36	911.42	986.34	980.64	974.25	967.08

12.0% Loan Rate

Loan Term	Payment	Prepaid In					
		1 year	2 years	3 years	4 years	5 years	6 years
7	17.65	902.94	793.58	670.34	531.48	375.00	198.68
10	14.35	944.87	882.74	812.74	733.86	644.97	544.82
12	13.13	960.25	915.46	864.99	808.12	744.03	671.82
15	12.00	974.61	946.01	913.77	877.45	836.52	790.40
20	11.01	987.18	972.73	996.94	938.11	917.44	894.15
30	10.29	996.37	992.28	987.67	982.48	976.63	970.04

12.5% Loan Rate

Loan Term	Payment	Prepaid In					
		1 year	2 years	3 years	4 years	5 years	6 years
7	17.92	904.60	796.57	674.24	535.70	378.83	201.17
10	14.64	946.34	885.58	816.77	738.86	650.62	550.70
12	13.44	961.59	918.08	868.82	813.04	749.87	678.33
15	12.33	975.74	948.26	917.15	881.92	842.02	796.84
20	11.36	987.99	974.39	958.99	941.55	921.80	899.44
30	10.67	996.75	993.06	988.89	984.17	978.82	972.76

13.0% Loan Rate

Loan Term	Payment	Prepaid In					
		1 year	2 years	3 years	4 years	5 years	6 years
7	18.19	906.24	799.54	678.11	539.92	382.65	203.68
10	14.93	947.79	888.37	820.75	743.80	656.22	556.56
12	13.75	962.89	920.65	872.58	817.88	755.62	684.78
15	12.65	976.82	950.45	920.43	886.27	847.39	803.15
20	11.72	988.76	975.96	961.40	944.83	925.97	904.51
30	11.06	997.09	993.77	990.00	985.70	980.82	975.26

13.5% Loan Rate

Loan Term	Payment	Prepaid In					
		1 year	2 years	3 years	4 years	5 years	6 years
7	18.46	907.86	802.48	681.96	544.12	386.48	206.19
10	15.23	949.20	891.11	824.67	748.68	661.78	562.39
12	14.06	964.15	923.15	876.26	822.63	761.29	691.44
15	12.98	977.87	952.55	923.60	890.49	852.62	809.31
20	12.07	989.48	977.45	963.69	947.95	929.95	909.37
30	11.45	997.39	994.41	991.00	987.10	982.64	977.54

14.0% Loan Rate

Loan Term	Payment	Prepaid In					
		1 year	2 years	3 years	4 years	5 years	6 years
7	18.74	909.46	805.39	685.78	548.31	390.31	208.72
10	15.53	950.59	893.80	828.53	753.31	667.29	568.19
12	14.37	965.38	925.59	879.85	827.29	766.88	697.44
15	13.32	978.87	954.58	926.67	894.59	857.71	815.33
20	12.44	990.16	978.85	965.86	950.92	933.76	914.02
30	11.85	997.67	994.99	991.91	988.37	984.31	979.63

14.5% Loan Rate

		Prepaid In					
Loan Term	Payment	1 year	2 years	3 years	4 years	5 years	6 years
7	19.02	911.03	808.27	689.58	552.49	394.15	211.25
10	15.83	951.95	896.44	832.33	758.28	672.75	573.96
12	14.69	966.57	927.97	883.37	831.87	772.37	703.66
15	13.66	979.83	956.54	929.64	898.57	862.68	821.22
20	12.80	990.81	980.18	967.92	953.75	937.38	918.48
30	12.25	997.92	995.51	992.74	989.53	985.83	981.55

15% Loan Rate

		Prepaid In					
Loan Term	Payment	1 year	2 years	3 years	4 years	5 years	6 years
7	19.30	912.59	811.13	693.36	556.66	397.98	213.79
10	16.13	953.27	899.03	836.07	762.99	678.16	579.70
12	15.01	966.74	930.29	886.82	836.36	777.79	709.80
15	14.00	980.76	958.43	932.51	902.43	867.50	826.97
20	13.17	991.41	981.44	969.87	956.43	940.84	922.74
30	12.64	997.14	995.99	993.48	990.58	987.21	983.29

15.5% Loan Rate

		Prepaid In					
Loan Term	Payment	1 year	2 years	3 years	4 years	5 years	6 years
7	19.58	914.13	813.96	697.11	560.81	401.82	216.35
10	16.44	954.57	901.58	839.76	767.65	683.53	585.41
12	15.33	968.87	932.55	890.18	840.76	783.11	715.87
15	14.34	981.65	960.25	935.29	906.17	872.20	832.58
20	13.54	991.98	982.63	971.71	958.98	944.14	926.81
30	13.05	998.34	996.41	994.16	991.53	988.46	984.88

APPENDIX E

Effective APRs Table

Increase in Annual Percentage Rate (APR) for each half point loan fee paid. For rates of half percentage increments, average the figures for the closest whole percentages.

Example
The effective APR for a 12% loan, 15 years, 2 point loan fee that prepays in 5 years:

$$12.0\% + (4 \times .146\%) = 12.58\%$$

Note: this table is approximate and becomes much less accurate for loan fees greater than 4 points. Other tables should be consulted for loan fees higher than 4 points.

8.0% Loan Rate

Loan Term	1 year	2 years	3 years	4 years	5 years	6 years	Maturity
7	.559	.310	.230	.191	.173	.162	.160
10	.547	.298	.215	.173	.150	.136	.120
12	.543	.291	.207	.167	.143	.130	.100
15	.539	.286	.201	.162	.138	.120	.085
20	.535	.282	.197	.156	.130	.114	.070
30	.532	.278	.193	.151	.128	.110	.055

9.0% Loan Rate

Loan Term	1 year	2 years	3 years	4 years	5 years	6 years	Maturity
7	.564	.313	.231	.195	.175	.166	.164
10	.553	.299	.216	.175	.153	.139	.120
12	.549	.294	.210	.169	.145	.130	.104
15	.545	.290	.205	.164	.139	.124	.088
20	.541	.285	.201	.159	.134	.118	.073
30	.538	.282	.198	.155	.130	.113	.058

10.0% Loan Rate

Loan Term	Prepaid In						
	1 year	2 years	3 years	4 years	5 years	6 years	Maturity
7	.566	.314	.234	.196	.178	.169	.165
10	.555	.301	.218	.178	.155	.141	.123
12	.551	.296	.213	.171	.148	.133	.106
15	.547	.291	.208	.166	.141	.126	.090
20	.544	.288	.203	.161	.136	.120	.075
30	.541	.285	.200	.158	.133	.116	.061

11.0% Loan Rate

Loan Term	Prepaid In						
	1 year	2 years	3 years	4 years	5 years	6 years	Maturity
7	.568	.316	.236	.199	.180	.170	.168
10	.557	.303	.220	.180	.158	.144	.125
12	.554	.298	.215	.174	.150	.135	.109
15	.549	.294	.210	.168	.144	.128	.094
20	.546	.290	.205	.164	.139	.123	.079
30	.544	.287	.203	.160	.135	.199	.065

12.0% Loan Rate

Loan Term	Prepaid In						
	1 year	2 years	3 years	4 years	5 years	6 years	Maturity
7	.570	.319	.238	.201	.183	.173	.170
10	.559	.305	.223	.183	.159	.145	.128
12	.555	.300	.216	.176	.153	.138	.113
15	.552	.296	.213	.171	.146	.131	.096
20	.549	.292	.208	.166	.141	.125	.081
30	.546	.290	.205	.163	.138	.122	.069

13.0% Loan Rate

Prepaid In

Loan Term	1 year	2 years	3 years	4 years	5 years	6 years	Maturity
7	.573	.320	.240	.204	.184	.175	.173
10	.561	.308	.224	.184	.161	.148	.130
12	.558	.303	.219	.178	.155	.140	.115
15	.554	.299	.214	.173	.149	.133	.099
20	.551	.295	.210	.169	.144	.128	.085
30	.549	.293	.208	.166	.141	.125	.074

14.0% Loan Rate

Prepaid In

Loan Term	1 year	2 years	3 years	4 years	5 years	6 years	Maturity
7	.574	.323	.243	.205	.186	.178	.175
10	.564	.309	.266	.186	.164	.150	.134
12	.560	.305	.221	.181	.158	.143	.118
15	.556	.301	.216	.175	.151	.136	.103
20	.554	.298	.213	.171	.148	.131	.089
30	.552	.295	.211	.169	.144	.128	.078

15.0% Loan Rate

Prepaid In

Loan Term	1 year	2 years	3 years	4 years	5 years	6 years	Maturity
7	.573	.322	.241	.207	.188	.179	.177
10	.563	.310	.227	.188	.165	.144	.135
12	.559	.305	.221	.182	.159	.142	.120
15	.555	.301	.219	.177	.153	.138	.105
20	.553	.298	.214	.173	.149	.133	.090
30	.551	.297	.211	.171	.146	.130	.080

APPENDIX F

U.S. Coast Guard Homeports

HOMEPORT DISTRICTS	TERRITORY IN DISTRICT
OFFICE OF DOCUMENTATION OFFICER U.S. Coast Guard 447 Commercial Street Boston, MA 02109 Phone: (617) 565-9030	ME, NH, MA, RI, VT (that portion not in New York, NY homeport)
OFFICE OF DOCUMENTATION OFFICER U.S Coast Guard 210 North Tucker Boulevard P.O. Box D-17 Room 1118 St. Louis, MO 63188-0017 Phone: (314) 425-4497	WV, KY,TN, MO, AR, IA, OK KS, NE, SD, ND, WY, CO, southwest PA (south of New Castle, west of Johnstown, approximately), southern OH (south of Akron, approximately), IL (except north of 41° north latitude and east of 90° west longitude), southwest WI (south of 46°20' north latitude and west of 90° west longitude), southern MN (south of 46°20' north latitude), northern AL (north of Gadsden, approximately), northwestern MS (northwest of a diagonal from the AR/LA/MS border through Tupelo, approximately)
OFFICE OF DOCUMENTATION OFFICER U.S. Coast Guard Battery Park Building New York, NY 1004 Phone: (212) 668-6435	CN, eastern NY (east of Utica, approximately), eastern NJ (east of a diagonal from the PA/NY/NJ border to Atlantic City, approximately) northwest VT (Orleans, Franklin, Chittendon, Addison, Rutland, Grand Isle Counties)
OFFICE OF DOCUMENTATION OFFICER U.S. Coast Guard 1 Washington Avenue Philadelphia, PA 19147- 4394 Phone: (215) 271-4876	DE, eastern PA (that portion not in St. Louis, MO and Cleveland, OH homeports), western NJ (that portion not in New York NY homeport)
OFFICE OF DOCUMENTATION OFFICER U.S. Coast Guard Norfolk Federal Building 200 Granby Mall Norfolk, VA 23510 Phone: (804) 441-3272	MD, VA, NC, District of Columbia,
OFFICE OF DOCUMENTATION OFFICER U.S. Coast Guard 155 South Miami Avenue Miami, FL 33130 Phone: (305) 536-4246	SC, FL (except west of Tallahassee, approximately), GA (except southwestern portion encompassing Columbus and Albany, approximately), Panama Canal Zone, Puerto Rico, Virgin Islands

U.S. Coast Guard Homeports

OFFICE OF DOCUMENTATION OFFICER
U.S. Coast Guard
1440 Canal Street
New Orleans, LA 70112-2711
Phone: (504) 589-2932

LA, southeastern MS (that portion not in St. Louis, MO homeport), southern AL (that portion not in Miami, FL homeport), GA (that portion not in Miami, FL homeport)

OFFICE OF DOCUMENTATION OFFICER
8876 Gulf Freeway
Suite 210
Houston, TX 77017
Phone: (713) 947-0314

NM, TX

OFFICE OF DOCUMENTATION OFFICER
1240 East 9th Street
Room 2029
Cleveland, OH 44199-2060
Phone: (216) 522-3945

MI, NY (that portion not in New York, NY homeport),northwestern PA (north of New Castle, west of Johnstown, approximately),northern OH (that portion not in St. Louis, MO homeport),northern IN (that portion not in St. Louis, MO homeport), WI (that portion not in St. Louis, MO homeport), northern MN (that portion not in St. Louis, MO homeport)

OFFICE OF DOCUMENTATION OFFICER
U.S. Coast Guard
165 North Pico Avenue
Long Beach, CA 90802
Phone: (213) 499-5535

AZ, southern CA (Santa Barbara, Kern, Ventura, San Bernardino, Los Angeles, Orange, Riverside, San Diego, Imperial Counties), NV (Clark County only), southern UT (Washington, Kabe, Garfield, San Juan Counties)

OFFICE OF DOCUMENTATION OFFICER
U.S. Coast Guard
Building 14 Coast Guard Island
Alameda, CA 94501
Phone: (415) 437-3101

Northern CA (that portion not in Long Beach, CA homeport), NV except Clark County), northern UT (that portion not in Long Beach, CA homeport)

OFFICE OF DOCUMENTATION OFFICER
U.S. Coast Guard
1519 Alaskan Way South
Seattle, WA 98134
Phone: (206) 286-5500

WA, MT

OFFICE OF DOCUMENTATION OFFICER
U.S. Coast Guard
6767 North Basin Avenue
Portland, OR 97217
Phone: (503) 240-9345

OR, ID

COMMANDING OFFICER
U.S. Coast Guard
Marine Safety Office
433 Ala Moana Boulevard
Honolulu, HI 96813
Phone: (808) 541-2066

HI

COMMANDING OFFICER
U.S. Coast Guard
Vessel Documentation
2760 Sherwood Lane, Suite 2A
Juneau, AK 99801-8545
Phone: (907) 586-7280

AK

APPENDIX G

Title and Registration Information

This appendix contains registration and titling information on all fifty states and the District of Columbia.

All registration fees are for initial registration which, unless otherwise noted, is for one year. No figures are given for renewal fees. Other fees may be assessed for duplicate registration and/or title, transfer of ownership, late registration penalties, etc.

"Motorboat", "motorized boat" or "boat with motor" refers to any mechanically propelled vessel, unless noted otherwise. "Sailboat" refers to a boat powered solely by sail (if a sailboat has an auxiliary motor, it is usually defined as a "boat with motor").

Where proof of sales tax or use tax payment is required, the term "use tax" generally refers to the tax offsetting payment of another states' sales tax if the boat is brought into the current state of registration.

The abbreviation MSO represents Manufacturer's Statement of Origin or Manufacturer's Certificate of Origin, whichever applies. The MSO is provided with any new boat sale.

Title and Registration Information

Boats subject to registration	Registration fees	Documents required for registration	Other special requirements for registration
ALABAMA All motorboats and sailboats.	Less than 16' $6 16' to less than 26' $10 26' to less than 40' $20 40' or over $40 Plus $1 issuance fee on all boats	Application for registration	None
ALASKA All boats	Any boat $6	Application for Boat Registration Number; proof of ownership (signature of past owner or bill of sale provided by current owner)	None
ARIZONA All boats	7' or less $7.50 $.50 additional for each foot, or fraction thereof, over 7'	Application for Arizona Watercraft Certificate of Number; evidence of ownership consisting of either endorsed Arizona Certificate of Number, bill of sale, or court decree. If previously registered in another state, title (if title state) or registration (if non-title state) is also required	Proof of paid sales tax required or else vessel is subject to use tax.
ARKANSAS All sailboats; all other boats with engines larger than 10 hp; all boats operating after dark or on waters designated as Federally controlled	Less than 16' $4 16' to less than 26' $8 26' or more $12	Boat Application Form; bill of sale and copy of MSO for new boat purchase; bill of sale for used boat	Proof of sales tax paid.
CALIFORNIA All sailboats greater than 8'; all boats with motors	Any boat $9 (Original registration)	New boat: MSO and completed Application for Boat Registration Number. Used boat: Prior registration/title and bill of sale	Sales tax must be paid or use tax is assessed. Title is automatically issued on all registrations.

Is titling available?	Titling fees	Title requirements	Where to register or title
No	N/A	N/A	Marine Police Division 64 North Union Street Montgomery, AL 36130
No	N/A	N/A	U.S. Coast Guard Marine Safety Office Attn: Boating Registrar 2760 Sherwood Lane Suite 2A Juneau, AK 99801-8545
No	N/A	N/A	Arizona Game and Fish Department 2222 W. Greenway Rd. Phoenix, AZ 85023
No	N/A	N/A	Arkansas Game and Fish Commission Boating Safety Section 2 Nat'l Resources Drive Little Rock, AR 72205
Yes	Included in registration fee	Same as registration	Any local Department of Motor Vehicles office

Boats subject to registration	Registration fees		Documents required for registration	Other special requirements for registration
COLORADO Any boat with a motor or sail	Any boat	$10	Application for Colorado Boat Registration; proof of ownership (bill of sale, prior registration, or sworn statement of ownership)	None
CONNECTICUT All boats with motors, and all sailboats without motors 19½' and over	Less than 12' each additional foot from 12' up to (but not including) 16'; each additional foot from 16' up to (but not including) 37'; each additional foot from 37' up to (but not including) 43'; each additional foot from 43' up to (but not including) 65' 65' and over	$7.50 $3.75 $7.50 $22.50 $7.50 $525	Application for Vessel Registration and Certificate of Number or Decal; bill of sale	Proof of payment of sales or use tax. If vessel is documentedor registered out of state, a Certificate of Decal is obtained instead. This also requires proof of payment of sales or use tax.
DELAWARE All boats with motors	Less than 16' 16' to less than 26' 26' to less than 40' 40' to less than 65' 65' and over	$5 $10 $15 $25 $30	Application for Delaware Boat Registration; notarized bill of sale; title if boat was previously registered in a title state	None
FLORIDA All boats with motors.	Less than 12' 12' to less than 16' 16' to less than 26' 26' to less than 40' 40' to less than 65' 65' to less than 110' 110' or more (Vessels that are registered between January 1 and June 1, which have never been registered before, pay only one half the registration fee for one half the year. A $2.25 service charge and a $1 fee will be added to the registration amount. Fees will be changing in June, 1989.)	$4.25 $8.25 $13.25 $33.25 $53.25 $63.25 $78.25	Form DNR 10-T-1 (16); MSO (new boat) or proof of owernship (used boat)	Proof of sales tax paid; vessels 16' and over must be titled.

Is titling available?	Titling fees	Title requirements	Where to register or title
No	N/A	N/A	Division of Parks and Outdoor Recreation Registration Unit PO Box 231 Littleton, CO 80160
No	N/A	N/A	Local Department of Motor Vehicles office
No	N/A	N/A	Delaware Department of Natural Resources 89 Kings Highway PO Box 1401 Dover, DE 19903
Yes	$5.25 ($6.25 with lien recorded)	Same as registration	County Tax Collector's Office in the county the vessel is located or in the county the owner resides

Boats subject to registration	Registration fees		Documents required for registration	Other special requirements for registration
GEORGIA Any boat with motor and any sailboat 12' or more	less than 16' 16' to less than 26' 26' to less than 40' 40' or more	$10 $24 $60 $100	Boat Registration Application Form. If previously registered in Georgia, prior registration or copy of bill of sale	None
HAWAII All boats with motors; sailboats without motors greater than 8' in length	Less than 20' 20' or more	$13 $25	Application for Vessel Registration and Certificate of Number; proof of ownership (bill of sale, valid title, or affidavit supporting the claim of ownership)	None
ILLINOIS All boats	Less than 16' 16' to less than 26' 26' to less than 40' 40' and over	$16 $19 $22 $25	Watercraft Application; MSO (new boat) or title and/or registration (used boat)	Title must be obtained at the time of registration. Proof of payment of sales tax required.
INDIANA All boats	Up to 16' 16' to less than 26' 26' to less than 40' 40' or more	$12 $14 $17 $22	Application for Watercraft Registration and Title; original MSO (new boat) or bill of sale and previous title and/or registration (used boat)	All boats acquired after January 1, 1986 are also required to be titled.
IOWA All boats	Less than 12' 12' to less than 15' 15' to less than 18' 18' to less than 25' 25' or more Any documented vessel	$9 $11 $13 $19 $29 $26	Application for Boat or Snowmobile Registration	All vessels over 17' must be titled. Documented boats must pay a "registration" fee.
KANSAS All boats	Any boat	$9	Application for Certificate of Number; bill of sale	Proof of paid sales tax required if purchased from a dealer. Private individual sales are tax exempt.

Is titling available?	Titling fees	Title requirements	Where to register or title
No	N/A	N/A	State Department of Natural Resources Boating Unit, Suite 100 2258 Northlake Pkwy. Tucker, GA 30084
No	N/A	N/A	Harbors Division 79 South Nimitz Hwy. Honolulu, HI 96813
Yes	Included in registration	Same as registration	Illinois Department of Conservation Watercraft Division PO Box 19226 Springfield, IL 62794
Yes	$9 (no additional fee for lien recordation)	Same as registration	Indiana Department of Natural Resources Law Enforcement Div., Titling Section 606 State Office Bldg. Indianapolis, IN 46204
Yes	$5 for title ($10 with lien recorded)	Application for Iowa Vessel Certificate of Title; proof of sales tax paid; MSO (new boat); bill of sale (used boat)	County Recorder in county of residence or, for non-residents, county where boat is principally used
No (bill pending to create titling act effective January 1, 1990)	N/A	N/A	Kansas Department of Wildlife and Parks RRZ Box 54A Pratt, KS 67124

Title and Registration Information

Boats subject to registration	Registration fees		Documents required for registration	Other special requirements for registration
KENTUCKY All motorboats	Outboards: less than 16' 16' to less than 26' 26' to less than 40' 40' or more Inboards: All boats	$10 $14 $20 $24 $24	Boat Registration Application; bill of sale or proof of ownership affadavit	None
LOUISIANA Any boat with motor	Any boat	$16	Motorboat Registration Application; copy of bill of sale	Proof of paid sales tax.
MAINE Any boat with motor	Any boat	$4	Maine Boat Registration Application; copy of bill of sale	Proof of payment of excise tax before registration will be accepted. Tax varies by municipality.
MARYLAND All boats with motors. Documented vessels must apply annually for a documented yacht validation sticker	Over 16' or with a motor of greater than 7.5 hp (Other vessels are exempt from registration fee)	$12	Application for Maryland Boat Certificates; original MSO for new boats (must be accompanied by a certified bill of sale if the assignment of the MSO does not include the total price paid); bill of sale and previous title and/or registration for used boats	If sales tax not paid, a 5% excise tax is levied on the gross sales price (less any trailer). All registered vessels must be titled first.
MASSACHUSETTS All boats with motors	All boats (Two year registration)	$30	Application for Certificate of Number; copy of bill of sale; prior registration	Proof of payment of sales tax.

Is titling available?	Titling fees	Title requirements	Where to register or title
No	N/A	N/A	Office of the Circuit Clerk in the county where the boat is principally used or in the home county of the owner
No	N/A	N/A	Louisiana Dept. of Wildlife and Fisheries PO Box 14796 Baton Rouge, LA 70898
No	N/A	N/A	Department of Inland Fisheries and Wildlife 284 State Street, Sta. 41 Augusta, ME 04333
Yes	$2 for title ($17 with lien recorded)	Same as registration	Department of Natural Resources Licensing and Consumer Services 580 Taylor Avenue Tawes State Office Bldg. Annapolis, MD 21401
No	N/A	N/A	Any Massachusetts Department of Law Enforcement office

Boats subject to registration	Registration fees		Documents required for registration	Other special requirements for registration
MICHIGAN				
All boats with motors; non-motorized vessels over 12', except canoes	Fees apply only to boats with motors.		Application for Certificate of Watercraft Title and/or Registration; MSO (new boat) or bill of sale (used boat)	Proof of paid sales or use tax; all boats 20' and over and all boats with a permanently affixed motor must be titled.
	less than 12'	$11.25		
	12' to less than 16'	$13.50		
	16' to less than 20'	$33.75		
	20' to less than 28'	$75		
	28' to less than 35'	$135		
	35' to less than 42'	$180		
	42' to less than 50'	$225		
	50' or more	$360		
	(Three year registration) Fees increase each year through 1991			
MINNESOTA				
All boats except non-motorized boats of 9' or less	Up to 19'	$12	Minnesota Department of Natural Resources Boat Registration Application	For any dealer sale, proof of paid sales tax for an in-state purchase or use tax for an out-of-state purchase. Private individual sales are tax exempt.
	Over 19' to less than 26'	$20		
	26' to less than 40'	$30		
	40' and over	$40		
	(Three year registration)			
MISSISSIPPI				
All boats with motors	All boats	$2.50	Application for Registration; Certificate of Ownership	Proof of paid sales or use tax .
MISSOURI				
All motorized watercraft and all sailboats greater than 12'	Under 16'	$10	Application for Watercraft Registration Number	Title must be issued at time of registration.
	16' to less than 26'	$20		
	26' to less than 40'	$30		
	40' or more	$40		

Is titling available?	Titling fees	Title requirements	Where to register or title
Yes	$5, no fee for lien recordation	Original MSO (new boat) or previous title and/or registration	Local Secretary of State branch office
No	N/A	N/A	Minnesota Dept. of Natural Resources License Bureau St. Paul, MN 55155 or any Department of Motor Vehicles office
No	N/A	N/A	Mississippi Dept. of Conservation PO Box 451 Jackson, MS 39205
Yes	$7.50	Application for Title; MSO (new boat); notarized title or notarized bill of sale and affidavit of ownership (if no other ownership document exists) (used boat); payment of sales tax plus local tax	Department of Revenue Marine Registration PO Box 100 Jefferson City, MO 65105

Boats subject to registration	Registration fees	Documents required for registration	Other special requirements for registration
MONTANA All motorized vessels; sailboats 12' and over; sailboats with motors, 10' and over	Motorboats 10' but less than14' $7.50 Sailboats 12' but less than 14' $7.50 14' but less than 16' $15 16' but less than 17' $32 17' but less than 18' $51 18' but less than 19' $54 19' or longer $4 per foot or fraction thereof. Plus $2 license fee, all boats	Application for Certificate of Title; proof of ownership, either previous registration, bill of sale, MSO, or builders certification	All registered boats must be titled.
NEBRASKA All boats with motors	Less than 16' $15 16' to less than 26' $30 26' to less than 40' $45 40' and over $75 Plus $2 issuance fee	Application for Boat Number and Certificate	N/A
NEVADA All boats with motors	Less than 13' $10 13' to less than 18' $15 18' to less than 22' $30 22' to less than 26' $45 26' to less than 31' $60 31' or more $75	Untitled boat: Proof of ownership (original bill of sale or subsequent bill of sale, MSO, or physical inspection by Nevada Dept. of Wildlife). Titled boat: Certificate of Title endorsed to new owner. Application must be made in person	Proof of payment of Nevada sales tax.
NEW HAMPSHIRE All boats with motors and any sailboat over 12'	Depends on boat length, horse power rating and model year. The state will not release registration fees except upon application for a particular boat	Application for Boat Registration; copy of bill of sale	Proof of "permit fee" paid (varies by county).
NEW JERSEY All boats over 12'	Less than 16' $6 16' to less than 26' $14 26' to less than 40' $26 40' to less than 65' $40 65' or more $125	Application for Boat Registration; Report of Sales Tax on Vessel; proof of ownership (bill of sale, MSO, previous boat registration or certificate of ownership by sworn affadavit)	Registered vessels must be titled.

Is titling available?	Titling fees	Title requirements	Where to register or title
Yes	$6	Same as registration	Registration and title application filed with County Treasurer in the county of residence
No	N/A	N/A	County Treasurer in owner's county of residence
Yes	$5	Same as registration	Nevada Deptartment of Wildlife 1100 Valley Road Reno, NV 89512
No	N/A	N/A	Any registered boat agent
Yes	$5 ($9 with lien recorded)	Application for Certificate of Vessel; same additional requirements as registration	Any Motor Vehicle Agency office in the state

Boats subject to registration	Registration fees		Documents required for registration	Other special requirements for registration
NEW MEXICO All boats with motors	Less than 16' 16' to less than 26' 26' to less than 40' 40' to less than 65' 65' or more	$28.50 $36 $43.50 $51 $66	Application for Vessel Registration and Title; MSO and dealer invoice (new boats); previous title if a title state or bill of sale if not a title state, and physical inspection (used boat)	Proof of paid sales tax; any boat over 10' must be titled.
NEW YORK All boats with motors	Up to 15' 16' to 25' 26' or more	$9 $18 $30	Application for Boat Registration; proof of ownership (either MSO, current title or transferable registration) and bill of sale	Proof of payment of state and local sales tax.
NORTH CAROLINA All vessels except sailboats 14' or less	All boats	$5.50	Application for Vessel Number	Proof of payment of taxes.
NORTH DAKOTA Any boats with motors	Under 16' 16' or more (Three year registration)	$6 $15	Application for North Dakota Watercraft Certificate of Number	None
OHIO All boats	Under 16' 16' to less than 26' 26' or more	$23 $31 $46	Certified Boat Registration Application; proof of ownership, (MSO or bill of sale with previous title)	Vessels 14' or larger must be titled before registration.
OKLAHOMA All boats	Varies depending on original purchase price and model year. Amount due decreases by approximately 10% for each year of vessel's age		Application for Registration; MSO or bill of sale (new boat); title or registration and bill of sale (used boat)	Proof of paid excise tax (varies, depending on purchase price and model year - one time fee).

Is titling available?	Titling fees	Title requirements	Where to register or title
Yes	$10	Same as registration	Any Department of Motor Vehicles field office
Yes	$2.50 ($5.50 with lien recorded)	Only vessels 14' and longer and built in 1987 or later are eligible for titling. If issued, title replaces registration certificate	Any Deptartment of Motors Vehicle district office
No	N/A	N/A	Wildlife Resources Commission Archdale Building Raleigh, NC 27611
No	N/A	N/A	Game and Fish Dept. 2121 Lovett Avenue Bismark, ND 58505
Yes	$3 ($6 with lien recorded)	Proof of payment of state and local sales tax	Department of Natural Resources Division of Watercraft Fountain Square Columbus, OH 43224
No (title provision becomes effective January 1, 1990)	N/A	N/A	In person, any Motor License Agent

Boats subject to registration	Registration fees		Documents required for registration	Other special requirements for registration
OREGON All boats with motors and sailboats 12' or more in length	Less than 12' 12' to less than 16' 16' to less than 20' 20' or more plus $2 for each additional foot or part thereof over 20'	$11 $17 $21 $21	Application for Boat Title; MSO (new boat); previous title or previous registration and bill of sale (used boat)	Must title all registered boats.
PENNSYLVANIA All boats with motors	Up to 15' 16' or more	$4 $6	Application for Boat Registration; copy of MSO (new boat); notarized bill of sale (used boat); notarized dealer purchase agreement	Proof of sales tax paid.
RHODE ISLAND All boats	Under 16' 16' to 25' Over 25' to 35' Over 35'	$10 $15 $25 $35	Boat Certificate of Number Application; MSO or Builders Certification and bill of sale (new boat); previous registration or title, whichever applicable (used boat)	Proof of paid sales or use tax on net (after trade) price of boat. All boats bought after Jan. 1, 1989 must be titled.
SOUTH CAROLINA All boats mechanically propelled	All boats Any outboard engine (I/O and inboard engines included in vessel registration fee)	$10 $3	Watercraft Application; MSO (new boat); registration and title if available (used boat). If no title, then notarized bill of sale	Proof of paid sales tax. All watercraft over 14', not hand powered, must also be titled.
SOUTH DAKOTA All motorboats and all non-motorized craft over 12'	Non-motorized boats Motorized less than 19' Motorized 19' or more	$5 $10 $15	South Dakota Boat Registration Application	None
TENNESSEE All boats except hand powered	16' and under Over 16' to less than 26' 26' to less than 40' 40' or more	$4 $8 $12 $16	Application for Boat Certificate of Number	Proof of paid state sales tax.

Is titling available?	Titling fees	Title requirements	Where to register or title
Yes	$7	N/A	State Marine Board 3000 Market Street, NE #505 Salem, OR 97310
No	N/A	N/A	Pennsylvania Fish Commission Boat Registration Div. PO Box 1852 Harrisburg, PA 17105
Yes	$10 ($25 with lien recorded)	Same as registration	Department of Environmental Management Boat Registration and Licensing 22 Hayes Street Providence, RI 02908
Yes	$3	Same as registration	South Carolina Wildlife and Marine Resources Boat Titling and Registration PO Box 167 Columbia, SC 29202
No	N/A	N/A	Department of Game, Fish and Parks 412 West Missouri Pierre, SD 57501
No	N/A	N/A	Tennessee Wildlife Resources Agency Boating Section PO Box 40747 Nashville, TN 37204

Title and Registration Information

Boats subject to registration	Registration fees		Documents required for registration	Other special requirements for registration
TEXAS Any motorized vessel	Less than 16' 16' to less than 26' 26' to less than 40' 40' or more	$12 $18 $24 $30	Application for Certificate of Title for Motorboats; MSO (new boat); previous title or registration and notarized bill of sale (used boat)	All motorboats in excess of 14' must also be titled.
UTAH Any boats except hand powered	All boats	$10	Application for Boat Title and Registration; MSO (new boat); notarized bill of sale and last registration (used boat)	Proof of payment of sales and/or property tax on used boats. Must title any boat newer than 1984 model year.
VERMONT All boats with motors	Less than 16' 16' to less than 26' 26' to less than 40' 40' or more	$5 $10 $20 $50	Application for Motorboat Registration; original MSO and bill of sale showing purchase price (new boat); original title or last registration with all subsequent bills of sale showing purchase price (used boat)	Must title any boat 16' or more with motor greater than 10hp if model is 1989 or newer. Proof of sales or use tax paid.
VIRGINIA All boats with motors	Any boat	$11	Application for Boat Registration Number/ Certificate of Title; MSO (new boat); bill of sale and previous registration (used boat)	All boats over 15' with motor over 25hp and all sailboats over 18' must be titled.
WASHINGTON All boats with motors and sailboats 16' and over	Any boat (plus initial filing fee of $5)	$6	Notarized Vessel Title Application; MSO (new boat); "proof of ownership" (used boat)	All registered vessels are automatically titled.

Is titling available?	Titling fees	Title requirements	Where to register or title
Yes	$5	None	Texas Parks and Wildlife Department 4200 Smith School Road Austin, TX 76744
Yes	$6	No titling available for 1984 or older boats	Local Department of Motor Vehicles office in the county of owner's residence
Yes	$5 ($8 with lien recorded)	Same as registration, plus visual inspection of Hull Identification Number by a certified law enforcement officer	Agency of Transportation Dept. of Motor Vehicles 120 State Street Montpelier, VT 05603
Yes	$7	MSO; proof of Watercraft Tax paid; sales invoice (new). Previous title or registration; bill of sale (used)	Department of Game and Inland Fisheries Boat Section PO Box 11104 4010 W. Broad Street Richmond, VA 23230
Yes	$5	Proof of payment of vessel excise tax ($\frac{1}{2}$ of 1%)	State Parks and Recreation Commission 7150 Cleanwater Lane Olympia, WA 98504

Title and Registration Information

Boats subject to registration	Registration fees	Documents required for registration	Other special requirements for registration
WASHINGTON D.C. All boats	Boats with propulsion machinery: Under 16' $10 16' to 26' $20 Over 26' to 40' $30 Over 40' $40 Boats without propulsion machinery: (used boats) Any size $5	Application for Boat Certificate of Title/ Registration Number. MSO (new boats); notarized invoice for boat that includes the purchase price, boat description and date of purchase registration.	Payment of Title Tax (6% of purchase price or fair market value). All vessels are automatically titled at time of
WEST VIRGINIA All boats with motors	Any boat with engine of 3hp or more $5	Application for registration, MSO (new boat); out-of-state title or registration or W. Va. registration with notarized bill of sale	Payment of 5% Privilege Tax on purchase price of vessel. Boats bought after July 1, 1989 must be titled.
WISCONSIN All boats with motors	Sailboats over 12' $6.50 Motorized: less than 16' $6.50 16' to less than 26' $8.50 26' to less than 40' $10.50 40' or more $12.50	Boat Registration & Titling Application; MSO (if purchased out of state, a bill of sale is also required) (new boats); previous title or registration, or dealer statement (if bought used from dealer) (used boat)	Title issued automatically on boats 16' and over. Proof of payment of sales tax, or its equivalent from another state.
WYOMING All boats equipped with motor of 5hp or more	Any boat $5	Watercraft Application; copy of bill of sale (new boat); notarized bill of sale (used boat)	None

Is titling available?	Titling fees	Title requirements	Where to register or title
Yes	$2 ($3 with lien recorded)	Same as registration, except that vessels registered prior to March 14, 1984 do not require titling unless ownership is transferred	Harbor Branch Special Operations Division Metro Police Department 550 Water Street SW Washington D.C., 20024
Yes	$5 ($10 with lien recorded)	Same as registration. Vessels bought before July 1, 1989 may be optionally titled	Division of Motor Vehicles 1900 Kanawha Blvd. E Building 3 Charleston, WV 25317
Yes (effective February	No fee as of yet	Same as registration	Department of Natural Resources Boat Registration and Titling Box 7236 Madison, WI 54707
No	N/A	N/A	Game and Fish Dept. 5400 Bishop Blvd. Cheyenne, WY 82002

APPENDIX H

Charter Equipment List

Quantity Description

Anchor equipment: Estimated cost = $700.00
6-10'	Anchor Chain (size depends upon boat length)
1	Spool 3/8" Nylon Line 3 Strand
1	Danforth 12 lb. Anchor
1	Danforth 20 lb. Anchor
6	7/16" Anchor Shackles
4	1/2" Thimbles
1	Chain Deck Pipe

Safety devices: Estimated cost = $860.00
2	Adult Safety Harness (sail)
6	Life Jackets - Adult
2	Life Jackets - Child
1	Horseshoe Buoy & Steel Holder - w/labor
2	Ring Buoy & Bracket - w/labor
1	Flare Kit
1	Distress Flag
1	First Aid Kit
1	Fire Extinguisher
1	Halon System - w/labor

Electrical: Estimated cost = $400.00
1	Spotlight & 12v Deck outlet - w/labor
1	Anchor Light
2	Floatlite
1	Hubble 30 amp shore cable
1	Hubble 30 amp to 15 amp adaptor

Electronics: Estimated cost = $5900.00
1	Depthsounder - w/labor
1	Knotmeter - w/labor
1	Wind Machine - w/labor
1	Loran-C - w/labor
1	VHF - w/labor
1	Antenna - w/labor
1	Chart Lighter
1	Stereo AM/FM - Cassette - w/labor
1	Clock
1	Barometer

Engine room: Estimated cost = $4300.00
- 1   Racor Fuel Filter Mod. - w/labor
- 1   Battery Charger - w/labor
- 1   Air Conditioner/Heater - w/labor
- 1   Sea Water Strainer - w/labor
- 1   Manual Bilge Pump - w/labor

Canvas: Estimated cost = $2400.00
- 1   Bimini Top - w/labor
- 1 set   Privacy Curtains - w/labor
- 1 set   Interior Screens - w/labor
- 1   Dodger w/Helmsman Awning - w/labor
- 1   Windscoop

Exterior deck and cabin: Estimated cost = $2770.00
- 1   Cockpit Table
- 4   Yacht Chairs
- 1   Deck Table
- 1   Bell, Chrome
- 1   Horn
- 1   Boat Hook
- 1   Bar-B-Q Grill & Rack - w/labor
- 1   Bar-B-Q Tool Set
- 1   Zodiac - Tender Var.length Teak Rub Rail - w/labor
- 2   10" x 26" Par Fenders
- 1 pr   Fender Guards
- 1   Stainless Steel Stern Mount Swim Ladder - w/labor

Interior cabin: Estimated cost = $650.00
- 1   Fan/Stateroom - w/labor
- 1   Electric Heater
- 1   TV- B/W 12" Sony
- 2   Bean Bag Ash Trays
- 3   Rubber Maid Plastic Trays
- 1   Mirror Mounted in each Head
- 1   Shower Curtain & rings
- 2   Towel Racks in Head
- 1   Toilet paper Holder
- 1   Toothbrush rack
- 1   Cabin oil Lamp
- 1   Smoke Bell

Furniture: Estimated cost = $1700.00
- 1   Salon Hide-a-Bed
- 1   Stuffed Chair
- 1   Lamp - AC

Galley equipment: Estimated cost = $1100.00
- 1   Electric Coffee Pot
- 1   Toaster
- 1   8 place set S.S. Flatware
- 1   8 pc Table settings
- 8   10" Dinner Plates
- 8   8" Sandwich Plate
- 8   Cereal Bowls
- 8   Coffee Cups
- 8   Yachtware Tumblers

8	Insulated Mugs
1	Tea Kettle
1	5 pc kitchen knife set
1	Standard Coffee Pot
1	Silverware holder
2	Salt and Pepper Shakers
1	Ice Pick
1	Wiskbroom & Pan
2	Pot Holders
2	Hot Plate Pads
1	Plastic Spatula
1	Corkscrew
1	Bottle Opener
1	Can Opener
1	Vegetable Peeler
3	Wooden Spoons
1	Deli Cutting Board
1	Wisk
1	Dishrack & Drainer

Navigation tools/charts: Estimated cost = $630.00

1	Ritchie Navigator Compass - w/labor
1	Hand Bearing Compass
1	Dividers
1	Parallel Rule
1	7 x 50 Binoculars
1	Binocular Rack
6	Local Charts
1	Ships Log Book
1	Engine Log Book

Sails and equipment: Estimated cost = $2500.00

	Genoa Sheet
	Jib Sail
	Mainsail with one row of reef points
	Mainsail Cover
	Winch Handle Holder
2	Genoa Track Cars for Boom Vang
	Spreader Boots, Large Oval - w/labor
	Jib Roller Furling System
	Boom Vang
1	Bosun Chair

Tools: Estimated cost = $250.00

1	Plastic Tool Box
3	Assorted Slot Head Screw Drivers
3	Assorted Phillips Head Screw Drivers
3	Adjustable Wrenches 6", 8", 10"
1	Large Channel Lock Pliers
1	8" Vise Grip Pliers
1	Set of 6 Open End Wrenches
1	Set of 6 Metric Wrenches
1	Needle Nose Pliers
1	Regular Pliers
1	Hacksaw & Blades
1	Stubby Screw Driver
1	Large Slothead Screw Driver

1	Ball Peen Hammer

Clean-up gear: Estimated cost = $92.00
1	Hose
1	Hose Nozzle
1	Mop/Bucket
1	Handbrush
1	Yacht Mop
1	Deck Brush
1	Large Sponge

Total Estimated Cost = $????????????

Sail	Power
$19,500	$19,932
- Air Conditioner	- Windmachine
- Furniture	- Sails
	- Knotmeter

APPENDIX I

Charter Survey Results

1. The total number of Charter Company respondents is 14 out of the 50 (28%) to which a survey request was sent.

2. The areas represented are:

   ▶ United States - Florida, Mid-Atlantic, and California

   ▶ Caribbean - St. Thomas, Bahamas, and Belize

   ▶ Mediterranean - Greece and Turkey

   ▶ Southeast Asia - Singapore

3. The types of charters include both crewed and bareboat.

4. The average number of years in operation is 8. The oldest is 35 and the youngest is 3 years old.

5. Owner financial programs include both management (10) and lease back (2). The owner's share varies from 50 to 85%, and the lease back percentage is 8.

6. Maintenance is provided by all the companies. Seventy-five percent also allow owner participation, and most discount parts but not labor. The labor rates range from $9/hr-$30/hr (skilled), and from $5/hr-$18/hr (unskilled). Annual maintenance costs for sailboats vary between $1,000 and $5,000, and between $1,500 and $6,000 for powerboats.

7. The charter fleets consist of predominently sailboats by an 8 to 1 margin. Each company has a principle location, and some may operate in as many as three additional locations. The largest number of boats in any one respondent's fleet is 80, and the smallest number is five.

8. Fleet sizes range from twenty footers up to large yachts over 60 feet. Ninety percent, however, fall into the 30'-50' sizes, with equal numbers between the 30-40' and 40-50' size ranges.

9. The weekly rates follow:

Location	20-30'	30-40'	40-50'	50-60'	>60'
Caribbean	$700	$1575	$2080	$3775	$5200
Florida	-	$1000	$1500	-	-
Mid-Atlantic	$550	$750	$1400	-	-
California	$550	$1050	$1200	$2000	-
Mediterranean	$700	$1000	$1750	$3000	$5000

10. Charter seasons are divided into high and low periods depending on the weather and climate. The survey covered the following:

Location	High		Low	
	from	to	from	to
Caribbean	December	April	July	October
Florida	November	April	May	November
Mid-Atlantic	April	November	-	-
Mediterranean	April	November	-	-

INDEX